WATERS UNDER BAGHDAD

ZAID BRIFKANI

For the mothers, wives, and sisters who stay behind in times of war and hold the line against hate: Your silent cries are louder than bombs, your tears heavier than oceans. Don't let go of love.

1

Minsk, Belarus
November 2021

After three cold nights in the open courtyards and streets of Minsk, another chapter of my twenty-day journey begins. Or shall I say *our* journey? There must be at least a couple thousand of us migrants, most like me with sad stories to tell but desperately attempting to run away, even if that meant crossing borders illegally.

We have gradually drifted onto a long street surrounded on either side by colorful old brick buildings. There is little sign of recent development, but the more we walk, the more the urban transformation becomes visible: modern buildings, mostly uniform in color and style but much cleaner and better organized. It is as if we are transitioning from one world to another, yet I still feel lost, as if I'd never the left the dark streets that expelled me.

Although most of the migrants appear to have come from Iraq and a smaller number from Syria, I hardly know anyone personally. I've mostly kept to myself. The only two guys I came to know when we first acquired a Belarus visa and plane ticket in Istanbul are from outside Baghdad. We've stayed together so far. We don't talk about anything other than the one and only goal on our minds: to find a way to cross the Belarus border into Poland, where the free land of the European Union awaits. Over there, there is no ISIS, no Al Qaeda, and no racial or sectarian infighting. To the many Syrian migrants around us as well, there will be no Bashar al-Assad.

Last night, we purchased SIM cards and food for the trip. My sleeping bag and my coat, which I bought back in Istanbul, should keep me warm in the freezing nights we are told await us in the forest separating Belarus and Poland. This morning, a Syrian man went around with tearful eyes, asking for money to help him purchase more insulin for his diabetic eleven-year-old son. Someone called him an idiot for risking his child's life, but the insults went right past him. He insisted and left us after securing a stash of dollar bills. I gave him a hundred-dollar bill, which reduced my reserve to only one thousand dollars. Seeing the tears of uncertainty in that man's eyes turn into tears of happiness made it all worth it.

It is now past eleven in the morning, and the local Belarusian police have stopped ignoring us and are actually helping us shepherd small groups into taxis parked at the edge of the city. They seem to be on a mission. They also appear to have done this many times. We are smoothly situated in a taxi, five of us, including the Syrian man and his son.

"I lost his mother and my two daughters during a Syrian army bombing in Aleppo," he says as soon as our eyes meet.

I don't say anything. He is sitting to my left, in the back seat and behind the driver. I keep my head down and close my eyes. The Syrian man continues. "I pray we reach safety. My son and I have seen a lot of tragedy."

The passenger in the front seat blurts out, "Can you shut up, man? We all have seen hell. Otherwise why would we be here. Just be quiet and keep to yourself and lay low to keep your son safe. Got it?"

Total silence ensues.

The Belarusian taxi driver, an elderly man with thinning gray hair, drives nonchalantly with his right hand on the steering wheel and the left extended out of the half-open window. The freezing air burns my face, and as much as I try to keep my eyes shut, I still feel winter piercing my eyelids, causing my eyes to run and my icy nostrils to drip. Who will be the hero and ask the driver to roll the window up?

We have not seen the sun for two days now. The road turns into gravel, making the drive bumpy and shaky. The driver finally grabs the steering wheel with both hands. The window, however, remains open. The cold air refuses to let go of our faces. The thick, dark, and heavy clouds overhead suddenly disappear behind the leafless trees as we enter a forest. Minutes later, the car comes to a sudden stop, and the driver motions for us to get out. We have each paid a hundred dollars for this ride. The payment was made to police officers, who claimed they would pay the driver once he had dropped us off safely and returned. It is all a scheme, but who cares? We are at the insertion point.

"One of the men points at several hundred migrants gathered under the trees in small, scattered groups. "What are these people doing there?"

"I don't know," another said. "I was told to get out of the car and keep going straight."

Soon we are on foot and heading straight into the ominous forest, where we are told it will eventually end in an open area at the border. A few hours later, we find ourselves in a large mass of people. Some have set up small tents, while others just lay on the muddy ground. While the drop-off point was eerily silent, here are the sounds of children crying, men chitchatting, and some teenagers challenging each other. I can see the edge of the barbed wire fence behind some trees in the distance but no military installations or patrol units. A middle-aged man is lying with his back against a tree and playing with an unlit cigarette. I approach him with careful steps. "How long have you been here?"

He gives me a long look, studying my clothes, and smiles. "You will soon look dirty and humiliated like the rest of us."

Now I am focused on his attire. Pants soaked with brown-and-black mud, a torn jacket, and a hat with a few spots of blood. When he adjusts his hat, I see a cut above his left ear. It is fresh and still oozing. Before I ask him again, he says, "We have been in these woods for three days now. They keep turning us back."

"Who does?" I say as I set my duffel bag on the ground and sit not too far from him, my sleeping bag still tied to my back.

"The police," he says. His accent is not Iraqi, but he is definitely a native Arabic speaker. I can't tell if he is from Syria or Lebanon.

"I thought they didn't mind us passing through!"

He shifts his body and faces me, then says with a grunt, "Sometimes they allow people to pass. Other times, they deny. Last night, they pushed us back."

I take out my water bottle, and he grabs it from me before I can open the cap. He nods with a smile as if asking me for approval. I nod back as he gulps it down to half within seconds.

"I think they're playing a game with the Poles," he says.

"Every move is calculated. We're just small bones that they throw around."

My exhaustion intensifies. I've been dragging since the day I landed in Istanbul. I can barely keep my eyes open. This man, whose name I still don't know, gives my foot a gentle kick and says, "Try to get some rest. Tonight, we're making another run for it."

Before dark, I walk around trying to find a private spot to empty my sick intestines. I find another group scattered a few hundred feet or so away. And then another and yet another. I slowly maneuver my way around the masses of people, and a hand grabs my left shoulder. I keep my pace, but the hand holds on to me with insistence and forces me to stop. I turn and find an elderly, heavyset woman speaking quickly and incoherently. She is distraught. Her voice is hoarse. I tune out the background noise so I can make out what she's saying. I know it's something in Kurdish, though I don't speak the language and only know a few words. Her wrinkled face has been ground down by suffering. She's wearing a blue scarf over her head and a thick fur jacket a few sizes too large. She stands there with bewildered eyes, out of touch with her surroundings. I greet her in Arabic, and she switches languages at once.

"Please, help me! I've lost my family!"

I look around. People are going about their business, the business of trapped migrants, as if they've been here for years. I try to avoid her pleading look, but she grabs my hand, bringing my attention back to her. "Please, mister, help me find them. I've been looking for them since early morning."

Something about this woman feels strikingly familiar. It's as if I have known her all my life. Hers is a face I have never seen before, I am sure of that, but I'm haunted by a sense of familiarity. But I'm already exhausted and have no energy left to rifle through my memories to find her in my past while dealing with her panic in the present.

All my attempts to explain to her that I have just arrived are in vain. I gently pull her to the side and try to calm her down. It's getting dark, but I don't mind. Her broken face terrifies me. I offer her some water and a piece of bread, and she sits down, shaking and crying. When she finally catches her breath, she stares at me desperately and says "My name is Gulistan. I am from Kirkuk. Do you know where that is?"

"Yes," I say. It is part of our broken Iraq, I want to say, but I decide to keep the drama at bay.

"Will you help me find my family? You are just like my son. Can you help, please?"

I inhale deeply and decide to put my lingering thoughts aside and ask her in a calming tone. "Sure, *khala*." Auntie. "I just need you to relax and tell me what happened to your family. Who are you looking for?"

She extends her legs and zips up her coat, then speaks in a more relaxed tone. "My daughter-in-law and her three kids. They are missing!"

"How are they missing?" I'm trying to keep her focused.

"I woke up this morning, and they were gone. No one seems to know where they are."

She slips into another crying jag, and I sit there, nervously playing with the cap of my water bottle, not sure what to say.

In an attempt to release the tension, I ask about her family's journey to Belarus, and my guess was correct: just like thousands of us here, they traveled via smugglers through Turkey.

I offer her some of my food and promise that I'll stay by her side until we find her family. Deep down, I hope she's psychotic, that there's no truth to her story, that she's just a lonely passenger on this lost train of migrants. It would make her less of a burden.

"What is your name, my son?" she asks between shallow breaths. "And what is your story?"

"My name is Faisal."

"Nice name," she says.

"I was named for my grandfather, who was born a hundred years ago outside Baghdad."

2

September 1921
Village of Sudah, thirty kilometers northeast of Baghdad

It had been a long day, an exhausting one, and one during which Haj Mohammad sweated more than usual. His mind was divided between his date palm farm, where he had been most of the day, and his home in the village, where his wife had been in labor since he left in the morning. She was attended to by the village *daya*, midwife, and a few other women. He couldn't stick around to offer support or comfort or even to be reassured that things would be fine. Men were not allowed to linger when women were in labor. They had to remain aloof and await word of their offspring's arrival and hope that it would be a boy. Boys! Future hands to help work the land. Future men to stand beside them and replace the men so often lost to diseases and wars.

"You look worried, Haj," one of the other farmers said as he walked past on his way to his own date palms. "It will be all right. You're acting as if this is the first time you're going to have a child."'

But this time really was different. This was not just any other pregnancy or delivery. This baby followed sorrow and trauma. Boy or girl, he didn't care. It was time for new life, and his young wife was soon going to bring it for him.

Haj Mohammad had arrived at the fields before everyone else. Since then, he channeled his anxiety and anticipation into work, and a lot of it. His fields contained at least two hundred palm trees in an area covered with thousands of them, exceeded in their number only by their counterparts deep in the south, in Basra. There were no fences or property lines. Everyone knew their own palm trees. They felt their touch and absorbed their scent. They lived with them throughout the seasons.

One farmer ordered his young son to climb a tree and check the ripe dates. A small crowd of farmers gathered to watch. The boy hesitated, then gave in to his father's orders after some thinking. Moments later, the boy was down on his back with the farmers bursting out in laughter.

"Even a mule can follow instructions better," his father said in frustration.

"I told him he needed to first stand next to the tree and let it feel his attachment," one of the men said.

"I've never even seen him walk near one," another added.

To the farmers, the palms were family members. They cared for them as they would their children, and they needed to have a special connection with trees in order to be accepted by them. They divided their time and attention between the palm trees and the orange trees, depending on the season. Now was date harvesting season.

Haj Mohammad was tall and thin with broad and prominent shoulders that seemed a mismatch to the rest of his body. He stood under a thick palm at least three times his height. He felt inconsequential next to the tree, which had survived all sorts of tragedies that had swept through the area over the years: wars, floods, diseases, migration. Haj Mohammad looked up and proudly acknowledged the sparkling dates. Their shades of yellow, brown, and orange stared down at him in reciprocal love, announcing the coming of another round of harvesting.

"Go get them, Haj," someone shouted nearby.

He pulled his long white *dishdasha* robe up to his waist and wrapped it above his pants, already brown from dirt and dust. With the harness around his midback, he approached the trunk and tightened the harness while leaving enough space to maneuver his body. At age fifty-six, he had lost a lot of his strength, but his mind was as sharp and as focused as ever.

"Let me help you," a young man said. He offered to climb up himself, but Haj Mohammad waved him away and started his ascent.

"They are my dates, and it's my job to harvest them," he said with pride. A faint line of dust obscured the top of his vision—his bushy eyebrows were caked in the stuff. "But you can stand under the tree and catch what I throw down."

Carefully adjusting his bare feet against the trunk and with the machete strapped to his back, he grabbed the triangular-shaped protrusions of bark and pulled himself up. After harvesting the dates this week, he would load them on mules and take them to the banks of the Tigris, where boats would take them to Baghdad to be packaged and shipped overseas. Each farmer claimed that his dates carried a special taste from one original seed that no one else had. All were equally convinced that both their date orchards and orange orchards had superior soil and the finest farming and harvesting traditions.

"Ten minutes later, Haj Mohammad cut the fifth stalk of ripe dates and was preparing to drop it to the young man below when another breathless young man came running. "Haj, Haj, your wife gave birth to a boy!"

He lost his grip on the stack of dates and watched it fall to the dusty ground and break and scatter to pieces. He slid down and ran toward the boy. Panting from the sprint he had made all the way from the village, the child said, "My mother sent me to deliver the news."

He was the midwife's son and surely wouldn't leave without some reward. Haj Mohammad handed him whatever money he had in his pocket, and the boy disappeared quickly, probably in case Haj Mohammad changed his mind about his generosity.

A few nearby farmers dropped what they were doing and gathered around Haj Mohammad, congratulating him from all directions.

There was something different about this particular birth and for this particular man. He had endured an entire village's share of loss and misery. Many years ago he'd moved back to the village from the city after losing his first wife and two daughters to a cholera epidemic that swept through Baghdad, killing tens of thousands of people. Years later, he lost his son, and only after the terror at the thought of living his entire life alone did he decide to remarry.

To the dozen or so men gathered under the palm trees, Haj Mohammad personified hope and perseverance. He had endured what they could scarcely imagine, and they seemed determined to make this moment a memorable one for him.

Next to a stream of water that cut through the palm orchard to bring water and life from the Tigris a half kilometer away, the men sat and enjoyed tea and some leftover bread from lunch.

One of the men turned to Haj Mohammad and said, "*Qurrat ainak.*" Let him be the light of your eyes.

Another refilled his tea glass and announced, "Lunch on me tomorrow. I will slaughter a sheep right here next to this water to celebrate our dear brother's son."

During the chitchat, Haj Mohammad mostly reflected on his life since returning to the village, not only his own inner turmoil but the turmoil in the outer world that crashed over him and his fellow Iraqis at the same time, the rocky transition between two eras: the collapse of the storied Ottoman Empire in the aftermath of the First World War followed by the British invasion and occupation.

"So, what are you going to call him?"

The question caught him off guard, pulling him back into the gathering. "Faisal. I'll name him Faisal!"

He sounded like someone who had contemplated his decision ahead of time. Knowing somebody would ask him why he chose that name, Haj Mohammad beat them to it and declared, "I will name him after our new king."

The previous weeks had been filled with celebration as the public anxiously lived through the first chapter of their brand-new country with the crowning of King Faisal, the first monarch of modern Iraq. But alongside the excitement were skepticism and dread.

"How can we be excited for a ruler who is not even from Iraq?" one of the farmers said. "A Hashemite from Hejaz!"

A young boy behind the row of men said, "He is from the family tree of the Prophet Mohammad."

His father yelled at him without even looking. "Who asked your opinion? When the grown-ups speak, you keep your mouth shut."

Haj Mohammad looked at the man with annoyance. "Let the boy talk. He's telling the truth. Our king is a descendant from Hasan, the grandson of the Prophet, peace and blessings be upon him, and royalty of Arabia."

The father gave his son an evil stare for weakening his own argument. "And brought to us by the British."

The debate continued with one side arguing that a person from outside Iraq 'didn't belong and others believing that a man with such a noble family lineage and experience with administration and leadership was just what Iraq needed now that the Ottomans had retreated.

The sun was gradually sinking below the horizon, and the meeting was brought to an end with Haj Mohammad declaring, "By the grace of Allah, we will stand behind our King Faisal and hope for times of prosperity and unity. I believe in him."

Someone laughed. "I hope you're not expecting the king to hire you as an adviser for naming your son after him."

There were chuckles all around as everyone but Haj Mohammed rose and headed through the dense, cooling orchard toward home.

Haj Mohammad remained behind in the orchard to clean up, and the others were long gone before he was finally ready to go home. The palm trees were looming shadows in the blackness. He maneuvered between them, keeping his eyes focused on the light of a small fire at the edge of the village. The darkness took him back to the night a British soldier killed his first son, the only thing still connecting him to his first wife. That was less than two years ago, and it didn't happen far from where Haj Mohammad was walking. His son was an infant when he brought him home from Baghdad in 1898, days after the disease killed the mother only a few hours after giving birth and less than a week after both of their daughters were taken by the illness as well.

Haj Mohammad was born near Sudah, and his family had later moved to Baghdad. But when disease took his family and left him with only an infant son, he had to return to the enchanted land of his forefathers to heal his sorrow and replace his loss.

He'd watched his son grow and saw in him every bit of his lost family in Baghdad. He took pride in watching him enlist with the volunteer army during the Great Revolution against the Ottomans, pushed and encouraged by the Brits, who promised the Arabs a country of their own. It was King Faisal's father who was fooled and played, of course, but Haj Mohammad never felt that his son's efforts or the efforts of thousands of other volunteer fighters were wasted until two years ago when two British soldiers passing through the village flirted with a local girl and tried to touch her. The scene outraged the villagers. Haj Mohammad's son, twenty years old at the time, jumped one of the soldiers and stabbed him in the arm. Before anyone could intervene, the other soldier shot the young man dead before running away and disappearing.

Haj Mohammad's world collapsed around him, and his rage against the English was born and continued to brew. But then he married Batul from the neighboring village and vowed to continue his lineage on the land of orange orchards and palm groves.

She was beautiful and young, more than thirty-five years younger than Haj Mohammad. From the first day, Batul was determined to erase the sorrow from her husband's face. While she was mostly unsuccessful at healing her husband from the inside, she did manage to get him to smile again, especially when she told him she was pregnant.

Haj Mohammad continued his hurried walk home with a

timid smile on his face in the darkness on the narrow trail. He couldn't wait to meet Faisal, the new king of the house and the hope that had appeared among the ruins of what had been a vanished life. He had not told Batul about the name he had chosen, but he was sure she would like it. As much as he had reassured her that he would be as happy with a girl as he would with a boy, he knew she would embrace him at the door with joy on her face.

3

Belarus

In the middle of Gulistan's frenzy last night, I found myself backing slowly into the crowd under the trees. Temperatures dropped precipitously after midnight, and it wasn't until we lit a fire that I was able to warm up enough to get a short nap. This morning, Gulistan woke up anxious and edgy, as if a switch had been turned on in her head.

"It was around this time yesterday when I woke up and my grandkids and their mother were gone," she says in a broken voice as she inspects every face that comes and goes.

I have a feeling she has not told me the full story, but I'm not about to dig deeper into her fragile mind. I have serious doubts about what she's saying to start with. Now she's barging into nearby makeshift tents, sticking her head inside with total disregard for privacy. A woman yells from inside a small tent, and Gulistan pulls her head out nervously. I stand there watching as she sits in the mud and weeps.

A man sitting nearby stares at her with contempt on his

face. "I've seen you yell at that poor young woman and berate her so many times that I'm not surprised she picked up her kids and left you and your vile mouth."

And just like that, my hope of Gulistan's story being a bout of psychosis evaporates. I quietly withdraw to the opposite side of the camp and try to find a signal for my phone.

"What are you trying to do?" a man asks as I wave the phone in the air.

"I can't seem to get an internet connection here."

He approaches and leans over to look at my screen. With a chuckle, he says, "Whoever sold you the SIM robbed you. You don't get internet coverage with this service."

After a few unsuccessful international call attempts, the phone indicates insufficient funds. Most of the people have packed up by now, folded their tents and sleeping bags, and gotten themselves ready for another attempt to cross the fenced border.

Two young men are standing in front of me and speaking in Kurdish. I approach them and ask in Arabic how long they've been here. One of them turns and gives me a puzzled expression, but the other one slowly says without looking, "We've tried to cross to the other side of the forest for three days now. It seems the police are selective in who they allow to pass through."

"I don't understand," I say.

A few drops of rain hit my face, and I look up. The sun is beginning to appear from behind the clouds. Maybe today we'll have some good luck.

"The young man gives me a dismissive look. "What is it you don't understand?"

I get closer and whisper, hoping it will ease the tension a bit. "I figured that since the police rounded us up back in Minsk and sent us here that we'd be free to go."

The other young man, who seemingly doesn't speak Arabic, says something I don't understand. His partner soon produces a cigarette and hands it to me. I take it from him, although I don't smoke. I keep the cigarette in my hand, hoping to fit in, still waiting for a response.

He seems annoyed. "Man, you seem lost. This is a political game. They're using us to mess with the Polish forces. All I know is that we're about to make a run for it."

Gulistan suddenly appears behind me again. How is it possible that among this mass of people, many of whom speak her language, she's managed to find her comfort only in me? I reassure her that I will help her to the best of my abilities just as long as she stops creating a scene.

It suddenly hits me, and hits me hard: my mother! *Mama!* *Yumma!* This woman reminds me of her, of her scent, her energy, her looks, her heart, and her eyes. A flood of emotions overtakes me when I notice Gulistan take her thick coat off, revealing her black dress underneath. She is *Mother* wearing layers of black over her aged body, her heart carrying more layers of sorrow while her eyes are draped with thick layers of sadness. Gulistan is probably double the size of *Mama*, but every footstep of hers and every facial expression reminds me of her. *Yumma!* How much I have missed you. How much I would love to fall in your arms now and feel like a little kid all over again. Gulistan gently pulls my shoulder before I step into a mud puddle and says, "Are you OK, my son?"

No, I am not OK. I am broken into pieces all over again.

We start our walk out of the woods and into the open area again. Some five hundred feet or so later, the trail leads to a narrow road that's covered with small ponds of mud. What we thought was the beginning of the border fence is only partially true. The fence overlooks a steep hill that's impossible to cross without risking a fall down at least a few hundred feet. There is no way we can cross from here. How stupid of us to think the border fence would be abandoned like that. So we decide to continue our walk on the dirt road. Every few minutes we pass pockets of clearly exhausted people. I do my best to avoid interaction with Gulistan, especially when she aggressively approaches new groups of people and asks them about her missing family.

A dozen or more Belarusian soldiers appear in front of us, pointing guns in our direction. The crowd gradually comes to a stop, forcing the armed men to take a few steps back before finally standing firm. A few moments pass, then another group of soldiers appears, followed by a few dozen migrants who look as frustrated and as worn-out as we do. The soldiers round us up in a circle, and one of them yells in English for us to turn around and start walking back where we came from. With the guns pointed at us, we have no choice but to obey and get moving.

Walking behind us, the soldiers engage in conversations among themselves, often giggling and nonchalantly messing around with total disregard for our sense of urgency. Periodically, a loud voice comes through a walkie-talkie barking orders in a language we don't comprehend. Soon, a small military truck shows up in front of us and without coming to a complete stop makes a sharp turn. The driver extends his hand out the window and motions for us to follow him across a narrow road covered with gravel and mud. He eventually leads us to a large warehouse at least three hundred feet long. The walls appear to be metal painted with a variety of military signs and other foreign writing. Inside the warehouse, dozens of rows of empty metal shelves extend along the length of the walls and in the center. The air is freezing, making each breath feel labored. We disperse through the walkways, passing hundreds of other migrants who seem to have settled on the bare concrete floor.

Of course, Gulistan is by my side, and of course she recognizes someone here. She rushes toward a woman sitting next to three young children and a man. She asks her about her grandkids, but the woman shakes her head. She returns and says, "This family was staying close to us the night before my family disappeared. They didn't see them leave. I don't understand how four people can just vanish. God, oh God!"

I motion for Gulistan to sit down, and I address her straight: "You have to tell me more about your family and what happened if you want me to believe your story and to help you search for them."

She coils with her back against a metal post. She's shivering, which only makes me feel colder. Freezing air continues to flow into the warehouse through the wide-open door.

"I had a disagreement with my daughter-in-law, and she got mad at me."

"*Khala*, people don't just pack up and abandon family members over simple disagreements." She is hesitant to tell me more, so I try a different angle. "How many grandkids do you have?"

"Three. One girls and two boys. The youngest is sick. She's the reason we're here to start with. I told her we should never have taken this wild journey, but she never listens."

I'm sucked into the world of mother-in-law and daughter-in-law, the eternally challenged relationship that leaves so many boundaries unset and so many expectations unsettled. Our conversation is abruptly brought to a halt when two men in the opposite aisle get into an argument that leads to fist fighting and intervention from the guards. The warehouse is suddenly filled with armed men who secure every corner by parading with pointed guns. At least the front door is finally shut, and the wind is blocked from our tired bodies.

Over the next three days, more unfortunate people like us are rounded up and forced into the warehouse. The Belarusian officials, much to our surprise, provide regular meals in addition to blankets and other supplies. People find opportunities to connect more, share stories, and bond. While we started off as a fragmented group full of traumatized individuals, we bond over our common struggle and a willingness to listen to each other and help those in dire need. During this time, I dig deeper into Gulistan's story. She confesses to accusing her daughter-in-law of providing sexual favors to a relative of hers back home in exchange for arranging their travel and fake documents.

"He was her lover before she married my son. Everyone knew he wanted her and was courting her. I told my son to find someone else, but he was hell-bent on her." Gulistan's eyes tear up again. There is so much pain behind those nervously twitching eyelids and so much trauma etched into her wrinkled face.

I mull over my next question for some time, then decide to let it out without looking at her. "Where is your son?"

She sobs and faces me. It is her way of forcing me to listen to her heart and not just her words. In a broken voice, she says, "My boy, my son, my only child was killed in the war against ISIS."

She coughs and draws a deep breath. I managed to compartmentalize my trauma and sorrow and set it all aside, but since I met this lady a few days ago, all the chaos I left behind has come rushing back into my mind. She erupts into a bout of violent coughing, and with her face covered by the right sleeve of her jacket, she gently grabs my shoulder with her left hand and asks, "How about you, son?"

What about me? I remain silent, hoping she isn't too curious. "Where is your family? What is your story?"

I sigh and sit up when I spot two guards pushing a large
cart full of boxed meals. For the next hour or so and over a
cold, old, and uninviting meal amid the freezing air of the
warehouse, I answer the barrage of questions Gulistan asks
about my family and background. I am from Baghdad. I come
from an Iraqi family that was shaken up by war, hatred, injus-
tice, and cruelty. We are no different from thousands of other
Iraqi families interwoven in a web of misfortune, sorrow,
letdowns, and conflict for generations. I would rather learn
more about Gulistan's son and how he was killed. It was either
that or tell her how my own shattered like a vase thrown at a
wall.

4

Sudah was a village of less than three hundred citizens. All sixteen homes were made of clay and lined up across from each other in two parallel rows. In its current location, the village was not near any main pathways or on any secondary roads. Most villagers maintained cottages between the village and the palm tree orchards.

Five decades earlier, the village was elsewhere and had a different name. Elders gave accounts of two disasters that happened within two years. First, a major Tigris flood swept through, uprooting homes and killing half the population. When they made efforts to rebuild it, a wave of typhoid hit the area and killed most of the rest, with the exception of a few families. That was when the survivors decided to move the site of the village away from the reach of the Tigris. And to keep the dark memories alive, they named the village *Sudah*, The Black.

Haj Mohammad was not there when these events took place, but 'his ancestors had lived in the previous village, and when he moved back from Baghdad, the new location was proving to be a source of more stability and prosperity. When he landed in the village as a widower with his infant son, he was well received and embraced. A distant relative helped him raise his son until she passed away. There was a lot of land to claim and a sea of palm trees to attend to, and the land belonged to whoever cared for it. That was the idea that drew ownership. And so Haj Mohammad easily slipped into his new life in Sudah and claimed his share of the land with the treasures of palm and orange trees.

Sudah maintained easy access to the Tigris for transportation, but it remained a hidden jewel. There was no mosque in the village, but the neighboring village was less than a kilometer away with a larger population and a deeper history. That was where Haj Mohammad later married Batul.

Though he quickly developed a personal connection to his land, something still called him to Baghdad. As much as he tried to put it behind him, the city continued to haunt him. During those first years of King Faisal's rule, he kept up with news about development projects in the big cities of Baghdad and Basra and to some extent Mosul. New roads were being opened and bridges built. There was continuous talk of expansion projects to cut new roads through the rural areas, such as their village, and connect them with the surrounding cities.

When the main road was built along the Tigris and the outskirts of Sudah, one of the citizens of a nearby village opened a small hut on the roadside. He started by bringing basic home supplies from the city, then developed a business exchanging crops for those goods and taking them to the city to sell for large profits. The man knew how to read, so he always kept copies of newspapers he brought back with him from Baghdad. He hung them on the wall, but no one ever bought them or asked about them. Few knew how to read, and even fewer showed interest in reading.

Haj Mohammad soon became a regular customer. He didn't know how to read either, but he made weekly trips to the market, mostly in search of anything that would resonate with his connection to the city. He stood by the door of the shop and stared at the newspaper pictures and highlights.

"What's the latest news?" he asked the shopkeeper.

The man laughed and shoved the newspaper at him, knowing Haj Mohammad couldn't understand a word. The images, though, intrigued him. Eventually the shop owner said, "Come on in. Let me read you the news over glasses of tea." Tea was the magical pleasantry.

It was Haj Mohammad's way of staying in touch with city life. It was also his way of measuring the progress of King Faisal's rule.

"Your favorite king is making strides, and I'm sure you're proud," the shopkeeper often said after a lengthy reading session. He was deeply invested in the new era and what it had to offer for a land torn by war, diseases, and lack of political identity.

Haj Mohammad always looked at his son Faisal when he wanted to appreciate the progress of young Iraq. The boy had turned nine, and Haj Mohammad felt he could remember every day of those previous years. His son meant the world to him, and he was determined not to let anything take him away. Not this time. He couldn't afford to lose another child, now his only child. Batul had given up on having another after six failed pregnancies. She initially wanted to keep trying, but the village women persuaded her that the spirit of her husband's first wife was swarming around and thwarting her. Just one child was all she was entitled to. Just one to give Haj Mohammad something to look up to. Anything more would be a luxury, they said, and Haj Mohammad was not entitled to luxuries.

~

Haj Mohammad finished eating his early lunch and insisted that Faisal go with him to visit the shop despite the boy's pleas to stay behind and play with his friends. The children were going to swim in the Tigris that afternoon, which was even more reason for Haj Mohammad to keep his son by his side. He could not risk losing him to drowning or any other accident from careless childhood games.

Faisal was nine, but he often said he felt five because of the way his father treated him. He was the best-dressed kid in the village, and boys often mocked him for being a weak, spoiled brat. He often complained to his mother, unhappily asking for freedom. Batul took every opportunity to allow Faisal to go out and play with the boys, but she was also afraid. Her husband had warned her that he would divorce her on the spot if something ever happened to his son due to her carelessness.

The shop owner was taking a nap when Haj Mohammad and Faisal arrived. In the far distance, the soft and wavy Tigris positively glowed in the sunlight. The water moved quickly enough to carry boats, but it was not forceful enough to overturn them. Faisal's white dishdasha still looked neat and spotless even after nearly a two-kilometer walk. He observed the Tigris from afar, and Haj Mohammad could tell that the boy wished he was there by the river, half naked and barefoot and jumping in to swim with his friends.

"Wake up, lazy man!" Haj Mohammad yelled.

The shop owner 'didn't depend on foot traffic. His presence was more for the establishment of the franchise as the original and still main source of villagers' contact with the city beyond the Tigris River. He adjusted himself in the wooden chair and frowned. "Old man, you're disturbing my afternoon nap. Don't you have anything better to do?"

Haj Mohammad stepped inside and motioned for his son to follow him into the shade. He inspected the shop for any new products and said, "I'm here to pick up the soap my wife asked for."

The shop owner shook his head in disappointment. "The shipment hasn't come yet. But ... here, I have something you'll like." He stood and walked to the back of the store and picked up a rolled newspaper and opened it.

"Here." He pointed at the front page and said, "Fresh news you will like. Have a seat!"

Iraqi newspapers were black and white in both writing and content. Articles either majestically praised the king or fiercely criticized his shortcomings. They looked at new events as extremely hopeful or terrifying and dire. There was no in between, no reasonable middle ground. Haj Mohammad yearned for progress, but he felt nearly alone among a small minority of Iraqis in a sea of people polarized with extreme ideologies and positions.

The man sat back down and started reading the top story on the front page. Every corner of that page had something to say about the recent developments in the ongoing struggles with the British: scattered violent clashes, organized protests, and openly voiced disapproval of their presence. King Faisal had finally been able to reach an agreement with British officials to allow Iraq limited independence from their direct rule, but the writing was as much on the wall as it was on the front page of the paper: Iraq would continue to be under indirect control of the Brits.

The shop owner put the paper down and grinned. "Isn't it funny?"

"Isn't what funny?" Haj Mohammad asked.

"How naive Shareef Husain, the father of our king, was to believe the promise of the *Engleez* for Iraq's independence from the Ottomans only to then become a colony of the Brits. They're even stranger than the Ottomans. It's just stupid and funny that we're now celebrating getting only partial freedom from them."

This man came from a family with deep roots in the Ottoman civil offices in Baghdad. Naturally his opinion would be skewed, but even Haj Mohammad recognized the irony. And yet there was progress. There was hope. Sparks of it. That was all he really wanted. It kept his dreams alive and going.

He turned to Faisal and said, "Son, let's go. If we stay here any longer, this man will make me change your name."

The shop owner chuckled and gave Faisal a small, wrapped cookie. "It's filled with dates," he said. "From a recently opened factory. Another one of King Faisal's achievements."

Haj Mohammad couldn't tell if the man was being sarcastic. While Faisal ate the cookie, the owner picked up the newspaper again and turned to the middle, where he located a small article in fine print. He pressed his finger on it. "This, right here, is something you should not be proud of the king for. Taking land away from the farmers and giving it to the feudal lords."

Haj Mohammad thought of a large house near their village on the banks of the Tigris. The owner was a mysterious man who liked to be called Bul Khair, the father of blessings.

Bul Khair had risen in power after the coming of the king and somehow built a name for himself as the leader of a dozen or so villages on the west side of the river. He had power, men, and money. He showed up in the area one day with orders from the government to manage the land and its crops. At first, he sold himself as a facilitator and promised to help the farmers get what they needed. He vowed to help them efficiently get their crops to the city and outside the country and with a better return. But that's not what happened. A few years later, he had total control of the land and micromanagement of the returns. Farmers saw little of what their land produced. Bul Khair's men were in every village, and they made sure that everyone followed orders.

As Haj Mohammad waved goodbye, the man yelled, "Tell you what, Haj. If you enroll your kid in school, he could learn to read, and that way you won't need to put up with my negative opinions." He was chuckling and probably not being serious, but Haj Mohammad stopped and turned. He thought to himself for a few seconds, then said, "There are no schools around here. The nearest is three kilometers walking."

"They opened one on the other side of the river. My sons are going. They'll be taking the boat."

"No, thanks. I am not going to make my son risk crossing the Tigris twice a day for some education I know little about."

"It is the education your favorite King Faisal has initiated." He smiled with his usual sarcasm.

Haj Mohammad cleared his throat. "I am not sending my son to government schools unless they open one in the village." He grabbed his son's hand, and as they started walking he said to him, "But I will send you to the next-door village where you will learn reading and writing at the hands of the imam."

But Batul convinced him to enroll Faisal in the government school across the river, and it only took her one night to do so. She would ride the boat with him back and forth every day and would guarantee his safety as long as she was alive.

5

1932
Village of Sudah

The place that sparked Faisal's passion for learning soon became his sanctuary. He walked in his free time, with or without a reason. He took his books to the shop and read. When his homework was finished, he asked the owner for a newspaper. He started by staring at the pictures, fascinated by the prestige of King Faisal and the royal presence in the various images, some of them amid the background of political struggle. He grimaced with hatred at images of British soldiers and officials.

Faisal didn't fully comprehend the reason for his father's utter disdain for the *Engleez*, but he knew there were valid reasons. Haj Mohammad was the kindest man, and if he hated you, it was probably your fault.

Men in the village often beat their wives and children, taking out their frustration on their helpless families. Not Haj Mohammad. Faisal's father lovingly and caringly attended to his wife's needs. He never laid hands on her. Nor did he even once yell at Faisal. And yet he hated the English. The contradiction gave Faisal yet another reason to learn how to read, so he could learn enough to understand his father's hatred of foreign men.

"The *Engleez* and the French made the Sykes-Picot agreement to divide our land and our hearts," the shopkeeper told him. Faisal didn't fully understand what that meant, but it was enough to know that the agreement, whatever it was, was not good for the land or its people.

One afternoon, Faisal came home carrying a newspaper.

"Where have you been all day, son?" his father asked.

"Why do you make us worry about you?" his mother added from the small open kitchen.

Faisal sat across from his father while his mother remained in the kitchen washing dishes but presumably listening closely. He unfolded the newspaper and pointed to an article with a large image of King Faisal in his neat, white military uniform and a circular helmet, his right hand grasping a sword. Faisal placed his index finger on the first word of the article and started reading aloud. Haj Mohammad listened and watched without breathing.

"Our son is actually reading the newspaper for us!" his mother shouted from the kitchen." "Congratulations, Haj."

School had indeed paid off.

According to the article, Iraq had officially declared independence from Britain. Faisal's father wept happy tears. Faisal understood this much at least. Not only had Faisal the king liberated Iraq from the British, Faisal the young village boy had liberated his father from the shopkeeper.

On a hot September day in 1933, Faisal returned home exhausted from swimming in the Tigris River with his friends. His mother had begged him to spend only a brief time there and come back before his father returned. He saw his father hurry out of the house without even looking at him. That was unusual. Almost stunning. What was going on?

His mother appeared.

"What happened? Baba looked upset!"

"Oh, my son. He is very upset. They're saying King Faisal passed away from an illness."

Faisal froze in place, unsure how to process the news or his father's reaction. He turned around when he heard two men rush past their house. One repeatedly yelled "King Faisal, King Faisal!"

"Go check on the news, son, and come back to me with details," his mother said. "Everything you hear and see." She sent him on his way with a pat on his back.

He hurried until he was a few feet behind the two men and followed them down the road to the largest house in the village. It was isolated from the rest of the homes as a statement of superiority. It belonged to Bul Khair's right-hand man, the lord's fist in this village and its surroundings. A group of villagers gathered in front of the house, and the news of the passing of King Faisal was confirmed by the tears of women and the broken faces of men. Faisal's father was there too, visibly upset, perhaps the saddest of them all.

They spend an entire evening in front of that house discussing the era of the first king of modern Iraq.

"We'll hold a memorial here tomorrow to mourn the passing of our beloved king," said the owner of the house. He spoke slowly for emphasis. When the crowd began to disperse, he raised his voice and added, "Our village will be honored to host our beloved Bul Khair at our funeral gathering."

Faisal's father accompanied him to the funeral the next day. Faisal wanted to see inside the big house he often walked past but never dared scrutinize. Being the only structure with stone walls and large windows, it silently screamed of status and power not to be reckoned with. The home belonged to someone important, his mother always told him.

Inside, men were engaged in casual chatter. Faisal timidly took a seat next to his father in the far corner of the guest room.

He scanned it with a hesitant gaze, realizing the room alone was larger than his family's entire house.

"Is Bul Khair here?" Faisal whispered to his father while scanning the faces of the men.

"Be quiet, son," his father replied while gently pushing against his shoulder.

"The big man," the man to Faisal's left said, "is not coming."

There was going to be meat, and a lot of it, and who would want to miss that? Enough food was being prepared outside to feed everyone in the village. Faisal's father told him to go with the rest of the young men and help get everything ready. When the men were invited to start the feast, Faisal found himself left out. The circle of men grew larger and tighter, and he was gradually pushed to the back, near where the food was being prepared. He stood there for a few minutes until his father noticed him and called for him to come and sit next to him. Before Faisal moved, the house's owner yelled for another plate of meat. Faisal was close to the food prep area, so he headed that way.

Two hands held out a steaming plate of meat. Faisal's eyes followed those hands to the eyes of a young girl. He grabbed the plate and held on to it while the girl's eyes lingered on his. It happened in moments: her watery eyes twisted his stomach into a knot. Faisal had never experienced anything like it. Never had he seen such beauty.

He dropped the plate upside down on the ground. He

faintly heard his father calling his name and a woman's voice calling out, "Maryam! What happened? Did you drop the plate?"

Faisal the king may have died, but Faisal the village kid had experienced some kind of birth. There was only one complication: Maryam was the daughter of Bul Khair's right-hand man. Faisal couldn't eat. Not one bite even though there was more than enough meat to stuff him full twice.

Every time he closed his eyes that night, he saw the girl. Maryam, the tall village girl with beautiful brown hair to her waist, had swept Faisal off his feet more swiftly than the mighty Tigris could sweep house away during a flood year. He could not purge her deep black eyes from his mind.

For almost a year, Faisal only saw Maryam from afar. One day, she randomly appeared at their house with a plate of dates and cookies from her family. It was the first day of Eid. Faisal felt his face flush hot.

After she left, his mother smile and said, "Do you think she's pretty?"

He wanted to say yes, to speak like a man who knows when he's in love, but he was only thirteen, and he remained silent and squirreled himself away from his mother's attention.

After that, he made a point of walking past Maryam's house over and over again until he saw her. When their eyes met, they exchanged looks of innocent admiration, but that was the extent of their interaction for another two years.

6

Sudah
1930s

Faisal's father loved Baghdad and visited any time he could think of a reason. The roads were more accessible now thanks to the infrastructure work started during the reign of King Faisal. When the shopkeeper with the newspaper passed away, his children lost interest in the business, so it was time for someone else to manage the transport. Boats were more sophisticated now and had greater capacity. Trucks also facilitated the movement of goods into and out of the city.

Everything had to go through Bul Khair's right-hand man, who also happened to be Maryam's father. Faisal watched his own father follow orders in broken spirits and vent barrages of insults in the friendlier waters of Baghdad. Yet Faisal felt joy at the mention of anything and anyone that reminded him of Maryam.

Every time they went to the city together, they got off the boat, unloaded their goods, made the exchanges, and declared what needed to be taken back to the village. He and his father then took strolls around the city. Walking over the shaky wooden bridge spanning the Tigris proved to be the beginning of every fun trip in Baghdad. It was not clear whose feelings were stronger, his father's longing for the city or his own fascination with everything new in a world he so much wanted to fully absorb and make his own. Faisal envied the boys he saw running around the busy alleys of Baghdad and swarming between cars, even those who were barefoot, dirty, and wearing torn clothes. He so wished he could trade places with them even though he was better clothed and almost certainly better fed.

One of his father's favorites stops was a coffee shop on the other side of the river. Men gathered there at all times of the day and early in the evenings to sip hot coffee and tea while sharing and arguing about the latest political news. His father liked to show off by handing Faisal a newspaper and having him read it.

Most of the regulars at the café were happy with the progress the country was making, but they dreaded foreign interference that always seemed to hover above the horizon. And it seemed like every time Faisal visited Baghdad, there were new faces in the various government cabinets.

One afternoon while they were walking down Al Rasheed Road, Faisal heard an angry voice over a nearby radio. "Dignified people, we *must* acknowledge the grave threat to our nation from the British Empire. It is time for us, the Arabs, to unite as one hand to stand up for the rights of all Arabs, especially the Palestinians who are being driven out of their land."

Faisal walked alongside his father as he took in the charged words from the radio. His father handed him half a piece of warm cake he had bought from a nearby stand, and before Faisal took a bite, he asked, "Who is the man yelling through the radio?"

"That is King Ghazi, the son of the late beloved King Faisal."

Faisal knew about King Ghazi but had never heard his voice. He didn't think it would be possible to randomly hear the king speak so casually and nonchalantly on a radio station.

"He has a habit of taking to the microphone and speaking his mind," his father said as he swallowed the last bit of cake and looked around for a place to get some water.

Faisal asked if Iraqis liked King Ghazi the same way they adored his father.

"We love our King Ghazi, but he will never be at the level of his father."

Faisal also wanted to know why there were so many new people at the top of the government and why the king allowed such instability.

"Because the country is moving forward, people think more intelligently and demand more than they used to."

During their repeated visits to Baghdad, Faisal often spotted protests, large and small, in various parts of the city, and he wondered what it meant that so many people were voicing displeasure about their miserable living conditions.

His father took his hand, pulling him in the opposite direction, and said, "Those are misled, stupid people. The king has enemies, many within the military ranks, who would benefit from disrupting the rule of law in our kingdom and open the gates for the *Engleez* to ride again on our backs." Faisal tried his best to absorb his father's words as he continued what sounded more like a rant. "When the people who divided our land come back to undermine the king, he has no choice but to work with new allies, even Adolf Hitler in Germany."

Faisal was fascinated every time he spotted a military truck or a uniformed soldier. There were more of them lately, and when Faisal asked why, his father told him that King Ghazi came up in the army and believed that a powerful armed force was key to Iraq's future.

W hen Faisal finished elementary school, the only school in their rural area, he asked his father if he could continue his education in Baghdad, but his father bluntly refused. It was not up for discussion. They had no relatives or close friends in Baghdad. The idea of a fourteen-or fifteen-year-old boy moving from the village to live alone in the big city was totally unaccepatable no matter how many other families allowed it. Not even Faisal's mother could change his mind.

So Faisal had to content himself, at least for the time being, with furthering his education at the mosque school in his mother's village. He had nearly finished memorizing the Quran and had studied over a dozen books of Arabic poetry, language rules, and Islamic teachings. The imam told him he could earn a certificate to give religious sermons in a few years if he remained focused. Faisal, however, wanted more. He wanted the city life in Baghdad, the same city his father so often longed for.

Crops were down in both quality and quantity. Faisal's father was one of many farmers frustrated with the crushing control Bul Khair imposed over every detail of farming, from planting and harvesting to selling and returns. On October 29, 1936, Faisal and his father arrived in Baghdad by boat with a fresh harvest of dates, and they noticed that the bridge was almost deserted. Streets were empty of shoppers and merchants alike. On every corner and in every direction they looked, they saw an unusually heavy military presence. Two soldiers angrily approached, and one of them barked out orders: "Leave everything behind and get off the streets."

This was no time to ask questions or delay following orders. Fierce punishment would certainly follow. So they hurried to the nearby warehouse where the owner was expecting their date harvest. They would not leave for two days.

General Bakr Sidqi had overthrown Prime Minister Yasin al-Hashimi and his government. Faisal tried his best to keep up with the fast-moving and often contradictory news. They were saying King Ghazi was indirectly behind the coup, but why? Why would the king support a military coup against a ministry cabinet he had originally approved?

"You still have a long way to go, my son," his father kept saying.

Once the army loosened civilian restrictions, Faisal and his father returned to their boat and made their way back up the river toward their village. And Faisal kept asking questions.

"Yasin al-Hashimi has been attempting to undermine the role of the king and the army," his father told him. "He was sowing chaos and undermining the rule of law. Ousting him was the right thing to do."

Faisal had kept a collection of newspapers from each of his visits to Baghdad. He'd managed to collect multiple photos of both King Faisal and King Ghazi in military uniforms, and he hung them on the worn-out clay wall of his bedroom using sharp wooden sticks. He also flipped through papers, hoping to find the photo of a girl that looked like Maryam so he could hide under his blanket and stare at it each time he thought of her, but the newspapers only showed well-dressed and serious-looking men from the military and government.

7

1930s

As Maryam's body became more mature, Faisal's fascination only grew stronger. Neither of them ever dared more than smile from a distance. Her pronounced cheekbones turned red every time she saw him stealing a look.

They did not speak to each other. Boys speaking with girls outside their immediate families were considered outlaws and risked a beating from anyone on the street.

Faisal stared at the dark walls of his room at night and swore that he loved her. She was in all his dreams, day and night. He was certain she was fascinated by him as well, but he couldn't understand why. She was pretty, the prettiest girl on earth. He was just another village boy.

Nearly everyone spoke of Maryam's beauty. It was a remarkable thing. Her father, though, was as nasty and ugly-hearted as she was pretty.

One day, Faisal was walking with three other boys when he spotted Maryam among a dozen or so women and young girls near the clay fire pit used to bake bread. Kids usually gathered around, waiting for their share of warm flatbread. Older boys typically found it unworthy of their time and status to just stand there, but Faisal didn't care. Not this time. Not with fire reflecting in Maryam's black eyes.

She used her stick to grab some hot bread and wave it around with a wide smile. One of the boys next to Faisal elbowed him, wickedly urging him to make a move for it. None of the other women were paying attention, or at least that's what Faisal wanted to think, so he slowly walked toward Maryam for what must have felt like an eternity to her. She almost gave up and took it away before Faisal finally confronted his fear and took the bread without even daring to look at her. He forgot all about his friends. That part of the world no longer existed. He hurried back toward home, silently playing a popular song in his head.

> *Um Al Eyoon Al Sood Majoozan Ana*
> Bearer of the two black eyes I am overtaken
> *Khaddikil Qaimar Wana Atrayag Mina*
> I would rather have your cheek as breakfast
> *Min Wara el Tanoor et Nawishni el Regheef*
> From behind the pit she offers me a loaf
> *Ya Ragheef el Hilwa Yekfeeni Sana*
> A loaf from my love is enough for a year

Faisal realized that his parents knew he liked Maryam. She'd certainly passed the eye test, and she was kind and thoughtful enough to knock on their door just to say hello and ask if his mother needed anything.

There was just one big problem: his father detested her

father. Faisal didn't dare mention her name around him, nor did his mother. They all seemed to understand that there was no way Maryam's father would ever agree to let a mere village boy marry his daughter. Faisal and his mother also realized that the man of their house, as simple a farmer as he was, had too much pride to allow himself to beg the powerful man of the village to accept the marriage of Maryam to Faisal.

Girls were marrying quickly in the village, and parents were rushing to establish new young families to maintain their claims over land. The girls were almost always younger than the boys. Most of them at the age of seventeen and eighteen could run an entire house. Faisal was seventeen, and many of his friends had weddings coming up.

Faisal wanted to tell his parents about his interest in Maryam, but he couldn't. His mother had hinted at it a few times, but Faisal remained silent. His mother even said something to Maryam once, how her beautiful face would glow even more if she were a bride in their house, but her face turned red, and she disappeared.

Faisal's father went through a rough patch. He fell from a palm tree, and although he didn't break any bones, he was bedridden for weeks. Then he developed a mysterious disease that made him short of breath, with chest pain at the slightest movement. The acute stage lasted over a month, and he never fully recovered afterward. His ability to care for his farm took a major hit, and while Faisal attempted to fill in for his father, only Haj Mohammad knew how to care for his palm trees, his children.

~

F aisal ate his breakfast and changed to get ready for farm work.

"Your father is very proud of you for filling in for him," his mother said. She stood across from him in the doorway. "It was always his dream to see you take over." She gently ran her fingers over his collar, wiping away some of the dust. She always wanted him to look his best, even when he was getting ready for work. "I can't wait to see you married and take over the farm while I and your future wife care for a house full of children."

Faisal looked at his feet. Every time he thought about Maryam, he remembered how much his father hated hers. It pulled his dream from the sky to the ground, where his eyes remained.

Somebody knocked on the door, and Faisal opened it. Two men were outside asking for his father. They looked deadly serious. His father emerged from the bedroom and seemed to recognize them. He invited them in while Faisal stood there watching with anticipation.

After a round of tea, one of them cleared his throat and said, "Haj, we're here to tell you that Bul Khair has decided to take control over the daily operations of the farms in our village."

"What does this mean?" his father said with a frown as he adjusted himself to get comfortable.

The second man put his hand on Faisal's father's knee. "We're sorry to have to tell you this, but we're only doing as we're instructed. We have no more power or money than you do."

His father drew a deep, slow breath.

"Only certain men will be allowed to farm from now on.

The landowners can help, but only within boundaries. The men will be strong, well built, and handpicked by Bul Khair."

Some servants had already been hired from nearby villages to take over farming and harvesting duties. They'd start with his father's land under the pretext of his inability to care for it due to his illness.

Faisal wasn't stupid. He knew they wouldn't relinquish control even if his father fully recovered, and he knew that Bul Khair would soon encroach on neighboring land. He started to protest, but his father waved his hand at him to be quiet.

Before they stepped out the door, one of the two men turned and said, "While this is not ideal for most farmers, Bul Khair thinks it's a more efficient way to take care of the farms and crops."

"Are we supposed to pretend this is a good thing?" Faisal said.

The guest put his hand over Faisal's shoulder. "Son, you're still young, and the real world of today is not as simple as you think. Just do as your father does."

"Will they at least allow us to sell our products?" his father asked.

"The idea is that they will farm and harvest, and then we'll have some involvement in transportation and sales, but to what extent, I don't know." The man nervously rubbed his head.

With his father's lingering health issues and slow recovery, Faisal stepped up to care for the farm as much as he could and was allowed to under the new rule. He took extra pleasure in making visits to Baghdad to conduct whatever business his father needed him to take care of. Some of his visits lasted for days, and he made some new friends.

One chilly day in early March when he returned from Baghdad after a four-day trip, Faisal passed by Maryam's house and noticed an unusual commotion. Two armed men, both of them Bul Khair's, guarded the door. Faisal stood there for a few moments trying to discern what was happening. Then an entourage of men emerged from inside the house, one of them Bul Khair, another a well-dressed young man behind him. Bul Khair offered words of praise to his host, his own right-hand man, and moments later, Faisal heard loud ululations coming from inside the house.

He ran home and found his mother in the kitchen. She told him her father was out attending to the land after finally recovering enough to be active again.

Faisal felt pale, cold, shocked. His mother studied his face. It was like she could read his mind.

"She was not meant for you. *Qadar*"—fate—"wrote her for somebody else."

Faisal withdrew to his room, his mother following him and desperately trying to console him or get him to say something, anything. But Maryam was gone. Nothing good could come from talking about it. It certainly would not bring her back. It wouldn't even make him less angry. It was one thing for *qadar* to take Maryam from him but another to hand her over to none other than Bul Khair's son.

Later that night, Haj Mohammad couldn't sleep even though he was exhausted from a long day of work. Batul lay next to him and attempted to comfort him.

"Your son wanted the girl," she said. "He was madly in love with Maryam."

Everyone knew about Maryam's engagement, but Haj Mohammad couldn't bother to be interested. He sat up and looked up at his wife, trying to measure her seriousness in the faint lantern light.

She spoke quietly, so Faisal couldn't hear, and told Haj Mohammad how their son had been attracted to Maryam for years.

"And you wait until the day she's engaged to tell me all this?" he finally said. Why, of all the girls in the world, did Faisal have to pick the girl of his nemesis?

"We both knew he liked Maryam, but the moment was never right," Batul said as she rubbed her husband's sore neck and shoulders. "Besides, I figured you'd never ask for kinship with that family."

"You mean they'd never agree to give us their daughter."

The room was silent. A cold breeze slipped through the half-open window. In the distant background, stray dogs were barking at something. Haj Mohammad shifted to his other side, grimacing with stiffness and pain. He let out a deep sigh. "We could have asked for her hand and let them reject us so our son doesn't live the rest of this life thinking *what if*."

"*Wallah*, I am surprised. I was certain you'd bring hell down over my head for even suggesting any connection with that family, but please don't tell Faisal. He'll feel even worse."

Batul's massage had eased some of the stiffness from Haj Mohammad's neck, and he rose from the bed and went to the window, staring into the blackness. It was right there on the other side of the palm trees: Bul Khair's gigantic house. "That man's son isn't fit to be a mule."

Batul sighed. "But he has a powerful father with lots of influence and money."

Haj Mohammad turned and faced his wife. "Did Maryam want Faisal? This is women stuff. I can't figure it out."

"It's not like she had a choice or would ever be asked. You know that as well as I do."

8

Belarus

It's our fifth day inside this godforsaken warehouse, and our numbers are growing rapidly by the hour. The number of soldiers and cops inside has been surging since early morning. At noon they order us to line up and head to the main exit. A young woman anxiously squeezes past people, holding her hand over the mask she's been wearing since I first saw her step inside the warehouse.

Gulistan is with me. People around us are coughing and sneezing, and they've been at it all night. I turn to one side to avoid someone who's obviously ill. The young woman shouts something in Kurdish.

"What's she upset about?" I ask.

"She's asking everyone to cover their cough," Gulistan says.

The woman shouts more loudly, and Gulistan elbows her and shouts back in her face, but she pays Gulistan no mind.

"What did you say?"

"I told her she's in the wrong place if she thought this would be a rosy trip with chocolates and candy."

Gulistan's breathing is labored as we head toward the exit.

"Are you OK?" I ask.

"Yes, my son. It's just dusty here." I'm not convinced. Her breaths are shallow, interrupted, but I let it go while carefully watching her.

At the door, two soldiers ask every man to empty his pockets. They take some money and hand the rest back. Those who resist are sent to the end of the line to start the process all over again. There's no physical violence, no yelling, no insults, but the fear of the unknown compels most of us to obey.

We're all outside in less than an hour, and the armed men push us back into the woods. Nobody asks questions. Our minds can't muster thoughts just as our bodies are unable to resist the long line of humans being channeled into the forest.

At around three in the afternoon, we clear the dense forest and emerge onto the open steppe. A kilometer or so away, another sea of migrants has washed up against the fenced border separating Belarus and Poland. The policemen and soldiers are gone. We're on our own again.

A Kurdish man from Erbil whom I met at the warehouse points toward the border. "The bastards had a plan for us all along!"

He's panting, and I can hear Gulistan behind me coughing even worse than before.

"They want to drive as many of us as possible to the border area to create a pressure point so we can cross," I say to the man, still trying to catch my own breath."

"The Poles won't be happy about it."

We've all been keeping up with the international news coverage of the two European sides, one aligned with Russia, the other with the European Union. And here we are, chess pieces being moved around on the board for no reasons that have anything to do with our lives. We are sacrificial pawns, it appears, on a board controlled by hands distant from our dire human needs.

People begin to scatter across the field. Some continue walking, others rest. Gulistan asks for a break. She's obviously tired. It will get dark soon, so I set my sleeping bag on the ground and help her lie down. Families that are fortunate enough to have secured tents back in Minsk start setting them up. I'm down to the last piece of bread and cheese plus half a bottle of water. Gulistan hasn't eaten since last night, so I share most of what I have with her.

She gulps all the water at once, ignoring the bread. She launches into another bout of coughing, then says in a weak voice, "You promised you'll help find my grandkids, right?"

"Yes, of course," I say, unsure if I'm more sympathetic toward her or more resigned to the fact that I'm the one person among all these thousands of people that she's turned to.

"What is the mother's name?"

She stares at me blankly while trying to suppress her cough.

"Your daughter-in-law? What's her name?"

"Oh, I'm sorry. I am light-headed and can hardly even hear. Her name is Nasreen."

I can tell that she wants to go on another rant about how Nasreen has done her wrong, but exhaustion gets the best of her. With Gulistan resting, I walk around and ask if anyone remembers coming across a tall young woman accompanied by three young children. All I get are shaking heads. No one knows a woman named Nasreen. I retreat back to our spot and rest my head as darkness settles in. More people are coughing repeatedly and violently. I start to regret not wearing a mask during our stay inside the warehouse.

Sometime after midnight, Gulistan's muffled voice awakens me asking for help. I turn on my phone's light and find her shivering and coiled up inside the sleeping bag. Upon closer inspection, I find her face and neck soaked with sweat. I fetch some water from a nearby group, and when I return, she's barely awake. I shake her arms, and she grimaces. Her breathing is labored. I anxiously call a few friends over to help.

A commotion builds up, and someone calls out, "Doctor! There is a doctor here. Make room."

The doctor, a middle-aged man from the Kurdish city of Sulaimaniyah, cuts his way through the crowd of mostly men and shouts at everyone to disperse and wear masks.

"COVID-19 is no joke," he says angrily. After some positioning, Gulistan opens her eyes, but her breathing remains shallow. She tries to cough, but she's so weak that her head falls in the arms of a young woman who seems to be related to the doctor, perhaps his wife.

Someone yells, "There's an oxygen tank inside one of the tents." He runs to get it while someone nearby whispers to his friend that the tank belonged to an elderly man who died two days ago. COVID-19 also? I can't think about it. Will I have to bury Gulistan in this miserable corner of earth?

Before sunrise, I count five times when we're almost certain that Gulistan has departed this world, but she keeps proving that she isn't ready yet. She still looks terrible, but the doctor rounds up some medicine and a bunch of inhalers, and with the oxygen supplementation, Gulistan's oxygen level reaches above 85, a number that the doctor indicates is a cutoff for panic.

I check Gulistan's oxygen level again later through a small finger monitor I borrowed from the doctor, and it shows 84. I'm not going to report that. There isn't much difference between 85 and 84, is there? And what would we do? The camp would become panic stricken again. Gulistan slips in and out of episodes of fever, cough, and wheezing. A few nearby families bring in rounds of hot soup and hand it to me to feed her. By now, people assume I'm a family member.

From afar, I can see crowds of people gathered against the fence. A large military unit is lined up by the fence on the Polish side, extending the length of the crowd of illegal migrants. Back by our spot, one of the men helps the doctor start a fire in anticipation of another cold night.

The sun sets faster than I want it to. I've quickly grown weary of the heavy darkness of this open land, far away from any city lights. It's the darkness that concentrates our worries, pains, and exhaustion, then drapes it over our tired souls in the thickness of the night. A bad feeling burrows deep into my heart, making me dread closing my eyes.

Gulistan manages to sleep intermittently, but as the long night stretches deeper into the darkness, she starts to talk in her sleep. "I'm going to die. This is my end. My life was meant to end here."

I pour a small cup of water for her, and she grips both of my hands with surprising strength.

"If I die," she says, "please ask my daughter-in-law to forgive me. Tell her I didn't mean what I said."

I gently rub her hand, feeling the dry creases, as I try to reassure her.

She continues after gasping for air for a moment. "She's always been dear to me, but damned be Satan. He put bad thoughts in my head."

"Try to get some rest, please," I urge her.

"Now I'm going to die here without getting a chance to make amends."

No, Gulistan, you are not going to die in my hands. I am not going to carry that miserable load on my shoulders.

9

In less than forty-eight hours, dozens of others fall sick with symptoms ranging from sore throat and simple cough to severe fever and hypoxia. An elderly disabled woman succumbs within hours. Those of us left behind face the dire responsibility of doing something for the sick. Of the five of us young men who've been caring for them, two have started to exhibit symptoms themselves. I have a sore throat as well, but I can't tell if it's the beginning of COVID or just my paranoid mind telling my throat to itch. Even the doctor is starting to cough and sneeze under the mask that has not left his face since I met him.

I turn to the guys around me and suggest we go back to the warehouse and try finding some medicine.

"The warehouse?" one of them says and chuckles.

"The warehouse is where we got COVID," says the other.

I check on Gulistan one more time and feel somewhat reassured by her stable oxygen level, although fever and cough are still persistent.

"We must find a solution, or we'll be burying bodies out here," one of the men says.

The doctor turns his cell phone toward us and points at something on the map. "There's a town nearby."

"Then we'll go and check it out," someone behind him says and gets up.

We ask the doctor to write down a list of medications and supplies we need, and we head through the forest toward town. My guess is that it's about an hour away.

It turns out to be three hours away. And when we get there, nobody speaks any language except Belarusian, and we can't understand a word of it. The people, however, seem to know what we want and need. Perhaps this isn't the first time they've been visited and approached by migrants?

We follow an old man into a small shop attached to an old house. At first, we're hesitant to enter, but the man shouts something, and an entire family emerges from inside. They take us into multiple rooms stocked with the kinds of supplies we're looking for.

Six hours and five hundred dollars later, we return with three boxes of antibiotics, a dozen inhalers, fever medicine, four portable oxygen tanks, face masks, and some food and water. We could not, however, find SIM cards for our phones. Nobody had them in stock.

Gulistan slowly improves. She gave us a few scares after we brought the medicine, but thank goodness the doctor thinks she no longer needs oxygen. We're one step closer to resuming our trip.

Out of thirty-three people who fell seriously ill with

COVID, so far we only lost two. I feel ashamed even thinking that. There's nothing fortunate for any group whose members, even one of them, have to return home dead after their war-torn homelands couldn't kill them. Then again, how alive are we really? I felt half dead already before I even left.

10

Sudah
1930s

M aryam knew that everybody in the village was talking about her.

Word got around about how devastated Faisal was that she was marrying someone else. Other boys wanted her too before Bul Khair's son crushed their dreams. Maryam's mother visited Batul one morning, urging her to put an end to the rumors so she wouldn't end up under the fire from Bul Khair and his men, including Maryam's father himself.

Batul was infuriated, and she threw Maryam's mother out.

The worst rumor of all was that Bul Khair initially refused to accept Maryam. He had wanted someone from his own class, but his son insisted. Things escalated to the point where Bul Khair's son, Hussam, left home for over a week to protest his father's refusal.

While her father was proud of the status and glory his daughter would provide through this marriage, Maryam withdrew to her own world of silence, only finding solace in the times she spent with her friends and doing her household chores.

"Run away with him," her friend Su'ad said during a trip to haul water.

Maryam rolled her eyes, but another girl added, "Yes, go and live your life away from this godforsaken, suffocating village."

"Do you really think it's better elsewhere?" Maryam said. "I'd be killed if I tried to do such a crazy thing." The very idea of turning against her family was a nightmare. "My mother would die of shame."

Another girl joined the conversation and asked, "Do you know for certain that Faisal loves you? You two have never even had a conversation beyond greetings. It would be dumb to pass on someone of high status for a bottom feeder like the rest of us only to later realize he had never wanted to marry you in the first place."

Maryam slapped her wrist and hissed. "The only dumb person here is you. I'm certain he loves me. And I love him too, but what good does that do?"

They had reached the edge of the village, and Maryam could see Faisal's house in the distance. How she wished that was where she'd be getting married in a couple of weeks. She stopped with the water jug still fixed over her shoulder and fought back a tear or two. Her girlfriends noticed and stopped with her in silent solidarity.

"Have you talked to your mother about this?"

Maryam sighed and wiped her face with her hand. "She told me that if I even think about protesting this marriage, my father would lose his mind."

She took as much time as she could to get home.

Weeks later, she left home for good when she married

Hussam. She did not kiss her father's hand at the wedding when she left to live with her husband, her way of silently protesting. She doubted her father even knew about Faisal. He would have mocked her heart's choice if he found out. From his point of view, she was entering a kingdom any village girl would have dreamed of. To Maryam, though, she was heading into a new home that was more of a grave than a nest.

11

Sudah
Late 1930s

Faisal woke to his father barging into his bedroom after the *Fajr* morning prayer. "I'm making a trip to Baghdad, and you're coming with me."

Faisal didn't even lift his head from the pillow. His mother walked in with hurried steps and yelled at him to get up and get dressed.

It was still dark when he and his father left the house. By the time they reached the river banks, the first glow of sunlight appeared behind the palm trees.

Faisal followed his aging father's slow steps. The old man appeared frailer and weaker than ever despite all his attempts to look strong. His wide shoulders had coiled in, having lost much of the muscle mass that decades of hard work had built. Yet he walked the streets of Baghdad with unwavering pride, pointing out to Faisal all that had been transformed during the royal era: roads, bridges, schools, and markets. He gestured at new buildings replacing the worn-out wreckage that had once littered the banks of the Tigris.

Faisal kept thinking to himself that it was only a matter of time before his father decided to return to Baghdad. His longing for the city was obvious.

They turned onto narrow Mutanabbi Street. Faisal's father pointed at a tea shop and said, "That, right there, is my favorite place to visit in this city."

"You've brought me here before," said Faisal.

At the door, Faisal scanned the large rectangular room steeped with smoke and chatter. The shop had gradually transformed over the years. There were more well-dressed men now in the traditional Baghdadi *effendi* hat. They, the *effendis*, sat at tables far from the *ammi*, the simple workers. The *effendi* didn't necessarily look down on the *ammi*. They simply lived in different worlds, with one group exquisitely dressed, and the other dirty, tired, and simply ... simple. The *effendi* appeared relaxed and spontaneous, while the *ammi* were focused and serious. But they all spoke of politics and war.

Faisal's father knew men in both groups, though as a village man wearing a common dishdasha and a white scarf over his head, he didn't quite fit in either, but he was clean-shaven and neatly dressed.

Faisal walked behind his father as he made his way between the full tables, greeting other customers and exchanging pleasantries. Everyone seemed to know Haj Mohammad.

Faisal quietly took a seat next to his father at the far end of the shop. Moments later, a middle-aged man in a military uniform stepped inside. Everyone turned in his direction, offering respect and a warm reception. The man walked with pride and declined all offers to sit, choosing instead to take a seat next to the poorest-looking man in the entire tea shop, who stood up and hugged the officer.

"Look at that acting job," somebody whispered at a nearby table. "Next he's going to kiss the officer's boots."

"Would you stop, man?" his friend said. "We're supposed to show respect."

The poor guy was now nervously adjusting his chair to make more room for the officer. Faisal imagined himself one day standing at that door while everyone admired his presence. He'd behave similarly, but he could do it more authentically because he'd base it on real passion to help the poor.

That evening, the shop owner announced the start of a new tradition for loyal customers. He introduced a man named Sultan, who carried a flat, triangular, stringed instrument made of wood, and he placed it between his knees as everyone watched in anticipation.

Faisal's father whispered, "That is called the *qanun*. It is one of the oldest musical instruments."

Someone yelled, "Finally, you honored our wishes!"

Faisal fixed his eyes on the instrument.

"We've been asking the owner to bring this guy in here for the longest time," his father said. "He kept making excuses about the cost."

Sultan positioned the pick over his index finger and played the strings. The melodies silenced the crowd. Tea glasses froze in midair.

Faisal's mother was visiting her brother for a few days, so he and his father extended their stay in Baghdad. They were staying at a *khan* near the river that hosted merchants and traders from all over the area and even from far away. His father knew the owner from decades ago, an acquaintance who usually offered a room for free.

They were enjoying a warm meal to offset the chilly morning when the owner rushed in and shouted, "King Gazi died! Our king is gone!"

His guests shouted questions.

"They're saying his car crashed into an electric pole."

The gathering quickly descended into a frenzy of shock, sadness, and chaos. Some men left the inn to find more details, but where else could one get more fresh news? The *khan* itself was a hub for news, spice, and details thanks to the handymen and servants working in the warehouse next door. There was no appetite remaining for food, arguments, or business deals. When the shock settled down a bit in the evening, the few remaining customers chatted among themselves.

"The Brits must've had a hand in his death."

"Yes. Gazi's close ties with the Germans finally got him killed."

"Gazi was known for heavy drinking, so who's to say he wasn't drunk and got himself killed?"

Shouting ensued, and the owner ordered the room cleared. Faisal had had enough anyway, and it seemed like his father did too, so they went to bed early.

As Haj Mohammad returned home with his son Faisal, the loss of King Gazi was quickly overshadowed by his succession. The royal constitution of the Hashemite monarchy gave the throne to Gazi's son, Faisal II.

"But he's only three years old," Batul said when Haj Mohammad relayed the news to her.

He extended his sore legs on the mattress after a long day

of travel. "Yes," he said. "But his mother, the queen, testified under oath that King Gazi had indicated on numerous occasions that if something were to happen to him, Prince Abdililah, the queen's brother, would be appointed as guardian until Faisal reached the legal age to take over as king."

"So, what happens now?" Batul asked.

"The regency has been set up under Prince Abdililah, and the cabinet has already been given the royal stamp of approval."

Batul was hardly a typical village housewife. She enjoyed discussing politics and history with her husband, especially as he had years of experience with it before she even married him. A brutal war was escalating in Europe, and Iraqis fretted about which side they'd come down on. The late King Gazi had been close to the Axis. The English had a long history in Iraq. And Prime Minister Nuri Pasha al-Said was strongly pro-British. The Anglo-Iraqi Treaty of 1930 required Iraq to side with the Allies and compelled Baghdad to deport German nationals.

Batul worried about a military draft to supply the Allied forces in Poland. "Do you think they'll round up our young men?"

Haj Mohammad didn't know and didn't answer. He sat by the front window, enjoying the early morning breeze. It would soon be time for the farmers to advance to their fields like an organized army. Even when Bul Khair brought in outside workers, the local farmers still hung around and remained involved as they could. Haj Mohammad, however, barely had the strength to even walk there anymore let alone care for the crops and trees.

When the sun rose, he imagined the younger version of himself, decades ago, striding with powerful steps toward the palm trees with determination and grit. With each step the younger Haj Mohammad took away from the house, the older Haj Mohammad, the real one, saw his life recede farther into the distance.

He heard Faisal somewhere in the house, moving about and getting ready to go for some random business that had nothing to do with their palm trees. At least he seemed to have forgotten about Maryam.

Batul approached and repeated her earlier question. "Haj. What are your thoughts? Do you think the government will announce a draft?"

"Leave me alone, woman. Nuri Pasha may be pro-British, but he's not stupid enough to send Iraq's sons to death in faraway Europe."

12

Sudah
Early 1940s

Faisal sat with his parents for lunch in the living room. It hadn't been upgraded since he was too young to even remember it. The winter had been a dry one, so April was starting out hot, which meant bad crops and a possible drought.

His father had not even been to the farm for months, and Faisal only sporadically worked there. Mostly he focused on getting goods from the village to Baghdad by truck now that new roads had been paved.

Sudah had grown in population over the previous decade. Over a dozen new families had moved there or been forced to relocate, mostly to satisfy Bul Khair's labor needs. It was the first-year anniversary of the death of King Gazi, and with the Germans making advances on European front lines, many were counting the days until the Allies would crumble and hand the reign of Europe to Hitler.

Faisal flipped through pages of the newspapers he'd brought from his latest trip to Baghdad and gave his father a summary of the news. Now nineteen years old, he did his best to skip the controversial subjects and bad news. His father's eyes had become so weak that he could no longer see the images on the pages, so he had no idea if Faisal was skipping articles or not.

"Why can't Iraq openly side with the Germans since it's obvious that Hitler will win?" his mother asked. "What if he gets mad and comes after us once the war is over?"

"Woman, this is politics, and you know nothing about it," his father said and snatched the newspaper from Faisal's hands and scrutinized a large image of Nuri Pasha al-Said.

"Mama," Faisal said, "none of this is as easy as it appears. Our leaders have a thing for the Brits and won't dare go against them."

"But didn't King Gazi openly oppose the Brits? What's changed?" She insisted on staying engaged.

"What changed is that King Gazi is no longer alive," his father said. "Now, will you stop asking stupid questions!"

Faisal turned to his mother and smiled. She was getting used to his father's more-frequent outbursts. "I don't think anyone has a good grip on what happens in our country anymore." He then excused himself and slowly got up.

For years, the boys of Sudah chose a day in advance for the first swim in the Tigris after winter. As soon as the weather became warmer and the water level was reasonable, dozens of boys and young men jumped in the river at the same time. Faisal asked his father if he wanted to accompany him, hoping he'd agree to get up for a change of scenery, but his father lay down and shook his head.

"Can I come with you?" his mother asked.

"What are you going to do there among men?" his father barked.

"I'm not going to be around men. Many women go. I'll be with them and watch from afar." He didn't seem convinced. "What if something happens to my son?"

Faisal had always been impressed with his mother's ability to convince his father of anything any time and with few words.

They walked down the dirt road leading to the edge of the village. The sky had cleared up, with the heavy clouds from earlier having moved farther north. As they turned the corner near the clay fire pit, Faisal spotted her, Maryam, standing in front of her family's house. She was near the front door and holding a baby in her arms, looking side to side as if waiting for someone. Her silky hair emerged from under the scarf she had tied over her head.

Their eyes met, and a monster of emotions awakened within Faisal. The deep wound opened up all over again. He froze in place with his mother next to him. Neither of them seemed to know what to do or say. At that moment, Maryam's husband appeared from behind the house, accompanied by her father and a few other men. Her husband walked away with little regard to his father-in-law and ordered his wife to move.

Maryam walked behind her husband while Faisal remained frozen, the old beast scratching mercilessly against his emotions. He could swear Maryam almost turned her head to look at him a couple of times, but she hesitantly straightened up again and followed her husband.

Batul shook her son's shoulder. "Let's go, son. They must've started swimming already."

Ignoring his mother, Faisal turned around and walked toward their house, slowly picking up his pace. Batul's attempts to catch up with him failed.

Nobody said much at dinner that evening. Faisal's father knew about the encounter with Maryam, if it could even be called that. His mother had tried to make him feel better, but his disdain for the village and all that it represented it was brewing. With the loss of Maryam, his hatred for Bul Khair, Maryam's father, and every powerful person whose existence came at the expense of the poor and helpless had calcified. He even hated their farm, the land, and the soil. Just as Maryam didn't belong to him, nothing else truly belonged to him either. He had lost her to an undeserving heart just as his father and the villagers had lost their land to undeserving hands.

13

1940s

In the morning, Faisal was already dressed when his parents woke up. He had a bag of clothes in his hand, and he waited by the door, anxious to leave, to break the news to them: He was leaving for Baghdad, and for good.

He'd decided to enlist in the military academy. The idea had been swirling in his mind for some time, but ultimately he made the decision overnight and finalized it in the morning.

It caught his parents off guard. They weren't even fully awake when he dropped the news on them while standing at the front door as if unwilling to waste another minute in the village.

His father sat down heavily on the couch, unable to verbalize his shock.

"Why, my son?" his mother said. "How can you go so far away from here?"

"Mama, I am twenty and can take care of myself."

"We're not worried about that. Who will be here to watch over us?"

"You can join me in Baghdad. We have no place here." Faisal saw his father's disappointed face from the corner of his eyes as his mother gripped his shoulders.

"Where is the military school?" his father asked, doing his best to sound nonchalant.

"How will we join you if you are going to be in military school?" his mother said. "Why did you decide this without talking to us?"

Faisal sat in a chair across from his father, a wave of guilt washing over him. He'd thought about joining the military several times, but because of the lingering prospects of the country being pulled into the European war, he wouldn't voluntarily enlist in the army. The academy would be different. His time there would last two to three years, so the odds that he'd be sent to Europe were slim.

"The school is outside Baghdad, and I checked it out during one of my previous visits. They'll cover the cost of living plus a small stipend for expenses."

His father drew in a heavy breath and shook his head.

Faisal put his hands on his father's knees and pleaded. "I can't stay here. I don't feel good here. There's no place for me on this land."

"Why, son?" his mother said with a breaking voice. "Why do you say that?"

Faisal turned to her and narrowed his eyes. "Look at us. We live like peasants."

He expected his father's face to turn red with anger, but he seemed indifferent. He couldn't tell if his father agreed with him or was already past the point of resisting. Things appeared settled, and everyone in the room knew it regardless of what they said or did.

"I promise that I will come back and take you with me to Baghdad when I get settled. Our life will be much better after I earn the rank of an officer and not just a soldier." Faisal kissed his father's hand, hoping for his blessing.

"But how can you just get up and go like this?" his mother asked. She was crying now.

"I'm only going to spend a few days in Baghdad to get my papers ready, then I'll be back. School doesn't start until June."

After nearly a year in the military academy, life had been everything Faisal had expected and hoped it would be. The intense training kept his mind off Sudah. Confined within the walls and fence of the academy, he'd been able to forge new friendships with young men from various backgrounds. By June of that year, 1941, they were going to transition from classroom learning to hands-on experience.

But April brought chaos that made June seem impossibly far away. England demanded that Iraq sever ties with Italy, which had entered the water against the Allies, and Iraq refused. Even Prince Abdililah had grown tired of British demands.

Then the country woke up to the news of a military coup led by Rashid Ali al-Gaylani. The revolting group of army leaders vowed to create a new system that was not aligned with the British.

Faisal sat in a wooden chair with his back against a concrete wall with a group of his academy comrades. It was past bedtime, but all rules were out the window under the circumstances. Everyone was on alert, and political arguments were heating up in that room. Prince Abdililah, Nuri Pasha, and the rest of the ousted officials had already fled.

"I hate the *Engleez* and would love to see every last one of their men out of this country," Faisal said.

"But we don't want to end up siding with Hitler," one of his comrades said.

"Who cares about Hitler, Germany, Italy, or Europe?" Faisal said, infuriated by the mere mention of foreign interference. "We just want to live in peace and dignity, without foreign lords stepping on our foreheads every day."

Everyone appeared angry, on the streets and on the radio. Everyone was mad at someone, and no one seemed to know exactly how to channel their emotions or demands. But Faisal knew two things: he hated the Brits, and foreigners could never bring peace.

A few days later, he and his fellow students were urgently called to mobilize and head to the city. A mob was attacking businesses and homes belonging to Jews. This was their first formal duty call and a painful introduction to reality in the military.

When Faisal arrived at Al Rasheed Street along with five of his fellow soldiers, they found dozens of stores with broken doors and shattered windows, their contents thrown outside. Looters wandered about, picking up whatever they could with total disregard to their surroundings or possible consequences. Faisal attempted to stop a man carrying a long expensive-looking rug, but the man pushed him away and yelled, "The Jews are enemies. They control all the money and will soon own our lives."

"We have to be smart and do what Hitler has done," another yelled.

A well-dressed, middle-aged *effendi* turned to Faisal and said, "Leave them alone. The military has unleashed these animals. It's all going to collapse on our heads."

Before Faisal could say anything, the *effendi* walked away in defeat.

Faisal and one of his comrades did their best to maneuver their way through the mob, which was now attempting to make its way to the balcony of the second floor of a large residential building, where a large number of women and children stood looking down in horror.

The soldiers, along with a group of caring citizens, finally secured the premises and provided protection to the Jewish citizens trapped upstairs. A nearby loudspeaker broadcast a message from the army: there would be no place for British intervention and enslavement of the Iraqis, and no room for mobs and chaos.

A skeptic in the crowd said, "I have a bad feeling about this. It's not going to end well."

And he was right. A month later, England invaded and toppled Rashid Ali al-Gaylani. The prince and the child king in line to the throne, along with Nuri Pasha and the others, returned. And unlike in the late 1930s, British-backed officials this time retaliated with the execution and imprisonment of the coup plotters.

By the following year,1942, the government took measures to weaken the grip of the military, limiting its involvement in national security and rendering it void of much of its previous political influence. Military units were cut down in numbers, which trickled down to affect the military academy. Faisal and his seventy comrades were not going to transition to high-class status in their second year as had previously been promised.

Faisal's uncle from his mother's side, Khalo Hakeem, showed up at his living quarters one day with terrible news. "Your father passed away. To Allah we belong, and to Him we shall return."

The news struck Faisal like a lightning bolt on a dry tree. It damn near cut him in half. His uncle had always been a cold person, but delivering the news so abruptly was harsh even by his standards.

His father's health had suddenly deteriorated, and he passed in his sleep, which was a blessing, Faisal supposed, but it hardly made him feel any better. On the contrary. Faisal wished his father had a prolonged illness instead. At least he would have been able to visit and possibly bring him to Baghdad for care.

F aisal stood at his father's grave at the edge of the village and as close to the palm tree farm as possible, where he would have wanted to be buried. He stayed behind after the burial, long after all the other men had left to set up the funeral area. His mother approached him and gently patted his shoulders without saying anything. Moments stretched like eternity, and Faisal drowned in a sea of guilt, unable to speak. He finally turned to his mother and buried his head in her arms. She rubbed his hair and knew just what he needed to hear.

"Your father loved you, Faisal. He was proud of you and never felt anything for you but love and admiration. You made us proud every step of the way."

"He left before I could say goodbye." Faisal's voice cracked, and his mother embraced him even closer.

A few days later, when funeral visitations were winding down, Faisal asked his mother to accompany him to Baghdad. He had less than a year left in his training and was eligible to live in a private house and commute to the base. She could live with him, and together they'd keep the family alive. But even after two days of deliberation and begging, Faisal failed to convince her. She was going to move in with her older brother in his village and live there. Faisal was welcome to visit her any time, and if he ever returned to Sudah, she would move in to live with him. Baghdad just wasn't for her.

"I don't know anyone there, and I would die of boredom and sorrow," she said.

"You will be with me," Faisal said, his softening voice pleading her.

"You pursue your dream, and your father's blessings will follow you everywhere." She sent him off with a motherly kiss.

14

Baghdad
1940s–1950s

Faisal's first post after graduating from the academy was guarding the main entrance of the National Museum built by the late King Faisal I. He was told it would be temporary, but Faisal quickly grew fond of the place. The collection of historic and archaeological pieces was exciting, but more than anything, Faisal enjoyed receiving groups of foreign journalists, scientists, and highly interested tourists.

One morning, when he stood in his military uniform, his gun at his side and his white cap on his head, an older Italian tourist approached him with a smile and took a photo. Faisal remained still, full of pride and style. Later, the man reappeared waving the photo, and Faisal couldn't help but be moved and break protocol. He held the picture and stared at his image. He looked so formal and elegant! Faisal invited the man to visit him at his mother's village, partly out of genuine hospitality but also so she could see how successful and connected her son was.

The tourist took pictures of the village and its people and joined Faisal at his father's grave, but that was as far as Faisal was willing to go. His mother said she was proud and delighted and asked if she could keep the museum photo Faisal proudly showed her.

"Come with me, Mama," Faisal pleaded. "Come live with me in Baghdad."

"No, son. I belong here. I can't leave this land."

"We can have a good life in the city," Faisal added, his eyes shifting between his mother and the door.

She kissed his head and said, "You go on about your life, habibi."

Six months later, Faisal's uncle appeared at the gate of the museum and in his usual cold demeanor dropped another bit of nerve-racking news. His mother had remarried, and Faisal was to accept her decision and respect it.

He clenched his fist, embarrassed that she was sharing her life with another man. "Who did she marry?"

"A man from the village. His wife died a few months ago, and he has no children to care for him."

Great, Faisal thought. Another old man needing a younger woman to take care of him until he dies and leaves her alone again.

Faisal's visit to his mother was anything but kind or loving. He arrived in civilian clothes, and once he located his mother's new residence, he barged in and shouted a barrage of insults at no one in particular. His mother attempted to calm him down, but he was not having any of it.

"Damned be the world that allows women to forget their husbands' legacies. Damned be the people who take advantage of such women."

His mother's new husband, Elias, grabbed Faisal by the arm and threw him outside.

〰

O n a cold winter day in 1946, Faisal sat in the security post in front of the museum observing traffic as people went about their business. Drops of rain were starting to fall at a faster rate, making him appreciate the recently installed roof, which he shared with another armed man. A bus stopped near the entrance, and in the middle of the mass of people struggling to get off or hop on, Faisal spotted a young woman extracting herself from the crowd and heading toward the museum. She was slim and of medium height. She carried a folder in her left hand, and her right shoulder barely supported what appeared to be a heavy purse. She was wearing a long skirt with her dark hair pulled to the back.

While Faisal watched, she suddenly tripped and fell face down a few feet away from the entrance. Papers flew all around, while her purse landed some distance behind her. Faisal jumped out of his post and ran in her direction. The woman, who looked to be in her early twenties, slowly got up and cleaned the dust and dirt from her face and clothes, showing little sign of embarrassment or shaking up from the fall. Faisal gently handed her the papers he had gathered from the ground as she grabbed her purse. As if nothing had happened, she looked up and said, "It's my first day on the job here. How do I get to the office of historical records?"

Her name was Asma. She was a new secretary in charge of filing historical records as part of a major government project to curate the National Museum. After that encounter, Faisal observed her every move and found every possible opportunity to meet her at the entrance. He often insisted on accompanying her all the way inside the building.

Months later, Faisal learned that Asma was from a family famous for its involvement in education and civics. Her father, originally from Istanbul many generations earlier, had been a civil servant in the Baghdad municipality during Ottoman rule. Her mother had roots in Damascus, but the family had settled in Baghdad across generations.

In January of 1947, orders came for Faisal to move to the Ministry of Military Affairs and work as a deputy assistant with a small unit in the outskirts of Baghdad. He had to find a way to tell Asma how he felt about her, his attachment, love, whatever it was called. He'd deal with her reaction in due time. For the first time in a long time, he found himself buoyed with confidence. And he knew he'd need that to impress a confident and classy young woman whose every step radiated tenacity and determination.

Initially, Faisal wanted to keep his mother far away from any marriage proposal. He was still angry at his mother for remarrying. Perhaps he found her as an easy target for his life's frustration, especially the disappointment stemming from not being able to see his father one last time before his death. But Asma's family made it clear they were not giving their daughter away to someone who was not forthcoming about his own family.

"You have to bring your mother and whoever has taken your father's place," Asma's father said in a classic fatherly voice. Faisal envied Asma for still having a father in her life.

"My mother is still in the village and isn't in the best health." He felt disgusted with himself for saying that, but he still hadn't entirely gotten over his anger with his mother for getting married again.

"Son, we're a family with dignity and class. We can't just

accept marriage like this. Bring your family, and God will bless this marriage with his grace."

His mother delightfully agreed to accompany Faisal to officially meet Asma's family, but Faisal refused to allow his stepfather to come.

Faisal and Asma married in 1948 and moved into a small apartment on the second floor of a new stone building in one of the upscale neighborhoods of Kadhimiya in the heart of Baghdad, far from where Faisal was stationed but close enough for Asma's commute to the museum. In Asma, he found a home for his wounded heart and in her arms a safe shore. He told her about his previous love experience, and she accepted his history but hoped he could forget his wounds and make her his one and only source for happiness.

"You will forever be my queen and love," Faisal promised her.

Asma was caring, kind, and understanding. She had a gentle heart that Faisal thought could never harbor ill feelings for anyone. She was outspoken and strongly opinionated, which Faisal later felt threatened his status as the man in the house.

Their first two experiences with children were heartbreaking. The first was a stillborn girl, and the second, a boy, died from a mysterious fever a few days after birth. Asma fell into a deep depression and quit her job at the museum. Faisal was then promoted and placed in charge of one of four tank units belonging to the main brigade guarding Baghdad.

In 1956, Asma was finally ready to try pregnancy again. This time, however, she vowed that she was not going to plan for another child until Faisal mended ties with his mother. "God is angry at you for cutting ties with her, and there will be no blessings from Allah as long as this abandonment is active."

It was not like Faisal needed more reasons to feel blessed

for being married to Asma, but that gesture in itself made him feel like the luckiest man on earth.

When he finally showed up at his mother's door, he was thirty-five years old and looked powerful decked out in his military gear. His mother was in her early fifties, but gray hair and wrinkles had transformed her beyond what Faisal could have imagined. When she opened the door, Faisal could not help but cry. She embraced him as he kissed her hand, broken and humbled.

"I knew my son would come back," she said. "You are Haj Mohammad's son, and you are my son."

The village had hardly changed, though his mother told him that Bul Khair had passed away and that Maryam's husband was in charge now. Faisal wanted to hear no more news. He wanted to bury his past and his memories. After spending some time with his mother and reading a few verses of the Quran on his father's grave, he headed back to the city, stopping only for a long look at the palm trees his father had once owned. He hoped to return one day with an army of soldiers hungry to retake the land on behalf of the poor people who were stripped of their rightful property.

A year later, Asma got pregnant. She took every opportunity to remind Faisal that the blessings of Allah had showered upon them since he had reconciled with his mother. When Faisal's stepfather died that year, right when Asma was in her last month of pregnancy, his mother finally decided to move in with them in Baghdad, the reunion that Faisal had always longed for.

Faisal's family may have been stable, but Iraqi politics weren't, not since the passing of King Ghazi. Every time Iraq got used to a new cabinet, the ministers seemed to vanish from history, and new ones appeared on the front pages of newspapers. The young King Faisal II, now in his early twenties, tried as best as a young and inexperienced ruler could to appeal to his citizens. He visited them in the deep south and the far north as modern infrastructure expanded beyond the urban areas and into rural Iraq.

"Why are people still unhappy?" Faisal's mother asked him over dinner as they watched a TV program showcasing a new factory being founded in the south.

"They're tired of all the unrest," Faisal said.

Asma joined in the conversation. "The divide is growing wider between the civil government and the military." She looked straight at Faisal when she said that.

"What are you looking at me for?" he said and smiled.

"Because you're in the army!"

"I'm just a simple officer," he said, unsure if his wife was serious. "The orders come from way over my head."

"There are a lot of poor people in this country, and the political parties and personalities are using their frustration for political gain," Asma added.

"Iraqis have always been difficult to please," his mother said before changing the subject to something more pleasant.

15

Baghdad
Late 1950s

F aisal was introduced to a group of fellow military men
who shared similar concerns about the political process
and dissatisfaction with the socioeconomic state of the country. Often, over dinner or tea at their respective homes and
away from feminine topics, they let pour their thoughts and
feelings.

Faisal, among all of them, was the most passionate about
change. A real change. "We need to bring back the status and
dignity of military men," he said.

Tea was being served, and clouds of cigarette smoke
hovered throughout the room, adding heat to an already
heated discussion.

"Since al-Gaylani's failed coup, the government has ripped
the army out, root and branch, from the circles of the government," one of the men added.

"Exactly," said Faisal. "They've only kept personnel blindly loyal to the civil government."

The host of the gathering, a passionate military officer, called for his son to bring another round of tea. When he returned to his seat, the discussion was still on King Faisal II.

"The young king is probably busy preparing for his royal wedding."

Six years earlier, in 1952, the Free Officers Movement overthrew Egypt's King Farouk in a military coup. He was offered a graceful exit on board a ship to Rome, and he accepted the voluntary exile. A couple of years later, Gamal Abdel Nasser, another military man, seized Egypt's reins and fulminated against the West, especially England, which he saw as the hegemon over the Arab monarchies. Nasser spread his Arab Nationalist and anti-imperialist fever across much of the Middle East, but the military men in Iraq were way ahead of him. If anything, Nasser and his Egyptian comrades took their inspiration from the first coup in Iraq over a decade earlier.

Faisal and his friends met again for dinner, chain smoking, and politics. The main subject of conversation: Nasser and pan-Arabism.

"Our government is terrified of his influence," one of the men said.

"They should be," Faisal said sarcastically. "Nasser was inspired by us."

"Exactly," someone else said. "We don't need Nasser to tell us how to care for our nation."

Faisal realized his friend had missed the sarcasm in his previous comment but decided to let it go. "So why is Nuri Pasha putting more restrictions on the press and political parties?"

"To contain the street and not let it out of their control."

The host offered Faisal a cigarette, but he passed. After a

few moments of reflection, he said, "We've had enough development under our kings that hopefully we won't need a coup,
but pressing on freedom of expression will only lead to more
frustration."

The group dispersed that evening feeling even more
uncertain about the direction their country was headed.

Faisal's close comrade Suhail introduced him to a secret
group of nationalistic officers that called itself al-Thubbat al-
Ahrar, the Free Soldiers. They apparently had long arms
inside the army, and their leaders were experts at concealing
themselves. The general consensus among them was that the
army needed to bring about more respect for the military.
Moreover, they wanted to see a more unified and nationalistic
agenda being forced on the ruling parties and against British
involvement, which had only increased after the fall of Nazi
Germany. At first, Faisal listened quietly and curiously but
passionately involved himself later. He wanted to be part of
the change. The Iraq that King Faisal I had founded was gone,
and Faisal intensely hated the existing social system. Poverty
was widespread, and the divide between the well-offs and
deprived was forever widening.

Anytime change was mentioned, Faisal saw Bul Khair
glaring at him in his mind. The ironic thing was that Faisal
had never even met Bul Khair. He just knew that the man,
although long dead by then, was nasty, ugly, and evil. There
were thousands of other lords, leaders, tribalists, sheikhs, and
rich merchants who maintained a thick curtain between the
royal family and the poor faces of thousands upon thousands
of Iraqis.

Asma was busy raising their infant son, Mustafa. Both
Asma and Faisal's mother became wary of Faisal's outings after
work and until the late hours of the night, when they knew the

coffee and tea shops were long closed. Asma didn't want him involved in any trouble. He swore to his wife and mother that he was not involved in any illegal activities. Just a group of military officers meeting at different locations to discuss the situation in the country and what some of their higher-ranking leaders were proposing behind the scenes as possible solutions.

"But we are safe," Asma said. "Everything's fine."

At which Faisal was surprised considering she came from a family with Ottoman affiliation and dislike for the British kings.

"The country has advanced so much since you were born," his mother said. "What else do you want? Look at Baghdad and its streets and buildings."

Faisal, though, was swimming in another world, deeper and deeper within the secret circle of al-Thubbat al-Ahrar, the free officers. His dislike for the Brits was the most valuable inheritance passed on to him from his father. That feeling was submerged in a sea of hate for the corrupt socioeconomic system and seasoned with bitterness from the brutal way Abdilllah and Nuri Pasha had executed the four major army generals who led the military coup of 1941, leaving behind a long-lasting friction. For Faisal, just as for so many other military men, a payback was due and would be served on a plate made in Hell.

In May of 1958, while in bed and fighting off a strong heat wave that kept Faisal and Asma from falling asleep, even with the windows propped open, Asma tried to get his attention for a night of romance and possibly another child. Faisal was distant, far away in his own mind. He turned to her and whispered, as if somehow the heat outside could hear them: "There will be a military movement in a couple of days to change the government."

"A coup, you mean?" Asma asked, her eyes wide open and staring at Faisal in the semi-dark room.

"Call it whatever you want, but they will change things. Iraq desperately needs a change."

Mustafa was squirming in the cradle, and Asma pressed Faisal's hand so he would stay silent and not to awaken their infant. She slid her leg to the side of the bed and gently pushed the wooden cradle with her foot, rocking it back and forth, until Mustafa's movements stopped and she was confident he was back asleep.

"Please, habibi, don't get involved in anything crazy. We have it good." She gently kissed her husband's hand.

"I won't. There will be no crazy stuff. But it's time for a change, and no we don't have it good. I won't sleep well until the day the feudal lords are brought down."

"So your problem is with them and the king!"

"Who am I to have an issue with the king? Does he know me, or have I met him?"

He wanted to tell his wife that peaceful change was on the horizon, just as it had been in Egypt six years ago, but Asma was already asleep. He held his wife's hand against his face and kissed it, returning the favor from earlier. He lay in bed, with his wife and son asleep, and imagined a parade of King Faisal and his entourage out of Baghdad and off to the north, where the Kurds would help him cross into Turkey, or west across the desert and into Jordan, where the last remaining members of the Hashemite ruling family would be standing.

People would quickly forget the king and turn to the soldiers and throw roses at them. Faisal envisioned himself in that crowd of soldiers, swallowed in a sea of pride and status.

That day, however, was delayed twice, first in May and then in June. The powers that be decided to wait until the right opportunity, when the three key figures of government—King

Faisal II, his uncle Abdulilah, and Nuri Pasha—were in a single location and couldn't resist.

On the morning of July 14, 1958, Faisal was sitting in a small office next to his closest comrade, Suhail, at their second base in Baghdad when a guard barged in, short of breath and panting. Faisal yelled at him for failing to salute, but all the guard could muster was, "Sir, I think you need to turn on the radio. It's urgent."

On the radio and in a loud and firm voice, al-Thubbat al-Ahrar leader Abdul Salam Arif announced the overthrow of the king. Faisal brought his ear closer to the radio, trying to absorb the breaking news, holding his breath so as not to ruin a single moment of the long-awaited announcement. Soon, more officers and soldiers gathered in the room as news of the revolution broke across the base. Only Faisal and Suhail had been part of the secret meetings and knew in advance about the upcoming move, but the sudden timing was a shock even to them.

As the two senior officers in the base, Faisal and Suhail demanded order and instructed a junior officer to watch over the unit and not allow anyone to leave the base unless first ordered to do so, then rushed outside themselves.

It felt surreal to ask strangers on the street what was happening. After all, they were the ones dressed in military uniforms. Their thoughts and ideas had merged with those of many other military men to create change. The first man they asked gave them a blank look. Another laughed. At the edge of the main road leading to Qasr al-Rihab, the royal palace, an elderly, crippled man was walking in the opposite direction and yelling to himself, "They've done it. The sons of Shaitan, the devil, have done it. They have murdered our king."

16

Baghdad
July 1958

The closer Faisal and Suhail got to Qasr al-Rihab, the thicker and rowdier the crowds became. Naturally, people saw Faisal and Suhail in military uniform and gave them the space to cut through. There were tanks scattered around with fully armed soldiers standing on all sides. People were haphazardly hurrying in all directions. The crowd gathering outside and around the royal palace was impossible to penetrate, so Faisal and his friend stood and watched from afar.

Sometime later, the crowd broke and went in two directions, one with facial expressions of sadness, disappointment, and fear, and the other much larger group stormed off in the opposite direction. It looked like a mob, and they were dragging or hauling something. When the entire crowd had left, more soldiers arrived and fully surrounded the royal palace. Faisal and his comrade, still shocked and speechless, followed the mob, maintaining a safe distance. Two men rushed past them. One stopped and said with a wide smile, "Good job, you brave sons of this nation. Long live your strong hands."

The second man yelled with excitement, "Yes, blessed be the hands that rid the nation of the dirty heads and tails of the *Engleez*."

In the late afternoon, Faisal left his friend and headed back home, his head spinning with images of chaos and paranoia. He realized that he had not eaten or drank anything in over eight hours.

The streets were filling up with people, yelling, screaming, shouting, and demonstrating. By now they had learned most of the details of the military operation or whatever the nation was trying to call it. A military unit under the leadership of Abdul Salam Arif had originally been ordered by the royal army commander to head to Jordan to provide protection against imminent threats from Egypt's Nasser. Baghdad was along its path. Abd al-Karim Qasim, the leader of another large unit stationed outside Baghdad, found it a great opportunity to convince Abdul Salam to redirect his unit and enter the heart of Baghdad. In doing so, they could take advantage of the fact that both King Faisal II and Abdililah were at the royal palace, making them an easy target. Abd al-Karim Qasim would then follow him and secure all entry and exit points of the city. The decision, as Faisal and many others later learned, was more or less unilateral from Abd al-Karim Qasim, which was how he ended up claiming ownership of the operation and later becoming the first president of the republic of Iraq.

When Faisal arrived home that evening, he found his mother sitting in the middle of the living room, her face red and her eyes full of tears. "Why?" she shouted when she saw him. "Why did you all kill the king? What had he done? The grandson of the Prophet. Still young. Still unmarried. He had barely tasted life! Why?" She was sobbing.

Faisal hadn't witnessed the scene at the palace, but he knew all about it. Soldiers had murdered not only the king but also the majority of his family, including women and young children. Faisal could not wrap his head around that. And that wasn't even the worst part. He had personally seen Abdulilah's dead body being dragged on the streets and then hung upside down, naked, from the balcony of a public building. Faisal wanted to tell his mother that a mob of civilians, not soldiers, had done that, but she'd already declared him guilty. The mob had even cut body parts off Abdulilah's corpse.

Faisal sat at his mother's knees, put his hand over her head, and kissed it. "Mother, it's chaotic out there, and I don't even know what is going on. All I know is there was a revolution against—"

"No," his wife said. "It was not a revolution. It was a military coup. Call it what it is."

His family was ambushing him before he even had time to process what was happening, mounting their own coup against him. He chose to avoid confrontation. Mustafa was asleep, and Asma didn't want him to be awakened. Faisal was light-headed and felt like the floor was tilting sideways. He drank three cups of water and crashed in bed, drenched in sweat and covered with dust and still wearing his uniform.

The next morning, he slept through loud protests outside, Mustafa's crying inside, plus the argument between his wife and mother, and he only woke when Asma shoved him. It was past nine, and he'd already missed the morning military shift, something he'd never done before.

Around ten, the heat from the sun through an open window finally made him uncomfortable enough to get up even though he didn't want to. Even after a long night of exhausted sleep, he still couldn't process what was happening.

His heart sank when someone banged on the front door. He strode past Asma's blank face and avoided eye contact with his mother and opened the door to find Suhail in clean military gear and as serious-looking as Faisal had ever seen him.

"What are you doing, man? You didn't show up at the base this morning. You can go to jail for that, you know." He seemed as relieved to see that Faisal was alive as he was concerned about him being a no-show.

"Come in," Faisal said and pulled the door open, but Suhail grabbed his arm and shook it.

"Are you not hearing what I'm saying? You have to change and get ready right away. I lied on your behalf and told them your son was ill, but we'll both be punished if you're not on the base by noon."

Suhail and Faisal went all the way back to the first year in the academy. He came from an extremely poor family, which had moved to the outskirts of Baghdad from the southeast and lived in tents along with thousands of others in an area known as Al Chawader, The Tents. Suhail always seemed to be privy to inside information that Faisal knew nothing about. He was the one who first explained the difference between Sunni and Shia Muslims after declaring that he was Shia when Faisal noticed that he was praying with his hands down instead of crossed over his chest. Until that moment, Faisal had assumed that everyone in Iraq looked, believed, spoke, and practiced like the people of Sudah. His parents had never spoken of different religions or sects. While studying religion at the mosque, Faisal learned of the various schools of thought in Islam, but never the Shia sect. Suhail never said anything with a discriminatory tone but more of an enlightening one, and Faisal enjoyed learning from his friend about the different sects in Iraq and about the various political groups. But the two never mentioned religious sects again except in the context of politics.

Walking through the busy streets and maneuvering through the chaotic crowds, Faisal was trying to make sense of what had just happened. He suspected that Suhail knew some details of the military operation that he wasn't sharing, but Suhail swore that he was as shocked as Faisal and thousands of other officers.

"But why was there so much bloodshed?" Faisal asked.

"I know, brother, that was unnecessary, especially since Abdililah ordered the royal guards to put down their weapons."

Later, when Faisal got home, his mother met him at the door. The radio had been broadcasting news that Nuri Pasha had been captured after moving around in disguise. But the talk of the town was how Nuri Pasha was killed and dragged through the streets. Faisal's mother heard from a neighbor that a bloodthirsty mob dumped Nuri's body, or whatever was left of it, on the road and let cars run over it until it was nothing but wet, bloody tissue. Faisal didn't even want to think about that. His mother, however, pulled him into the living room, handed him the Quran she had been reading from, and demanded that he put his right hand on it.

"I want you to swear that you had no involvement in these barbaric acts. Right now, or you are not my son, and I am not your mother."

Asma sat down and started breastfeeding Mustafa.

Faisal chuckled, but his mother shouted at him, which was enough for him to gather every bit of seriousness in his body. With pleading eyes, he looked at his mother, but she shook her head. She was not going to have it. With his hand on the cover of the Quran, Faisal swore that he was not involved in any acts of violence.

"I knew there would be a military operation, and I've been in favor of overthrowing the corrupt and broken system, but on Baba's grave, I'm as shocked at what happened as you are."

His mother's face softened a bit, but Faisal saw looks of doubt on both his mother's and his wife's faces every time he left the house early or came home late.

He kept a low profile as events continued to unfold. The army men were in charge. They hammered anyone who dared to question their authority, but most people seemed to be content. At least that was how it appeared. Some people were on the streets protesting, but not for or against anything in particular. They often didn't know what exactly was taking place, but the previous sociopolitical system had become like a still-water pond, smelly and stinky, and any source of fresh water was rejuvenating. At least that's what Faisal kept telling himself.

17

Baghdad
Late 1950s to Mid-1960s

One of Abd al-Karim Qasim's first orders was the dissolution of the Baghdad Pact, ending the three-year defense treaty Iraq had with Turkey, Iran, Pakistan, and Great Britain. Nationalists welcomed the move. Communists enthralled by the Soviet Union saw a stick in the eye of the West. Most others carefully observed and celebrated the army's bold moves, including attempts to nationalize the oil industry and liberate it from foreign control.

The hundreds of infrastructure projects originally started under the king's administration grew into thousands. Faisal was especially happy for his friend Suhail when the revolutionary government issued a mandate to build the largest housing project yet where the tent city Suhail had grown up was established. The new development was called Madinat al-Thawra, Revolution City.

Within the first few months of the new Iraqi republic, conflict arose between the two engineers of the revolution. Abdul Salam Arif, fascinated with Egypt's Nasser, wanted to pull Iraq into a united nationalist front with Egypt akin to the United Arab Republic that included Egypt and Syria. Qasim, however, strongly rejected this notion and repeatedly emphasized his commitment to maintaining Iraq's sovereignty.

When Faisal read about Qasim's orders to send Arif away on foreign diplomatic duties, he turned to Suhail and smiled. "Can you smell the paranoia here?"

"He'll be back," Suhail said. "There's too much power for either one of them to so easily give up."

When Arif later returned to Baghdad, Qasim's concerns about a potential effort to overthrow his power grew even stronger. He accused Arif of plotting against Iraq's national interests and sentenced him to death, though he later reduced it to a prison sentence. Despite not formally serving a sentence, Arif remained a thorn in Qasim's side. In the eyes of the majority of the public, Qasim was the father of the poor. Arif and likeminded Iraqis, however, saw him as a dictator.

What Faisal had so long wished for finally happened: the end of the rule of the feudal lords. Land was to be redistributed back to the farmers. They would own it, farm it, and earn every bit of its proceeds.

1960 was Faisal's time to ride the wave. He was in charge of a medium-size military unit with ten cars under his command and plenty of guns at his disposal. It was time to use the law to return his father's land, but somebody else took care of it before he could make a move.

The Communist Party entered the mainstream after years of building up its public support and feeding on the widespread frustration from the progressively worsening socioeco-

nomic conditions of the poorer classes. Mobs of farmers and
communists descended on rural land, calling for the heads of
tribal leaders, landlords, sheikhs, and anyone else who
enjoyed social status under the previous political system.
Maryam's husband, having inherited land, men, and attitude
from his father, chose violence. His dozen or so armed men
were no match for the hundreds of angry farmers and workers
purging decades of swallowed anger, frustration, and social
enslavement. By midnight, he and every one of his guards
were killed. Maryam's father, however, like many others,
escaped to Baghdad and burrowed into a hiding place.

She showed up at Faisal's house in Baghdad one evening,
draped in black and begging to talk to him. Asma felt threatened, but Faisal's mother invited Maryam in and offered
condolences. Maryam didn't seem to care much about her
dead husband. She wanted to talk to Faisal, but he was out at a
meeting.

"I need Faisal's help to protect my father," Maryam pleaded
with tearful eyes. "Just ask him to help my father come safely
out of hiding, and I will forever be indebted to all of you."

Faisal's mother gave her word that she would make him
protect their once-valued neighbor and treat him forever like
family.

Asma was jealous and terrified by the prospect of her
husband meeting with his former crush and now widow.
Faisal, however, was scared of turning over old stones and
resurrecting lost feelings, and he certainly had no interest in
meeting with Maryam's father. But he later agreed to make
arrangements for him to be moved somewhere safe, to a
distant small town in the far east near the Iranian border.
The man was to never return to Baghdad or even think about
contacting him ever again. Maryam collected whatever
fortune was left from the remains of Bul Khair's kingdom

and followed her parents with her children into the unknown.

~

etween the late forties and early fifties, a group of anti-imperialist Arab Nationalists forged the Arab Socialist Ba'ath Party in Syria and dreamed of a unified Arab nation under a single centralized government.

In the weeks following Qasim's coup by Abdulkarim Qasim in 1958, one of the Ba'ath Party's founders, Michel Aflaq from Syria, visited Baghdad and implored the Iraqi military leaders to join the burgeoning and expansionist United Arab Republic, the merger of Egypt and Syria, but they adamantly refused, openly reiterating their commitment to Qasim as the first leader of the Republic of Iraq. The Communist Party was powerful and influential, and as a token of appreciation for their support, Qasim gave them unprecedented power in both the political and social arenas. This, of course, didn't sit well with the Ba'athists, who were slowly garnering more support, especially inside the military.

Faisal had always been impressed with Suhail's ability to accurately perceive what was happening on the ground when others could not. He often kept his analysis to himself until he tested it and proved it before sharing it with anyone else.

Faisal always made his views clear to Suhail, and he repeatedly said he was appalled at the violence against the king and his family.

Suhail argued with him at first, noting that Qasim wasn't even in Baghdad yet when the murders took place. Rather, it was Arif, Qasim's close friend, who first entered the city and instigated mob violence with his rhetoric. They both knew, however, that an army officer fired the first shots against the royal family.Later, Suhail admitted to Faisal that Qasim could have issued swift orders to protect the royal family from violence.

Both Faisal and Suhail decided it would be best for them to carry on with their duties as respected officers without getting involved in anything that could force them to harm or oppress anybody. Even so, Suhail hinted at how he felt about politics, especially in Baghdad, given that it was the capital and a forever-boiling cauldron. On a few occasions, Suhail told Faisal that he had been speaking with some rising young members of the Ba'ath Party in Baghdad and was coming around to their ideas, but Faisal dismissed all that, claiming no further interest in new ideas. But deep inside, Faisal was constantly searching for a stable ideological foundation. In 1961, the Ba'ath Party in Syria mounted out a coup against Nasser's centralized rule from Cairo, terminating the short-lived United Arab Republic.

Asma and Faisal failed to conceive again, and his mother blamed the terrible events in the country for the absence of blessings. "There is too much hate in everyone's veins, and peace doesn't live where hatred grows its roots."

She constantly pressured Faisal to move the family back to Sudah, but Asma was not going to give up her job, not when she had been enjoying the luxury of full daycare from her mother-in-law and not after getting a promotion. Faisal made it clear that he wouldn't even discuss returning to the village, and eventually his mother gave in.

In November 1963, there was another military coup, this time against Qasim. Faisal's mother stood at the door, blocking him from leaving. "Neither you nor Asma are going out even if that means losing your jobs. That's an order."

Faisal was taken aback. He slumped onto the couch and closely listened to the radio.

"Don't you see what happened?" his mother shouted. "These army animals killed the royal family in cold blood, and Allah has since withdrawn his blessings."

Asma nodded, but Faisal shook his head.

"Are you seriously going to tell me otherwise?" his mother said. "Look at them. Qasim's own right-hand man turned on him."

Indeed, Arif had just declared the end of Qasim's rule on the radio. It was just like five years earlier when Qasim declared the end of the treasonous royal rule and the beginning of a new era of nationalism and rule by the common people.

"Mama, not every change is a coup. There are no tanks or army men marching on the streets. This is different."

But Arif ordered Qasim to be executed. When the news broke on the radio, Faisal withdrew to his room. He couldn't bear the I-told-you-so looks from his own wife and mother.

Mustafa turned six, but somehow Faisal always felt that he had not been part of his son's childhood. When he wasn't physically absent at work, he was consumed with thoughts he couldn't talk about at home.

Suhail had moved up in the ranks quickly after the last coup, and Faisal hadn't even seen him for six months. So he invited Suhail to join him for tea in his father's favorite shop. Faisal sat on one of the same wooden chairs that he'd so often sat on before, only this time he sat across from Suhail. The man looked, walked, and talked differently. He clearly had become someone important aside from his military rank. Somehow Faisal felt a sense of non-belonging. What would his father have said about the state of his son's life had he been alive and sitting face to face with his son, upon whom he had hung a great deal of hope and dreams? Would Haj have been happy with his son?

Little had changed in the coffee shop since the last time Faisal's father had been there, but so much had changed outside on the street and inside Faisal, who felt like he had become foreign to the place. The owner had passed away, but his two sons had done well keeping up with the tastes of various customers. The same man was still playing the same tunes on the qanun.

Faisal put his empty glass of tea down and leaned closer to Suhail so no one else could hear him. "I need you to help me get a better job. I can't keep leaving for the base early every morning for the rest of my career."

Suhail chuckled. "Man, I thought you brought me here to discuss a coup or something."

"God knows we don't need any more coups."

Suhail leaned back in his chair and motioned for the tea boy to bring refills. "What happened to Qasim had to happen. He served his purpose, and his time had come to move aside, but he wouldn't let go."

Faisal reminded himself that Suhail was now an established member of the Ba'ath Party and that the group of military men who overthrew Qasim included seasoned army leaders with strong Ba'ath ties. The second round of hot tea arrived, and Faisal attended to his glass with passion, savoring every sip.

Suhail sat quietly for a few moments, then said, "I could get you a job at the Ministry of Defense, but you would have to—"

"I'm not going to join the Ba'ath Party, or any other party for that matter."

Suhail burst out laughing and took out a cigarette, something Faisal had never seen him do. He went through the process of lighting the cigarette with as much formality as he could. He might as well have shouted that he was a professional smoker. It was time for the third round of tea. Less sugar this time, Faisal requested.

Suhail inhaled the thick smoke. "You don't have to join the Ba'ath, although that would be your best bet in the jungle of Iraqi politics. You will have my support, but you must promise me that you won't join any other groups or stand in the way of the Ba'ath plans."

Faisal didn't know what to say.

Suhail continued. "We are now everywhere. We have members in every ministry, every municipality, every school, and under every roof in this land."

Faisal listened attentively, ignoring the loud music from the qanun.

Suhail suddenly looked at his watch and anxiously said, "I have to get to a meeting. Look, Faisal, you are like a brother to me. I will work on getting you a well-respected position inside the Ministry of Defense. Just promise me you won't make me look like an idiot later."

"You know I won't do that."

Suhail stood up, and before leaving he leaned over and whispered in Faisal's ear. "It's just a matter of time before you and every other talented young Iraqi with a brain joins the ranks of our party. We will take over. Keep an eye out and watch."

Faisal sat there and decided to have another glass of tea, this time alone and with no sugar.

He slowly processed what his friend had said as the tea lost its steam and grew cold. He reminisced about visiting the tea shop with his father as a child, when he'd hoped that one day he would become someone important, that he'd stride into the shop with charisma and attitude just as he'd once witnessed an officer do. He could still do that. He still wanted to. He was going to land a new job at the ministry, and he was going to step up the ladder without the need of any political party affiliation.

Faisal did indeed secure a new job maintaining the communication of logistics among the various branches of the military. Now the two friends were back in the same building but separated by two floors of concrete and many levels of status. Suhail had just received a promotion to be an assistant to the director of military intelligence, who was also one of the founding members of Iraq's Ba'ath Party.

Faisal enjoyed a low profile at the new post. He was sharp and a quick learner. Beyond that, he also proactively suggested new ideas and programs to optimize efficiency within the department.

Barely a week went by without his mother repeating her promise that she would leave Baghdad if she found out he was involved in politics. "Nothing beyond what your military duties require," Asma added, underscoring his mother. Heads flew with every coup and every change of administration. They wouldn't tolerate the man in their lives becoming collateral damage in another political and military adventure.

Even in 1966, when president Abdul Salam Arif died in a mysterious helicopter crash in southern Iraq during an official trip, Faisal kept silent at work and at home. He had strong opinions about the thick carpet of political influence the Ba'ath Party had laid across the country. It even manipulated the system to appoint the dead president's brother, Abdul Rahman Arif, as a lame duck president so they could proceed with their quest for absolute and uncontested power. For once, Faisal found himself outsmarting Suhail in reading the political map. Or at least that's what he thought.

Suhail said to him in confidence, "See how welcoming we are of all views? Although the majority of the men in power, especially from the military branch, are from the Ba'ath, we let Abdul Rahman Arif take the presidency."

Faisal chuckled but kept his true convictions at bay.

He could see the upcoming fire from miles away.

18

Belarus-Poland Border
November 2021

The weather has decided to be a bit more accommodating as we hit the road. With the exception of some mud here and there, most of the land is dry, but it's the type of dry that's cold and hard. It feels like concrete if you fall on it. We're initially able to see a large crowd of people at the border, but the view is soon blocked when we enter a dense forest. The forest is spooky, so I pick up my pace but soon realize that Gulistan can't keep up and has fallen at least a hundred feet behind. I'm one of the few men at the beginning of a long line that extends for at least three hundred feet. Men, women, elderly, young, children, sick, and well are all walking with one goal: to reach the fenced part of the border where thousands of others have already gathered. The accounts of their experience there so far are not promising.

We turn the corner near the edge of the forest and reach a hill overlooking masses of people below. Looking down, we see people moving about in no particular direction. A large group is pushing against the barbed wire fence only to be met with water cannons. We make our descent down the hill, and when we get close enough to see the impact of the water cannons, we stop, each turning to their walking companion with looks full of concern. One cannon pierces the barbed wire, throwing a man back a few feet, then violently throwing him sideways on his left side. Another man rushes to take his place, and the water from two cannons meets above his waist, instantly bringing him down on his back, motionless. Two men surround him and a few seconds later pick him up after much struggle. There's screaming all around. I see a long line of blood stuck to his back when one man turns him over and carries him over his shoulder.

I can't tell how long Gulistan has been standing next to me, but I'm sure she's seen enough when she asks, "Can they do that?"

I remain silent as some people around us resume walking.

Gulistan adds, "We're refugees, for God's sake. How can they do this to us?"

She goes into a coughing spree, barely holding on to her wooden cane. I grab her arm and gently pull her toward me. "Let's get going. Let's walk toward human civility!"

Some Belarusian soldiers appear from behind the growing crowd of people. They head in our direction in a manner that appears to have been rehearsed. They guide us like a herd of sheep toward the action by the fence. It's no longer ambiguous. The whole game is clear. The Belarusians want to gather us into masses and push us over the fence, putting pressure on the Poles to accept us. In doing so, Belarus is striking back at Poland for siding with Western European nations and sanctioning the pro-Russian Belarusian government. We've been hearing about this chess match between the two sides on the radio for days now. But it feels different to finally realize you're a piece on this board, and a worthless pawn at that.

I hold Gulistan's hand, and we slowly slip out of the crowd and move next to a large tree where three small tents have been set up, maintaining a few hundred feet distance from the clashes. Darkness falls quicker than we expect, and I set up a small camp next to one of the tents after getting permission from the small family staying in it. They somehow think Gulistan is my mother, and I decide not to argue. I soon realize the amenities back at the warehouse are ancient history.

After midnight, Gulistan experiences another heavy bout of coughing and shortness of breath. The more our neighbors try to talk to her, the more anxious she becomes. Finally, when everyone disperses, she calms down and goes quiet. I take advantage of this precious moment of peace and try to rest while Gulistan is seemingly asleep.

The camp settles into relative silence long after midnight, and I sit up with my back against a nearby tree. Gulistan's muffled voice pulls my half-asleep mind back into the dreaded present.

"I saw my son's beheading!"

I remain motionless, assuming that she's talking in her sleep. Even the slightest move could wake her up and hurl me into another emotional storm.

"I saw a video of my son being slaughtered by ISIS."

Her body is motionless, but her words seem to move the ground underneath me.

I sit up straight and shine the light of my camera on her face to find it soaked with tears. Gulistan has been crying silently while I sat not too far from her, my mind far away from here, from her, and from her sadness, until she decided to cut through my senses like a sword slices bread. I help her sit up and drink some water. She cleans her face with her scarf and looks at me, desperate to pour more of her emotions on me. I stare at her with as empty a look as possible, but she somehow sees through my face and finds a corner in my mind that can still hear her.

"My son, Zeerak, was only twenty-four when he joined the Kurdish Peshmerga fighters. We needed help when his father passed away. God! My husband is another story. He was a seasoned Peshmerga himself back in the late seventies, but he then came down and settled near Kirkuk, where he and I got married and we both pursued teaching careers. My husband died from a heart attack, and Zeerak was all we had. No other children. He was our world, our soul, our hope. He was whatever legacy I had left from my husband. He became a Peshmerga because he grew up hearing his father talk about their legacy. Also because it was a way for him to support us financially while fighting to defend our land."

I listen, every inch of my body held hostage to Gulistan's account of her son's struggles to make a living for himself, his wife, his mother, and his three little children, one of which is ill and in need of regular doctor visits and treatment. Even a nearby commotion by the border fence doesn't stop her from talking passionately and me from listening attentively. A few warning shots go up in the air when some men attempt to cut through the barbed wire fence, and soon the Polish soldiers strike back hard, forcing the men to back up and back down.

Gulistan, meanwhile, doesn't take a break for even a second.

"He was captured with dozens of other Peshmerga in a unit near Sinjar, where the first ISIS attacks took place. They were ambushed and quickly overtaken thanks to the American Humvees and artillery the ISIS fighters had gotten their hands on." I'm listening, but I'm also watching the chaos around us in the haunting darkness pierced by gunshots and security lights.

I don't know what to say to Gulistan except, "I am so sorry for your loss. May Allah bless his soul in the highest levels of paradise."

But she is not done. "When I first heard there was a video of his beheading being circulated, I couldn't believe my ears. I thought it was war propaganda. In all the wars and armed struggles we'ad been through, we never experienced the kind of brutality ISIS brought down on us." She starts crying again but continues in her muffled voice. "Soon, the video of three Peshmerga being beheaded spread like fire on a dry farm. Everyone was talking about it. I resisted my urge to watch the video for three days, but I finally gave in." Every bit of her emotions is being squeezed into her words. "It is the heart of a mother. I had to see his last look. They stood behind him and started cutting through his neck like he was a ..." She breaks down while I'm still confined to my awkward silence.

19

Baghdad
1960s–1970s

Abdul Rahman Arif proved to be more difficult than the hidden hands had anticipated. His leadership and charisma conflicted with each other in many ways, generally in good ways. He was a seasoned and well-established military man, but he appeared civic-minded in public. Supposedly he didn't want power, but he exercised it to advance strong internal and external agendas, often despite the displeasure of many in his circle. He forged close ties with Syria and Egypt. The Jordanian royalty had been at odds with Iraq's leadership since 1958, when their immediate family members (both Iraq and Jordan were ruled then by the Hashemite family) were brutally executed and their crown disrespected. However, Arif was able to bring about reconciliation and made a formal visit to Jordan. Thousands of political prisoners and detainees were released on his orders, and he gave political parties of various interests and ideologies some breathing room. He met with the Kurdish leader Molla Mustafa Barzani and deescalated an internal conflict between Baghdad and Kurdish groups in the north that had been heating up since the days of Qasim. Many of those in the political and military arenas, however, saw Arif's charisma as weakness in a political jungle, something to be taken advantage of.

Faisal found in Arif's apolitical status an opportunity to advance his career without having to compromise or be forced to join a particular party. He was promoted to be one of four assistants to the top military adviser for Arif inside the Ministry of Defense. Suhail's visits with Faisal increased in frequency, and so did his urging for Faisal to join the Ba'ath Party. Faisal, however, held his ground and often used the excuse of his mother threatening to disown him if he were to join any party or participate in any violence.

"We are going to overthrow him," Suhail said over tea one night at Faisal's house.

"Who is *we*?" Faisal asked, forgetting his tea in the heat of the moment, something he rarely did.

Asma dropped a glass plate on the kitchen floor. Obviously she had heard what Suhail said.

"Arif is weak," Suhail said, "and he's letting all sorts of civilian amateurs enter the government. He needs to go."

Faisal was astonished at the audacity of a single person, just *one*, in the military, not even of high rank, delegating to himself the right to decide when a president needed to go or how he should be handled. Faisal wanted to ask him if this was the mainstream of the Ba'ath Party's pursuit, but he already knew the answer.

Suhail kept at it over another round of tea, this time with a thick cigar. "We have military heads outside the Ba'ath ranks who also agree with us and want to rid Baghdad of Arif. This might be a good time for you to join the Ba'ath. You don't want to be left out."

Faisal's mother came out of her room, walking gingerly, and called on Asma to get her a warm towel ready for her stiff back. She had yelled at Suhail and Faisal many times in the past for discussing politics, so her presence meant the end of the discussion. When she sat down and said little, that was her signal for Suhail to leave. One thing was clear in her house: adults are children when they discuss politics, and children have no idea what they want or what's best. And when children are about to go astray, mothers must take over. His mother was not going to let go of the reigns of her house.

Later that night, Asma wasted no time. As soon as Faisal lay next to her in bed she said, "You are going to report this, right?"

"Report what?" Faisal said, knowing perfectly well what she meant.

"What your friend said about a coup against the president!"

Faisal knew deep down that he wanted to report that information, and he was going to, but he first needed to free himself of the guilt of having to betray his friend's trust—or was it arrogance?

The next morning, Asma stood in front of Faisal after helping him fasten the last button on his clean and shiny military suit. After all those years, she was still as beautiful as ever. He had not totally forgotten his first love, Maryam, but for all the days, nights, months, and years Faisal had been with Asma, the beauty of her face and heart reduced all others to shadows.

Mustafa was at the front door outside, waiting for Faisal to walk with him to his school. Before Faisal moved, Asma stepped closer to him, took both his hands, and passionately kissed them. Faisal pushed his face into her hair and kissed her gently. Asma then whispered in his ear. "Remember, you would be doing your president and your country a favor, and that is far more important than any friend's loyalty."

Faisal gently pulled away and offered a reserved smile, then walked out with Mustafa, holding his hand and squeezing gently as Mustafa firmly held his small backpack and enjoyed his walk of fame next to his father. When Faisal dropped him off at the entrance of the elementary school, he watched as Mustafa excitedly interacted with his friends.

"Is that your father?" one student asked.

Mustafa turned and looked at his father. "Yes. I want to be an army lieutenant like him when I grow up."

Faisal walked to the bus station and felt a heavy knot in his stomach as he headed toward work.

He turned out to be just one of many who warned the oblivious leadership about a coup through the president's assistants and allies, although he may well have been the one who felt the heaviest guilt for breaking a friend's trust. Asma may have been proud of him, but he was terribly disappointed.

"What was the point?" he told her. "The president pardoned all of them. They're now back at work as if nothing ever happened."

"Well, what did you want him to do? Execute them all?"

"Listen, woman, you can't politically survive this zoo without an iron fist. Eat or be eaten ... Or get out of politics all together."

Asma smiled. "That's why your mother and I are glad you've chosen to divorce rotten politics for good."

Arif's pardon proved to be the cardinal sin in his career. Shortly after the pardoned men were back on the streets, they plotted again, this time with more sophistication. They surrounded the presidential palace with tanks and soldiers and offered the president a peaceful exit in return for guarantees of his safety. Arif and his immediate family were soon in London, and the Ba'ath men were finally, and exclusively, at the top of the hierarchy.

Another seasoned military personality and a respected leader within the Ba'ath Party, Ahmed Hassan al-Bakr, took over as president. There was no bloodshed this time, but Faisal confided in his wife his grave concerns about his life, especially after he found out that the presidential adviser in the Ministry of Defense who had delivered Faisal's warning about the coup turned out to be a trusted Ba'ath member planted inside the ministry. Suhail, however, vouched for his long-time friend and secured not only official forgiveness but also permission to remain inside the Ministry of Defense, although on a lower level.

Mustafa was an exceptional student. No teacher ever punished him, nor did any administrators complain. During his elementary and middle school years, he was often rewarded with extra cookies or bottles of milk from the free student meals provided in schools. He held onto them and brought them back to his grandmother. After all, Mama Batul was the one who had walked him to school on his first day of kindergarten. She held his hand when he received his school immunizations, magically blocking pain and fear while dozens of other kids screamed in terror on the streets whenever the mobile health department teams rounded up children of the required age. She had also contributed to Mustafa's childhood collection of toys, magazines, and newspaper clips featuring spaceships and replicas of satellites and other new advances in the world of aerospace and communication. Mustafa memorized the names of all American and Soviet astronauts and often fell asleep thinking about becoming a famous astronaut himself.

20

Baghdad
1970s

Mustafa's grades were good enough for medical school, and neither Faisal nor Asma had considered an alternative to Doctor Mustafa. When Mustafa said he wanted to apply to the military engineering college, Asma gasped in shock, and Faisal shook his head in firm disapproval.

His parents were not having it. Asma spent countless hours at night crying while Faisal brooded in silence, pouring one glass of hot tea after another into his empty stomach. He wanted their son to be anything but a soldier. Knowing how much his mother disliked the army, Faisal thought of turning his son over to Mama Batul and declared that whatever she decided would be final. But after less than fifteen minutes with his grandmother, Mustafa secured her blessings to apply to his school of choice. Her word may have been law, but she had always been inclined to let Mustafa get what he wanted as he reminded her so much of her late husband.

"Let the kid decide what he wants to do," she said as both Faisal and Asma stood there in disbelief. "It's a college, not the army."

Mustafa kissed the hands of his parents and said, "I want to study satellites and communication and make our nation safer and stronger."

And on the first day of college, Batul insisted on accompanying Faisal and Mustafa all the way to the door on Rasheed Base. On their way home, Faisal and Batul stopped outside Haj Mohammad's favorite tea shop in all of Baghdad. With great effort, Batul pointed her cane at the rusty and worn-out shop sign, showing every one of her seventy-two years. Thick clouds of smoke billowed out of the shop.

"I outlived your father," she said. "He belongs there, and I belong to the village where his grave is now."

Faisal gently took his mother's arm, and they slowly moved along. "Don't say that, Mama. Long life, *inshallah*." God willing. "And may you always maintain a tent above our heads as a blessing from Allah."

One morning in 1977, Faisal was busy reviewing some papers on his desk at the ministry when he heard a commotion down the hall. Three guards appeared in front of his office and instructed him and two of his assistants to maintain their positions. At the same time, more guards rounded up the people in every other office on that floor. The office had been randomly selected for a surprise visit from the vice president.

Saddam Hussein had been a regular face on national TV, and his photos were everywhere. Suhail had told Faisal a lot about Saddam's rising star, especially since his long-time mentor Ahmed Hassan al-Bakr became president. Both men were from the same town, Tikrit, and while there were dozens of others from within the Ba'athist ranks much better qualified for the vice presidency, Al-Bakr used all his efforts to push

Saddam Hussein to the forefront. Everyone knew that even though Saddam was vice president, he was the real ruler, having slowly and meticulously penetrated in every corner of the state with his eyes and hands. It was said that Saddam even spied on the president, but Faisal thought that was a stretch of the imagination on everyone's part, both those who adored Saddam and those who feared him.

Of the twenty-three offices on that floor, Saddam Hussein randomly chose to stop at Faisal's while making his rounds surrounded by heavy security and an entourage of officers. He walked through the door, full of charisma and confidence. Faisal was already standing, and given his inherent military training, he found himself giving the military salute to Saddam Hussein even though Saddam was wearing a navy-blue civilian suit. There were no cameras and no media. This was merely a surprise visit for purposes known only to Saddam Hussein himself.

When it was apparent to Saddam that Faisal was the man in charge in that office, he motioned for him to sit down, which Faisal nervously did. Saddam then took a seat across from Faisal and started asking what appeared to be random questions. How is the work environment here? Are you happy with the support and resources you're receiving? Are you noticing more support now compared to earlier years? Saddam then asked Faisal to show him some of the record keeping he had been placed in charge of, and Saddam seemed impressed.

At the end of what appeared to be an impressive exchange, Saddam asked, "So, what is your rank in the Ba'ath Party?"

Faisal's hands were shaking, his uniform drenched in sweat. "Sir," he finally said. "I am independent. I have never belonged to any political party, but I am forever a loyal son of this country and would offer my life to defend it."

Saddam had visibly lost interest the moment Faisal said " independent." Then he smiled and got up. When Faisal was himself up and straight, Saddam put his right hand over his shoulder and said, "Good job with all your efforts and your dedication to your comrades in this building." And he walked away and out through the door, followed by three guards with thick mustaches and the most serious facial expression Faisal had ever seen.

The visit happened on a Thursday. On Saturday morning, when Faisal arrived at his office, there was a letter for him demanding that he report to his supervising officer on the fifth floor. The officer thanked Faisal for his service and said it was time to honor him with retirement.

Faisal knew all too well why he was being forced out, and he exited the building without further questioning. He was home early that day, and his mother could not have been happier to hear what had happened.

Suhail had risen in the ranks of the Ba'ath Party as one of the local leaders, but he told Faisal he couldn't do anything to help, and Faisal knew better than to pursue the subject further.

Faisal was fifty-six and had spent most of his adulthood in the military. Now he was jobless and lost. Days started to stretch like eternity filled with boredom and disappointment. His visits to the coffee shop became more frequent, but every time he went there, he sulked more heavily than the last time. He preferred to sit at a corner and indulge his new habit of smoking, drink rounds of tea, and listen to men discuss various topics spanning nearly every issue but politics. His mother was barely ambulatory these days, Asma was still working, and Faisal felt as if his early and forced retirement was the beginning of a slow death.

In 1979, Saddam Hussein finally took over as president

after Ahmed Hassan al-Bakr announced his resignation. Hardly anyone dared to say it in public, but almost everyone knew that Saddam had forced al-Bakr to give up power. Shortly after taking over, Saddam summoned hundreds of top Ba'ath Party members and officers inside a closed auditorium. He announced that a plot had been exposed, and he accused the people involved of attempting to overthrow the government. Dozens of men, even some of the party founders, were yanked out of their seats and executed without an investigation, trial, or even questioning.

"Should we be worried?" Asma asked her husband nervously.

"Why? I've been out of sight for a while now. I'm more like a donkey whose days are numbered."

"Don't say that. You were lucky to get out of there in time. *Inshallah*, Suhail will make it out safely."

Suhail was not at that meeting, but Faisal learned the next day that his long-time friend had been snatched from his home by security forces and taken to a secret prison. Two days later, Suhail's family was ordered to retreive his corpse.

A week later, Faisal's family was awakened in the middle of the night by furious knocks on the door.

21

Baghdad
1970s

W ithin minutes, three armed security officers turned Faisal's house upside down while two guarded the door with only their eyes showing above red scarves wrapped around their faces. They were looking for something, and none spoke a word.

When they were satisfied with the chaos they'd created, one of them turned to Faisal and said, "Sir, we want you to come with us to the security building for questioning."

They gave Faisal a few minutes to change and be presentable for God knows what was coming. It was the first time that he seriously feared for his life. He didn't want to look his wife or mother in the eyes because he wouldn't be able to stand their worried faces. At that moment, there was nothing he could do to convince them that he had not been involved in any trouble. Instead, he chose to lower his head and follow orders. He walked out with the officers toward whatever fate awaited him.

They made him wait in a small room with dim lights. Some unknown number of hours later, after he'd completely lost track of the time, they called him into another room, where two heavy officers sat across from him while he remained standing for what seemed to be fifteen or twenty minutes. They finally motioned for him to sit down. The interrogation was detailed and serious, mostly revolving around Suhail, the terrorist, the traitor, the enemy of the people and the Ba'ath.

Faisal wanted to tell them that Suhail was as patriotic as any of them could ever be and that he had only one major problem: blind loyalty to the Ba'ath and constant praise of Saddam Hussein. But he didn't say any of that.

After hours of interrogation, one of the officers said, "There is no place in the government, the military, or the nation for someone who does not belong to the Ba'ath Party."

Faisal held his breath, realizing that Saddam had just killed some of his own friends and lifelong companions from the Ba'ath ranks. Who was Faisal to them? Now he regretted not looking at his wife and mother before leaving the house.

The officers put him back in the room for several more hours before finally summoning him again to the dimly lit and oppressive interrogation room, and this time they told him how much they knew about him and his family and specifically his son, Mustafa.

"Our files show that your son is almost finished with his studies and is on track to become a highly sought-after engineering mind." The elder of the two officers flipped through a stack of papers without reading any of them.

Faisal's head was getting lighter by the second, and at the mere mention of his son, he felt the urge to vomit.

"And so for that and other reasons, the government and its wise leadership are going to give you an opportunity to enjoy the rest of your life in peace, but with one condition."

Faisal immediately but softly said, "Yes." He'd agree to whatever they said so long as they left his family alone.

"You are to remain in home confinement. You are not allowed to leave, not even to visit friends." The officer drew a line with his pen on the last page of the file as if indicating a sealed deal. As if Faisal had a say in the matter.

But house arrest was almost as bad as a death sentence. Faisal pleaded with them to give him a chance for a more acceptable alternative. Choosing his words carefully, he said, "Please allow me to return to my home village to live there. I'll sign any paperwork that would guarantee I won't ever return to Baghdad or even leave the village."

To his amazement, someone higher up agreed to the proposal. "Your son can pick up your monthly retirement pension here in the capital, and he can visit you in the village, but you are only allowed to visit Baghdad with special written permission. And there will be a bounty on your son's head if you ever try anything that would jeopardize national security."

Faisal couldn't wait to get out of there and head back home. He was ready to leave everything behind and escape with his life and return to Sudah. There was nothing he could do that would risk national security anyway. Who was he? He was nobody. Nothing. A piece of dirt in a land full of sand that now belonged to one party and one leader, only one.

They gave him forty-eight hours to leave. Mustafa heard and hurried back home, shocked and disheartened. Asma packed whatever she could, while Batul paced back and forth and mumbled prayers. At one point she turned to Faisal and said, "This is a sign from Allah that we need to return to Sudah, to be close to your father and to our land."

At the door, before exiting the house, Faisal turned around and inspected the living room. His military hat was still on the black-and-white television set. He walked back inside, passed the TV, and entered the bedroom. From a deep corner of the old, wooden standing closet, he grabbed a dark-brown civilian Baghdadi hat and placed it on his head.

He then headed out and joined his wife and mother as they followed Mustafa into a large van he had hired to take them to Sudah.

Per Faisal's request, the driver first headed into the center of the city and drove around various streets and neighborhoods. Faisal looked through the side window in silence. Baghdad was not the same city he had first visited as a child with his father. It was as beautiful, clean, and developed as he could imagine. New highways stretched into the far distance. Older roads were now wider, heavier with traffic, and pleasing to the eyes and souls that considered Baghdad home and even to visitors. That was the effect Baghdad had on people. You could visit the city once and be forever a son to Baghdad. It grabbed your senses and burrowed into your heart. Baghdad was a page in the world's book of beauty. Once glimpsed, your soul was forever embedded in its mosaic. Baghdad was a model capital city, a thriving place bursting with life, will, and attitude. And just as it finally achieved all these things, Faisal had to leave, probably forever.

He wanted to ask why. What had he done to deserve such punishment, to be separated from his second mother? To be banished like an outlaw! But Faisal knew every moment was valuable, so he chose to remain present, to take in the view, to absorb every image of Baghdad, its people, its heat, its identity, and its beauty.

Sudah looked different but felt familiar. There were more homes and lots of new faces, and the land seemed more alive.

Palm trees had grown thicker and heavier with dates. Faisal had given one of the village men the responsibility to maintain his farms in return for keeping half of the proceeds. That was years ago, and he was not going to dissolve that partnership.

Some of his childhood friends who were still around welcomed him at the door of his house, his father Haj Mohammad's old house, which had stood strong through decades of change and abandonment. Their house was old and worn-out, and the smell of dust stuck to the walls and floors.

Asma shook her head. "We will get sick here."

Mustafa inspected the small house and quickly turned to his mother and grandmother. "Give me a week, and I'll fix it up. We'll rebuild it with concrete." He looked to his father for reassurance.

"Why wait?" said an elderly man as he firmly pressed his cane against the ground by his foot. "Faisal is the son of this village and one of us. We have memories together. We will all help."

Another man, whom Faisal remembered well from when he went swimming as a child, emerged behind the man and added. "Yes, Faisal and his family are in our eyes."

Faisal withdrew from the house and walked to the farm. He sat under the shade of a palm tree. Who knows? It could have been the same tree under which Haj Mohammad had received the news of the birth of his son. It didn't matter. All the farms shared one identity. It was time to get back to work, although Faisal felt disconnected from the land now, and his farming skills had atrophied. He'd need to leave the farm in the hands of his partner and work only as a helping hand.

Faisal, Asma, and Batul visited Haj Mohammad's grave, and when they returned home, Batul said, "I could hear your father inside his grave. He is happy for our return. He won't be lonely anymore."

As if she had just been waiting to return to Sudah so she could pack up and leave for the next world, Batul died in her sleep less than two months later. Asma found her in the morning. Her face seemed content, her body relaxed. With his mother's departure, Faisal lost his last connection to the past. He was unmoored in a present that didn't want him and didn't welcome him, one in which he felt like a stranger.

Mustafa was devastated and sat by his grandmother's grave for hours until the village imam finally forced him out of the cemetery, claiming he was violating the peace of the dead with excessive grieving.

22

Between 1978 and 1979 and toward the end of his college training, Mustafa was stationed at a military base in the northern part of Babil (Babylon) Province, which would also end up being home to the majority of his mandatory three years of military service. During his second month on the base, he came across a senior officer who had a sudden heart attack while on duty. Mustafa rushed him to the military hospital, and the doctors resuscitated him. Although unable to continue his full-time military service, officer Ahmed felt lucky to be alive and invited Mustafa to his house for lunch on a Friday afternoon. He was a lot more informal and open-minded off the base than when he was on duty.

At the house, Mustafa spotted a young woman around his age, who offered her sincere thanks for saving her father's life. She moved about the house carrying plates of food from the kitchen to the dining room. She and her mother, along with two brothers, were forever thankful, they kept saying. Her name was Huda, and she was a teacher at a local school.

Mustafa took every opportunity to visit the officer, now his mentor, and Huda at their house.

When Mustafa formally graduated and was stationed at the same base in Babil, he approached his parents about marrying Huda, hoping his mother didn't have anyone else in mind, but both his parents objected.

"Is it because she's Shia?" he asked.

Obviously rattled, his father said, "What kind of nonsense is that? We don't talk about this stuff in our family."

His mother's face had tightened with anger. "It's the outside world that corrupted your mind, not us."

"I'm sorry," Mustafa said, embarrassed. "I know you didn't teach me these ideas, but I thought it's why you're refusing."

"We just don't know the family," his mother said, "and we don't know anyone who does."

Mustafa wished his grandmother were still alive to make a pitch on his behalf. But his parents finally agreed to let him marry her after hearing good things about Huda's family. The next setback was the refusal of the security services to grant his father permission to leave the village to be present for the official proposal.

After Huda's parents blessed the marriage, her father took his sons and visited Faisal in Sudah. He knew Faisal's situation and appreciated the difficult circumstances. The visit was a gesture of a new family bond being forged, and he officially offered his daughter to Mustafa.

In 1980, war broke out between Iraq and Iran. The country was on high alert, and the TV and radio covered little else. Iran had transgressed, they kept saying, and had to pay. Some intimidating statements by the new Iranian leadership about exporting the revolution to Iraq only further fueled the heightened level of sensitivity. Hundreds of thousands of soldiers were mobilized to the front lines in the south and southeast.

Fortunately, Mustafa remained at the base in Babil, where he and Huda lived in special homes offered to officers. In 1981, Huda gave birth to their first child, a girl, whom they named Fatima. Before Fatima turned one, the family moved to Baghdad when Faisal was attached to the Ministry of Defense, focusing on satellite communication. Mustafa had an intermittent service stint on the front lines near the Al Faw Peninsula, the tiny patch of Iraq along the Persian Gulf between the Kuwaiti and Iranian borders. Small in size but huge in geographical significance. Mustafa returned home in 1984, just missing the birth of his second daughter, Hadeel.

"When will Allah grant us a grandson?" Asma kept saying.

Huda took that personally. Things took a more tortuous turn one evening while Asma and Mustafa were visiting his parents in Sudah.

"So, what will you do when your next child is also a girl?" Asma asked Mustafa, sidelining Huda.

"We will thank Allah for his countless blessings," Huda hissed back.

To add more salt to the wound, Asma said, "A man who can't get a boy from his first wife has the right to marry a second wife."

Huda's jaw dropped, but Mustafa motioned for her to keep her calm.

Faisal shook his head at Asma, then turned to Huda and smiled. "Girls are the joy of life. Our Prophet says girls are parents' door to paradise."

Huda cut that visit to the village short, demanding that Mustafa take her home and to never return to Sudah again.

Asma claimed she meant no harm, but Mustafa knew his mother meant it.

But the two women in Mustafa's life reconciled before a tragic turn of events: after a prolonged bout of coughing, shortness of breath, and uncontrolled weight loss between the end of 1985 and beginning of 1986, Asma was diagnosed with lung cancer. During that time, Huda was pregnant, and she took some time off from teaching to stay with her mother-in-law in the village. Asma refused to leave her husband for an extended treatment in Baghdad. The doctors told her that the chance of success was low due to signs of widespread disease. Mustafa managed to bring doctors to Sudah to check up on her, but he had to leave for the front lines when his name was called back to the war.

"Forgive me, my daughter. I love you." Those were Asma's last words. And she said them to none other than Huda, who held her head in her hands as she took her last breath. Faisal was away when it happened, frantically scrambling around nearby clinics to bring a doctor to save his wife.

Asma died just a month before Huda gave birth to twin boys who arrived just a few minutes apart. The midwife said that one of the twins looked like his grandfather, and so they named him Faisal. The other was named Sami, a name Faisal randomly suggested and that Huda agreed to. The twins were born in the village when Faisal the grandfather desperately needed this gift to help him cope with the loss of his beloved wife.

Mustafa had to return to his post in Baghdad.

"You are coming with us," Mustafa told Faisal. He'd secured an official letter from both the intelligence and security departments that gave his father permission to return to Baghdad with guarantees from Mustafa that his father, now in his late sixties and with a body more exhausted than if he was in his eighties, wouldn't engage in any political activities. Faisal initially refused, but he had no ground to stand on.

Life had been good for Mustafa and his family, and it became even better for them and for the rest of the Iraqis when the war with Iran ended in 1988. The economy flourished, and one could barely find a poor person on the streets. After eight years of war, every Iraqi family had sustained losses, directly or indirectly. Every household had witnessed trauma of some sort, but the country was slowly returning to stability. Victory parades took place in every city and town, and the TV screen pumped up the spirit of victory against the Iranians.

"What about the mothers of the martyrs and the wives and children of the missing?" Huda said while setting dinner in front of her husband and father-in-law.

"Be quiet, woman," Mustafa shot back. "This is not the kind of thing Iraqis are supposed to talk about."

"Who's going to hear us?"

"It's better to stay out of politics altogether," said Faisal and demanded the TV be turned off.

Who dared question the victory? Who dared question a war that started and ended with no obvious achievement other than exhaustion and tragedy? Nevertheless, those in the military were of two kinds. The first were those who served the mandatory requirement and counted every second until they got out. Then there were those, like Mustafa, who were born into military families and pursued military training until it became the air they breathed, the food they consumed, and the life that kept them going. They didn't know anything else, and their alliance deep down was to their land and the nation, regardless of who the president was.

It only took a few minutes before the discussion returned to what they had just decided to stop talking about. But what else could they talk about? The entire country had grown up on these discussions.

When Huda was attending to her babies in the other room, Faisal turned to his son and said, "Everyone is exhausted."

Mustafa sighed deeply. "*Inshallah*, things will get back to normal. The economy is already booming, and people are enjoying instant prosperity."

Faisal looked skeptical. "All the money we borrowed from the Gulf countries during this war will have to be paid back."

Kuwait alone had given Iraq over fifteen billion dollar's worth of loans, and in closed meetings, Iraq had failed to convince Kuwait to reduce its oil production to help raise the price of oil. The public knew little of this. People only saw celebrations, parades, and countless new presidential palaces being constructed all over the country, including in the beautiful Kurdish region up north. Life seemed good, and everyone went with the flow.

Mustafa had finally finished building his new house in the Haifa neighborhood on a piece of land given to him as a gift by the government, like many other high-ranking army engineers and professionals. Faisal helped him with some money after selling one of his farms. After three years of interrupted construction, they moved in. Mustafa made sure his father had a room upstairs overlooking the Tigris. That was the biggest priority for Faisal.

Their neighborhood was located on the west side of the river, off Haifa Street, conveniently located halfway between Bab Al-Moatham Bridge and Shuhada Bridge. Relatively new, it was small compared to other busy and crowded Baghdad neighborhoods. Most people knew each other and rarely felt the need to lock their doors at night. Who was going to steal from their neighbors, their families? And who dared mess with the law? Why steal when there were countless opportunities to make a good living with minimal effort?

Standing on the roof of their two-story house, Mustafa could see the other side of the Tigris, his eyes first spotting the well-known Qishla tower on the eastern bank.

Faisal, standing alongside Mustafa, pointed his finger in the direction of the Qishla and said, "The Ottoman governor Wali Midhat Pasha finished building it in the 1880s and used it as the governance palace."

Faisal had often told his son about the history of the area surrounding their neighborhood. Although not clearly documented in books as far as Faisal could tell, historical accounts of the elders often stated that the area on Haifa Street was once a strategic spot for trade and exchange during the Silk Road era. Baghdad back then was the center of the globe, Faisal often said. To Mustafa, Baghdad still felt like it, especially whenever he looked through the bedroom window and watched the Tigris from afar, glowing in slow motion whether it was sunny or cloudy.

With their combined salaries, Mustafa and Huda were able to save money to buy a car in early 1990. It was a dark-blue Volkswagen sedan, common on the roads everywhere in Iraq. Huda cracked three eggs over the hood to keep jealous eyes away.

Mustafa then took his family for a ride around Baghdad, first stopping for ice cream, then at a central supermarket to buy a camera to document their memories with the car. He stopped in front of the Freedom Monument and shot a picture of Huda holding the infant twins with Fatima and Hadeel on either side. Grandfather Faisal was holding

Hadeel's hand while she held her favorite cotton candy in the other.

Their next stop was the National Museum. Mustafa asked Huda to take a photo of him and his father next to the car and with the museum's entrance in the background. It would be a memory to match his father's moment recorded in his military uniform in front of the museum decades earlier. Things looked, seemed, and felt good, as they were for the general public. But that wouldn't last.

23

Fatima had finished second grade, and Hadeel was counting the days to the start of first grade. It was still summer, and Baghdad's punishing climate had unleashed the heat. Huda was physically worn-out from the hyperactive twins, now turned three, and their quest to explore every inch of every corner they came across. Between May and July of 1990, conflict had been brewing between Iraq and Kuwait, with Saddam openly accusing Kuwait of intentionally lowering oil prices to jeopardize Iraq's economy. When the media reported that Saddam was accusing Kuwait of stealing Iraq's oil, Mustafa whispered in his wife's ear and under the blankets (because in Iraq, walls had ears), "I am worried another war may break out."

Huda chuckled. "We, the large country with the massive army, will square off against tiny Kuwait?"

Mustafa, however, had heard that certain army units had been mobilized. "I just don't have a good feeling about this."

"Sleep, man, sleep. Military men feed off paranoia." She tapped him on the forehead before turning over for sleep.

On August 2, 1990, Mustafa was driving to his office at a Department of Defense annex building near the headquarters of the national television station, and the radio broadcast was interrupted with the familiar voice of war: "Our brave men in uniform have advanced into Kuwait and driven out the traitors." The tone was heated and daring. "We will not stop until every force of evil and treason is far away and out of our land."

Mustafa listened as he gathered enough focus to drive without causing an accident. In the parking lot, he turned the car off and pushed his head against the headrest and squeezed his eyes shut. He had so much to say, but neither talking nor listening mattered. Only one person did, and that was the figure of Saddam Hussein looming over the nation.

By that evening, Kuwait had been declared "fully liberated" by Saddam and officially annexed as the nineteenth governorate. The Kuwaiti army of less than twenty thousand was no match for the hundred and fifty thousand well-armed and highly trained Iraqi soldiers who invaded Kuwait. Mustafa was glad he had not been part of the invasion or even aware of the launch details. He had reached a level of seniority and service that allowed him to remain in an office in a communications supervision role. His expertise was both practical and academic.

That Friday, he took his father and the family to the village. Nobody mentioned Kuwait over lunch, but Faisal later took Mustafa's hand and walked with him to the river where the Tigris turned and splashed against rocks, creating enough background noise for the two men to comfortably speak their minds.

"Our man has led us into a corner of hell," Faisal said. "We won't make it out without getting burned."

Mustafa wanted to explain that he was scared of another long war, but his father understood what was happening well enough. He knew an earthquake was coming.

The entire country was shocked by the Kuwait invasion. A peaceful and quiet summer had turned into thunderstorm. The international community responded quickly, and hundreds of thousands of foreign troops were being mobilized to Saudi Arabia and other parts of the Gulf. Usually on summer nights, families gathered in their gardens or on rooftops to enjoy tea and fruit. That night, however, Mustafa and his father preferred to stay inside glued to the TV like everyone else.

The United Nations had just imposed economic sanctions on Iraq, to which Saddam Hussein responded by adding the words *"Allahu Akbar,"* God is Great, to the Iraqi flag, defying the Saudis and their allies.

Faisal sipped his hot tea and immediately put it down. He grunted and yelled, "The tea barely has any sugar in it, Huda. I may have high blood pressure, but I don't have the sugar disease."

Returning from the kitchen, Huda said, "I'm sorry. I've lost my mind. I totally forgot to put sugar in all our tea glasses. How can we not lose it with everything that's happening?"

She served a freshly baked cake, something she had learned from her mother and further perfected to the point that Faisal refused cake from anywhere else. Mustafa called on Fatima to bring sugar and raised the volume on the TV set as the broadcast showed images of President Saddam Hussein, the commander in chief of the Iraqi military, meeting with top military personnel in his gigantic presidential palace.

"You know he never received any military training and was given the highest title as a gesture," Faisal said.

"Baba, come on," Mustafa said. "How many times have I said let's steer clear of this talk."

"It is the truth," said Faisal, motioning for Fatima to pour another spoon of sugar in his glass.

"We don't want trouble, please," Mustafa said. "Let's watch the news in silence."

A fresh song was just released, blasting the Saudis for committing treason by bringing the foreign disbelievers and crusaders to walk over the holy land.

Faisal enjoyed his last sip of tea and said, "You know he'll go all the way to Saudi Arabia. If they don't stand in his way, he'll reach Riyadh in half a day. I've met that guy and seen the determination in his eyes. Nothing will stand in his way."

Frustrated, Mustafa turned the TV off and went to the front garden to smoke a cigarette. Huda followed him with a glass of water. He could still hear the others in the living room.

"A family in the neighborhood next to us was taken away after their daughter mentioned at her elementary school that her parents were complaining about the government," Huda said. "We need to be careful what we say in front of the kids."

Mustafa stood in the garden, drowned in deep, silent thoughts, trying his best to ignore surrounding voices and movement. Something was going on in his mind, something that terrified him but that he couldn't verbalize.

For the following month, Mustafa ramped up his chain smoking in the garden, something he hadn't done in a long time. He alternated between the cigarettes and alcohol, and while his family didn't like the alcohol, he was not going to quit. He compromised by indulging in both habits outside and away from the kids. Theirs was not a religious household by any means, but Huda didn't want alcohol normalized in front of the kids.

The more the TV showed Arab leaders and foreign diplomats visiting Baghdad and urging Saddam to withdraw from Kuwait, the quieter Mustafa became. The children started school, with Fatima in her last year in middle school and Hadeel beginning first grade in a highly charged environment, which didn't allow parents much capacity to share with the kids the excitement of a new academic year. By the end of November, Saudi Arabia had managed to bring together a coalition of thirty-nine nations, led by the United States, that threatened an imminent attack if Saddam refused to withdraw from Kuwait. And he continued to refuse. An ultimatum was given for a deadline of January 15, 1991, for all Iraqi troops to withdraw.

Two days after the ultimatum was announced, Mustafa returned home early from work and went straight to the garden and sat down. In his chair, he drank an entire bottle of liquor before Huda even realized it. She stood above him, her arms crossed over her chest and repeatedly shaking her head.

Mustafa dropped the news coldly: "I am going to Kuwait."

Huda's jaw dropped.

"All skilled military units have been called to the front lines."

Mustafa suddenly realized that his father had also been standing not too far behind him. "I *knew* he would do this to us."

"They've even called up retired officers," Mustafa said, then stood up and went back inside looking down at his feet.

Huda wanted Mustafa to disappear and possibly go to the north as a deserter. He could not go to the front lines, not when half the world's armies were waiting to swallow him alive. Mustafa refused the idea. Not only that, but he accused his wife of being a coward. Their nation was under attack, and it was his duty, as a military man, to defend whenever and wherever needed regardless how good or bad the leadership was.

Faisal walked down the stairs, shaking his head, and said, "One day, you'll learn how stupid this idealistic military sentiment is."

The truth was that Mustafa didn't want to go. He despised war, and if it were up to him, he'd send everyone calling for war to the other side of the earth, never to return. He'd lost faith in the military, the leadership, and in all their narratives. But he was not going to openly question authority. He'd graduated from the military school. They had grown up on the total submission mentality. He was to report in forty-eight hours, so he did. His duty, as he was told, was to supervise satellite communication for one of the large front-line units. Any duty past the border and into Kuwait meant suicide.

By the end of December, pressure was mounting on Iraq. The looming war was as close to every Iraqi citizen's chest as ever, disturbing every breath, every meal, every thought. By early January, all of Iraq was preparing for war. A war unlike any previous war. This was America they were facing off against. This was the West plus the unlimited resources from oil lords of the Gulf. George Bush was not playing around.

Faisal paced half of Baghdad before he finally found some oil for the gas heater at home. Food was scarce. Most of the shops were closed before the end of the day, and fewer children were playing outside. Schools had not resumed since closing for the midyear break.

The greatest concern was a chemical attack. Citizens were

given instructions on what to do during such an attack, and many were more terrified by the sight of gas masks than the idea of a chemical bomb dropping on their heads. Like millions of other households, Faisal's family began preparations for an imminent attack.

Huda seemed dazed most of the time, worried to death over her husband being at the front line. "What are we going to do?"

Faisal hauled in another box of dates for reserve in case they got stranded inside the house during the war. "The room opposite mine upstairs has the smallest windows, so we'll use it as our safe room."

He cross-taped all the windows. Deep in his mind, he thought that if such an attack took place, no tape would work. He was going through the motions more for peace of mind than anything else. And what peace of mind could he or Huda have when Mustafa was out there in Kuwait across from the allied forces waiting to engage?

January 15, 1991, approached, and Saddam Hussein gave no consideration to all the begging, threats, and diplomatic meetings and correspondence. Zero Hour arrived, and Baghdad was lying quietly in silent darkness, or dark silence. Faisal and Huda had already taken the kids to the safe room upstairs, and Faisal held his portable radio in his hand, anxiously switching from one station to another. Then sirens pierced the sky, followed by successive explosions. Huda and her children clung to each other as explosions continued, while Faisal stood by the window trying to find a corner from which to observe, but everything was blocked by houses and trees. Defying Huda's pleading requests not to go, he walked up to the rooftop, and halfway through the door he watched the sky light up. Glowing circles of fire extended from the ground up and from the sky down, in all directions.

Baghdad's sky became like a dark board covered with menacing green circles around red balls of fire. Faisal saw so many streaks of light from missiles that he started to think there wasn't enough space left in the sky for more of them.

A missile hit the other side of the Tigris, rocking their neighborhood. With the kids now screaming downstairs, Faisal had to run down and attend to them. What was he going to do to make sure Huda and the children were safe? And who was going to keep his son safe under a barrage of missiles on the front lines? What good would Faisal's protection of the children be if their father never returned? And what good would a safe return for Mustafa be if he found his family dead? He took hurried steps down to the first floor.

24

Baghdad
Early 1990s

Forty consecutive days of aerial bombardment by the allies left Baghdad numb and crumbling. The city had still not recovered from the biggest missile attack on the Amiriyah shelter, which left over four hundred dead and countless others injured. Then just like that, the Iraqi leadership agreed to withdraw from Kuwait through a ceasefire agreement at the end of February. Huda had been crying every day and night. Faisal made his rounds of the neighboring homes, desperately searching for news about the soldiers at the front line. No one had come back yet, but there was a tremendous sense of relief at the cessation of attacks, though no one trusted either side.

Faisal paced Haifa Street, once vibrant and full of pedestrians and cars, now a haunted, desolate road. At sunset, the city was quiet and comatose. Slowly, over the following few days, people began to feel more trusting of the ceasefire as there were no more sirens or missile attacks.

"I heard reports that the allied forces are bombarding our troops as they're retreating from Kuwait," Huda said over dinner, knowing all too well that even if her father-in-law knew about it, he wouldn't says much.

"The details are scarce and inconsistent," he said, offering no more, which only made Huda more worried.

It was an early day in March when she heard a knock on their door sometime after sundown. She rushed and opened it. Two armed soldiers greeted her, and one asked, "Is this the house of the hero Mustafa Faisal?"

Huda's heart sank, and she struggled to maintain her balance. With her weight against the half-propped metal door, she lifted her tired eyes and said, "I am sorry?"

The second officer repeated the question with more urgency. Huda wanted to know the context of their question before she could commit to a yes or no. Fatima and Hadeel were both standing behind her now, terrified, as she hesitantly nodded and sobbed. The two officers were trying to tell her something, but she couldn't make out what they were saying. Every tragic scenario of her husband she had imagined in the darkness of night was now swirling in her mind. Her grip on the door was loosening, and the weight of the earth and the hell underneath and above was pulling down on her knees. She heard Faisal's voice behind her and felt two hands picking her up. Her mind started to clear up at the voice of a third officer yelling at his two assistants, "You idiots scared her to death! Move aside."

Huda was rushed to the military hospital, where her husband was. He was alive, yes, but severely wounded. How bad? Well, you would have to see for yourself, they kept saying.

There was not much to see when she got to the room. Only

his eyes showed. His left hand was wrapped as well, and when she moved the sheets, she didn't see his legs. They had both been amputated below the knees.

A young male doctor stood hesitantly behind her and softly said, "He is heavily sedated and probably will be for a few more days."

Two days later, Mustafa had to be put back under sedation when he entered a state of hysteria after discovering he'd lost both of his legs. No one could tell Huda what exactly had happened to her husband that led to such severe injuries. He was reportedly rushed into a local hospital north of Basra by a few of his officers, and once stabilized, he was then transferred to Baghdad. Huda and Faisal took turns visiting the hospital as Mustafa slowly made a painful recovery.

While Baghdad was licking its wounds during the month of March, most of the other parts of Iraq had risen up against Saddam in ways that defied both the odds and reason. The Iraqi military had lost control of the majority of Iraq. Then in a shocking turn of events, George Bush declared that the mission of the allies had been accomplished by liberating Kuwait and that everything taking place in Iraq was an internal conflict. A few days were all it took for the Iraqi military to remobilize and crush the uprisings in the south and then in the north. Those in Baghdad had not experienced the uprising, but scraps of information arrived with accounts of utter brutality against unarmed citizens, especially in the south. They, unlike the Kurds in the north, had no escape routes.

∽

One night, Faisal heard a soft knock on the front door. Huda was at the hospital with Mustafa, and the kids were in their parents' room sleeping. Fatima got up and followed Faisal to the door. A man whispered, "Is this Mustafa and Huda's home?"

Faisal immediately opened the door, thinking this time it must be a soldier delivering more bad news. A middle-aged man barged in as soon as the door was open. Faisal yelled for him to stop, and Fatima was about to scream, but the man motioned for her to be quiet. Faisal took hurried steps in his direction, imagining the worst that could happen and contemplating the most effective way his weak and old body could contain the threat.

The man's voice was broken, and his breaths were quick and labored. With nervous steps, he approached Faisal with his hands in the air. "I'm one of Huda's cousins, and this is urgent."

Faisal ordered Fatima to go upstairs and lock the door. With the soft light of an oil lamp separating them, Faisal was able to make out the man's face. His hair was unkempt, his face pale and terrified. He was anxiously crossing his knees over each other when Faisal broke the anxious silence. "What's your story? Tell me now, or I'll call the police."

"No, please. No police. I'm running away from them."

Here we go, Faisal thought. Yet one more problem.

"Huda is my second cousin. I visited her and Mustafa a few years ago. I need help. I have nowhere else to go." He was still hyperventilating.

Faisal brought him a glass of water, which the man gulped at once.

"Another glass, please," he said. After that, he took a deep breath and resumed. "I ran away from Karbala after the uprising was crushed. They killed my wife and children along with my parents, who were inside the holy shrine. I … I couldn't get back to them in time." The man's voice was breaking, but he drew another heavy breath and collected himself. "We were stuck on the other side of town fighting back a tank unit."

Still unsure what to believe and very much terrified of getting caught harboring a fugitive, Faisal mulled his options. Fatima confirmed that the man—Abbas was his name—had visited the house with his family once before. Faisal, though, wanted to be sure, so at dawn he dropped the kids off at a neighbor's house and warned Fatima not to say a word about the man. He took a taxi and left for the hospital, leaving Abbas behind with strict instructions not to step outside or even open the blinds.

When Faisal returned with Huda, they went straight home, where Abbas was anxiously waiting. At the sight of Huda, Abbas broke down crying.

Huda prepared a breakfast from leftovers while Faisal went over various options with Abbas. "Your best bet is west. I have relatives in Fallujah who could help you get to the Jordanian border." Abbas was still shaking. "If what they say is true about the military loosening its grip on the border due to the internal mobilization, you might have luck crossing into Jordan."

Huda was obviously terrified, but she said nothing. Every minute that her cousin remained in their house, the entire family was in danger.

Faisal would have to deliver Abbas personally. "If I am not back in a week, take the kids and disappear," he told Huda.

They decided to take secondary roads using a public taxi. Faisal instructed Abbas to pretend to be an independent passenger and that if they were detained at a military or security checkpoint, he was not to indicate that he knew Faisal.

Faisal appeared at the front door on the afternoon of the sixth day, exhausted and still recovering from a serious case of nerves, after successfully delivering Abbas to safe hands in Fallujah.

"I didn't leave until my people returned and assured me that Abbas had been dropped off at the most remote point along the Jordanian border," he said, happy to see Huda's much relieved face.

The electricity was still out, and street traffic was scarce. There was still an element of the unknown, an unknown that many people initially liked since Saddam's brutal government might potentially fall at any moment. That was Faisal's thought, anyway, a feeling that he was certain that many others shared even if they didn't dare mention it, not even to their spouses. Slowly, however, that hope evaporated, and people started to slowly return to the streets like sleepy animals waking up from hibernation.

Mustafa eventually returned home, traumatized, minus two legs, and carried on shoulders. Faisal circled around the city for a day and a half until he found a wheelchair at a medical supply store.

The blue Volkswagen had been parked by the door since Mustafa had left for the war. Neither Faisal nor Huda knew how to drive. It would be a long time before Mustafa would accept the wheelchair as his new ride and even longer before he could touch the wheels with his hands to push it.

There was a lot of shouting, screaming, crying, and broken household items during the first few months of Mustafa's return. In all of Faisal's seventy years, he had never felt so sad and distraught. He sat in his room upstairs for hours, staring at the wide shoulders of the Tigris pushing against the eastern and western banks while another ocean swelled up inside the house. An ocean of sorrow drowning the hearts and souls of everyone, from Faisal down to the twin boys, little Faisal and Sami.

While Faisal sat silent and helpless in his room, the children wandered around the house looking for something to distract them from their father's state of mind. Huda ran back and forth, dutifully attending to her husband's needs and emotions, hoping he would reach a peaceful new shore. More than anything else, she wanted to know what exactly had happened to him on the front lines.

One night, she finally asked the questions Mustafa knew were coming: How did he lose his legs? What happened to him? What did he see there? What did he endure?

They were in bed, now moved to the bedroom on the ground floor. Mustafa lay there in silence, staring at the dark ceiling but seeing a burning field full of lights, bullets, and missiles. He heard everything but the silence. Mustafa gently took his wife's hand, something he had not done in months, and brought it to his face.

"We were returning from our posts deep inside Kuwait," he told her. "There were thousands and thousands of us in military trucks. There were thousands of trucks carrying heavy weaponry plus hundreds of tanks." His feelings were raw, though his words were slow and natural. "We were retreating. We were following orders. No one fired a shot. All we wanted was to cross the border and head back to Basra. We were just happy to be returning home. Then ... Then ..." His voice cracked.

Huda said nothing. She only kissed his right cheek and listened.

"Then their planes flew over our heads and targeted us from all directions. Bombs, missiles, and fire rained down on us. Trucks were flying, bodies were on fire, the sound of screams were mixed with the roaring of more planes and more bombs and more explosions. They attacked us. The allied forces attacked us when we were already retreating."

One of the girls was crying upstairs, and Mustafa went quiet.

When the crying stopped, Huda turned back to her husband and whispered. "It must've been Hadeel. She's been having nightmares since the first night the city was attacked."

Mustafa grunted while attempting to adjust himself in bed, then continued. "A missile hit the vehicle in front of us, and we were thrown out of our truck like dominos. I woke to the sounds of my friends screaming. They were on fire. I watched their bodies turn to ash and couldn't do anything but lay there and watch. When I was finally able to get up, I found dozens of our trucks attempting to escape, scattering in all directions. I ran and got the attention of one driver and jumped into the passenger seat. I was familiar with the area, so I told the driver to turn right and head toward an area thick with trees. Soon, many of the other trucks followed us. I saved ten or twenty of the wounded. I can't remember for sure. I picked them up and threw them into the truck bed. Then as we entered the farming area, a helicopter hovered above us and shot us. After that I was gone. I later woke up in the hospital half gone. No legs. I'm useless now."

There was a lot more crying that night, and a lot more sobbing, but for the first time since Mustafa had returned home, he felt like he was finally beginning to process what had happened and how he could manage in the future with his disability.

He was a local hero now. Everyone in the neighborhood spoke of him. His name was mentioned on television. Then he was invited to the Ministry of Defense and given a presidential Medal of Honor along with twenty other war heroes.

But life was never the same again. Not for Mustafa. Not for Huda. Not for the children, and certainly not for Baghdad. Mustafa felt racked by so much uncertainty that he seemed to age a hundred years every day. Nothing was going to go back to how it was no matter how much everyone tried to pretend.

25

Belarus-Poland Border

I have lost track of time. December sneaked up on us, but
who's keeping track? All our attempts to cross the border
have resulted in failure and beatings. Another outbreak of
COVID has occurred, mostly among those with the luxury of
having and sharing tents. Gulistan has already had it, and as
for me, I went through the ordeal back in Baghdad. So our
immunity, as they say, should be good now.

"We should leave this place," Gulistan says. "I am terrified
of corona."

I roll my eyes at her. "You just recovered from it. If anyone
should be worried, it's me."

"Please, Faisal. Help me get away from here. Let's find
somewhere else."

This has the quest to find her missing family written all
over it. There's another large gathering a kilometer or so away,
and more people are starting to head down there.

As we walk, the fence between Poland and Belarus separates and becomes double layered. Each country has installed its own fence, maintaining a distance of hundred feet or so, marking a neutral area where mutual hate is kept at bay. It's as if each country has violently expelled its hate for the opposite side and thrown it over the border to get its toxic wrath outside its land.

The crowd swallows us up when we arrive. Faces look paler, bodies visibly tired, and the body language even more broken. Belarusian soldiers are nowhere to be found. There are no journalists or ambulances. There's a large, flat, concrete building next to the fence on the Polish side, and it's heavily guarded. The rain is picking up, and the wind that was at our backs earlier is now swirling around us from all directions, making the already-cold weather more unbearable. A few kids are venturing around in the bushes, trying to find something to stay busy with. Several men stand with their backs against the trunk of a nearby tree, smoking cigarettes, their silence radiating hopelessness.

Gulistan and I slowly walk toward a dozen or so people gathered around a large fire, and they squeeze their shoulders against each other, making room for us, no questions asked. Soon she strikes up a conversation with two women around her age, both of whom also speak Kurdish.

We are out of water and food. When night falls, all the people near the fire start to make themselves more comfortable, some sitting, others lying down, and a few choosing to walk around to stay warm. Gulistan has mentioned her family three times so far, and as long as she isn't talking to me about them, I'm fine. We have bonded. We are like family now. But I'm also exhausted from the emotional rollercoaster I've been riding since the moment she invaded my life.

It continues to rain sporadically throughout the night, and somehow this camp is more at peace with the constant sounds of children crying, the sick moaning, and men randomly shouting at each other and at the fence. I turn to one of the men next to me and ask him how long he has been here.

"I haven't had anything to eat in three days. That is what you should be asking."

"I'm sorry to hear that. Where we came from, there were some opportunities to get assistance. You don't get anything here?"

He stretches his legs in the mud and pulls his blanket over his face. "You'd better get used to these conditions soon, or you are in for a big letdown."

I don't like his tone. I don't like the tone of this camp in general. I get up for a walk when another man next to me also gets up, holding a lit cigarette in his hand. He is from Zakho, a Kurdish city near the Turkish border, but he speaks fluent Arabic. We go for a stroll, and he says, "Don't mind that man. He's been bitter since the day I first met him back in Istanbul."

He takes a long draw on the cigarette and coughs as he exhales the smoke, causing the long column of cigarette ash to fall. We stand on a small hill and look down toward the camp. Cutting through its darkness are the flashing lights attached to the top of the fence. With each flash, the lights silently emphasize the power and control asserted over us and just how thin yet powerful this fence is. It's so little compared to the open, massive land, but it's powerful in its ability to not just separate us from the open land on the other side but also from the world of freedom, safety, and opportunity we have been dreaming of.

I have by now learned not to ask people about their stories and what brought them here. There are no good stories. I've encountered as many rich as poor. Those who were well-off back home and decided to leave are just as traumatized as those accustomed to struggling. This man, however, volunteers his story and claims that he killed one of his cousins in a conflict involving land, and that forced him to run for his life. I'm willing to bet my life that he's lying. It's probably the story he made up in his mind for immigration officials so he can get asylum. I think he has rehearsed this story so many times that he has started to believe it himself. He doesn't pass for a violent person. He needs to rehearse looking like a rough man if he wants anyone to believe him, but I've learned to keep my mouth shut around here.

In the morning it starts to snow, and a wave of anxiety and paranoia overtakes the camp. I keep referring to it as a camp, but it's just a large, open area that stretches for miles with no resemblance to a proper camp whatsoever. I notice groups of people stranded between the two fences. Hundreds of them are wandering about, moving back and forth between Poland and Belarus. My friend from Zakho tells me these people found a way to cut through the Belarusian fence. Once on the other side, they made a few unsuccessful attempts to cut the Polish fence.

"While they were engaged in chaotic exchanges with the Polish border guards, the Belarusians quickly patched up their fence, so now they're trapped."

We watch from afar as dozens of Belarusian soldiers line up against their fence, which is higher than the tallest person around.

"You know what the Belarusians are doing, right?" he asks, his eyes still fixed on the fence. Then he answers himself. "They want to keep the people stranded between the fences to pressure them to push against the Polish side. Any clashes with the Poles would make them look worse in the eyes of the media, something Belarus would enjoy."

"They're exploiting our vulnerability for political points," I say.

"Now you're getting a grasp of things, my friend." He shrugs.

Gulistan has been looking around and asking people about her family, and after each round, she returns disappointed, sometimes crying. Her grandkids are gone, and in her eyes, the last people that connected her to her late son have been taken from her.

Frustration mounts among our crowd, and we finally decide to make a run for it. We choose the weakest part of the fence where two poles connect through a recent patch. Some fifty or more of us men slowly gather near that spot and with one uniform run, we attack the fence. Some of us kick it, while others push it with their hands and backs. Portions of the fence start to swing, but the poles stand tall and strong. Those on the other side also participate by pulling the fence from their side. Soon, Belarusian soldiers gather around us and start to disperse the crowd with force. A few soldiers finally reach the fence and turn around, facing us with their guns pointed at us. We keep advancing while more soldiers arrive. Very soon, they start shooting in the air to scare us away. When that doesn't work, they start randomly hitting us with sticks and with the butts of their guns. A stampede is imminent, but something hits me on the forehead, and the world goes dark.

I wake up with blurred vision and a severe headache. It feels as if the weight of a mountain is pushing down on my forehead. Gulistan's faint voice gradually becomes clearer as her warm hand gently rubs my forehead. I sit up. A cup of hot tea has never tasted this good, and I am slowly up and awake. The crowd around me disperses once reassured of my safety. The ground is freezing, and a thin layer of snow refuses to melt. Gulistan checks up on me one more time before taking a walk with a few of her female friends. I enjoy the warm feeling inside the sleeping bag, and a Tylenol helps me fall asleep for a much-needed break from the lingering headache.

Later, I'm brutally pulled out of sleep when Gulistan violently shakes me.

"I found them!" she shouts. "I found my family, Faisal. I found them."

With shaking hands, she points behind her toward the fence. I see the same fence, the same migrants, and the same guards. Gulistan takes my hand, and I follow her some two hundred feet or so. She points toward a large group of people on the other side. As we get closer, Gulistan grips the fence and shakes it, anxiously calling out her daughter-in-law's name and then her grandkids one by one.

I don't see anyone in particular standing up or walking in our direction. "Where are they?"

She points in the direction of a small crowd in the space between the two fences and says, "She's over there, with her kids. She saw me, and when I called her name, she grabbed her kids and walked farther away. Please help me get to them."

26

Baghdad
Mid-1990s

Baghdad's infernal heat had always been infamous. If anyone wanted to give someone perspective about how hot the weather could get, they'd say, "You haven't been to Baghdad in the summer."

From noon until late afternoon, the air outside was thick, heavy, and charged. It made everyone want to hide indoors and wait for the early evening breeze. To Fatima, though, the air indoors was hotter than the punishing heat outside.

The fourth anniversary of the Kuwait war was approaching, and that meant the renewal of bad memories, the resurrection of depressed feelings, and more yelling and screaming. Her father had been planted ever deeper in his wheelchair, his hopelessness and distraught feelings embedded into every spot of the wheels. He constantly shouted, threw tantrums, demanded the impossible, and hurled his wrath at Fatima's mother, who silently absorbed the punishment until she was alone with one of her children, at which time she would explode for reasons or for no reason, over something petty or major. Whether it was their fault or not didn't matter. If her father yelled at her mother, someone else had to feel it as well. Fatima and her siblings often magically disappeared, leaving their mother's broken heart to swell without any release.

Fatima fell a year behind in school due to her heavy responsibilities at home and a million other problems while her mother desperately tried to make ends meet. Like thousands of Iraqi families in Baghdad and millions all over Iraq, theirs had suffered mightily from the economic sanctions imposed on Iraq after the Kuwait invasion.

Fatima was skinnier than ever, and her rapidly growing height made her look even more malnourished. They had not had meat for nearly two months. Their father's entire monthly pension barely covered two week's worth of cooking oil or rice. Baba Faisal also contributed with his retirement money, but it was even less than their dad's after he paid for his medicine. Their mother's teacher salary, unchanged in amount even after inflation, had plunged in value. While before she could have bought their entire monthly supplies of food, clothing, and even toys with her salary alone, now with the same money she could barely afford two weeks of basic supplies. Eggs cost ten times more than before the war. If they all shared four eggs on a plate in the morning, they felt fortunate. Fatima couldn't remember the last time her mother bought her a new dress. There was a lot of recycling going on at the sewing machine, which had reemerged from a hidden part of the house. The Volkswagen was long gone, sold to cover the cost of their father's medical treatment, rehabilitation, and a hospital bed, plus a concrete ramp in their garage for his wheelchair. They still owed the government money for the loan they took out to build the house.

Fatima was only twelve, but the sheer amount of emotional burden made her feel sixty.

"School is starting soon, and I haven't gotten your siblings any clothes or supplies," her mother said bitterly.

What about me, Fatima wanted to ask, but she reminded herself that she was the ground upon which her mother stood like a candle, burning its wax and dripping it on her until she, Fatima, would grow up one day to be a candle herself.

"I'll help you patch up the worn-out clothes from last year," she told her mother. "So all we need is some school supplies."

The previous academic year, Fatima had to share school books with two other students. She once went a whole week without getting her turn at the books. She offered her new notebooks to her younger sister and chose to make her own notebook from scratch paper. Her childhood had slipped away before she had fully lived it. Yet she still felt fortunate, especially when she looked at her seven-year-old twin brothers who had never experienced a moment of proper childhood.

As for her sister Hadeel, Fatima saw in her the dedicated student who only had one goal in mind: to become a doctor. It was all she dreamed of and talked about. Nothing seemed to distract her, not even lack of food on the table or the absence of school supplies. She always found a way to make it work. She always got a perfect mark. She always found a way to slip away into her study sanctuary upstairs.

～

The twins, Faisal and Sami, grew up in a world of deprivation. Faisal's earliest childhood experiences were tainted with loss. Loss of stability in the house. Not enough food. Having to wear the same clothes for months, often with patches on torn pants and jackets. He had some faint memories of good times in the old family car, but he couldn't make out the images. The memories were more about feeling joy and being the center of attention than about the car itself, and those memories were coming back as his mother kept talking about the great times they had before the Kuwait war, when the house was vibrant, the kitchen full of all sorts of foods, their cabinets and closets full of fancy clothing and brand-name shoes. Faisal found it hard to believe that there was a time when their refrigerator was always stocked with meat.

The common theme throughout his childhood memories was the wheelchair. It was everywhere, outside and inside. It was parked behind the main door at the edge of the ramp. It was folded and left against the wall in the hall, over time creating a small indentation. It was wherever his father was, silently screaming disappointment and noticeably atrophying with muscle decay. The damn wheelchair! A constant reminder of legs lost in war before Faisal was even old enough to understand why his father couldn't sleep. The wheelchair: Sinbad's flying carpet, except this time it magically flew his father's mind back in time to the days when he was a strong military engineer, walking in the neighborhood with attitude and poise, making him more detached from the present every time he rolled the wheels forward.

His father was still a neighborhood hero. Several men in the area had served during the war, but only one received a Medal of Honor for bravery. Only one was greeted with warm words every time someone walked past him. Faisal remembered a few times when he and his brother Sami were given candy for free at the nearby neighborhood market for being the sons of the hero.

The free candy stopped when the market closed. The

owner, a middle-aged man and a close friend of Mustafa's, was gradually forced to retire when his cash flow dwindled and fewer people came to shop.

Baba Faisal did not feel at home in the neighborhood when he first moved back from Sudah some years ago, but it didn't take long for him to acclimate and make acquaintances. There were many of them, such as the retired old men who sat on small stools on either side of the street.

Their house was two streets down from Haifa Street, the neighborhood's main artery. Wide sidewalks surrounded the well-paved street on both sides. Most houses had trees and large plants extending from the end of the sidewalk and were starting to compete with the height of the concrete walls in front of each house. Vibrant Haifa Steet was just a ten-minute walk away. Five minutes away was the elementary school. Most of the houses were modern and made of concrete with small-to medium-size gardens in the front courtyards, the concrete walls providing privacy. Almost all the homes were two stories, and some had their gardens above the garage, where the first floor actually started. The area was not wealthy by any means, but most residents were reasonably well-off when they first built their homes.

The area, though, gradually took a turn after the Kuwait war and the economic sanctions. The vitality on the streets plummeted, as it did everywhere else in Baghdad and other Iraqi cities. There were fewer cars parked in front of homes now. The cars that did survive were old, rusty, and worn-out much like their owners. The houses looked exhausted. But the streets themselves remained clean. Young and old still gathered on sidewalks, elderly men sitting and smoking and engaging in soft conversations, children running wild. Gone were the days of passionate arguments. They were tired of reminding each other about poverty, hunger, and the absence of luxury.

Baba Faisal, however, used all his will, power, and strength to push his son's wheelchair on the street and around the neighborhood, often in no particular direction, just to keep going. Staying at home meant staring at the wall for Mustafa, which led to more thinking and eventually crying or shouting. Faisal didn't want that for his son. Even at age seventy-three, his shoulders and arms still had enough strength thanks to the countless times he'd climbed up the palm trees to harvest dates, carry them down, and haul them around the farm.

He'd run out of his blood pressure medicine again, and that was a good excuse to extend their stroll from their own street onto Haifa Street. Sami was never around, so little Faisal was given the job of accompanying his father and grandfather. There they were two Faisals, three eras, and one wheelchair.

They turned left at the school, and the two Faisals took turns pushing the wheelchair, although Mustafa never took his hands off the wheels. His wife had sewed special gloves for him from leftover fabric and attached patches of leather from an old jacket. The patches fit perfectly over his palms and helped his hands grip the wheels. Traffic was heavier on Haifa Street. It was early evening, and being November, it would get dark before they knew it.

Ali's Pharmacy had been there, right at the corner, when the family moved into the neighborhood before the war. The owner of the shop had passed the reins to his son, who was also a pharmacist, but he was as indifferent about the profession as his father had been passionate about it, so over time the pharmacy had been reduced to a small drug store, mostly offering cheap pain medicine, heartburn cocktails, and other unsophisticated daily solutions.

They slowed down, but Mustafa motioned for his son to keep pushing. "There's another pharmacy a few blocks down. They'll have more medicine."

The larger pharmacy also had a depleted supply, so Mustafa said to his son, "Go with Baba Faisal across the street. There's another pharmacy over there that may carry the medicine, but be careful crossing."

Mustafa slouched deeper into his wheelchair. Night was settling in, and streetlights were reluctantly starting to turn on, some flickering, others half lit, and still others defying decay and overuse. Few passersby carried bags. Fewer laughed or conversed. But vehicle traffic was still fast and heavy. Where was everyone going in such a hurry? Were people in a rush to get home faster, where financial uncertainty, hunger, and whatever other hopeless thoughts awaited them?

None of the pharmacies had what Faisal needed.

"Why bother opening when your shelves are empty?" Mustafa said.

Baba Faisal hoped to change the mood. "When I receive my pension next week, I'll stop by one of the main pharmacies on Al Rasheed Street. Don't worry, son."

"And what are you going to do until then?"

"I just remembered. I have an extra packet stashed at home." He was lying, but he wasn't going to be the reason his son worried that night. He had an idea for a better change of scenery. He told his grandson to push the wheelchair and follow him, then reached into his pocket and felt the few paper bills. They were still there. They were all he had until the following week. They would probably lose even more value next week as the dollar was gaining even more ground against the Iraqi dinar.

A few blocks later, they stopped in front of Haifa Restaurant. Once a high-end establishment, it had turned into a fast sandwich shop as fewer and fewer people went out to eat. The restaurant had closed its large double-door entrance and opened a small window on the far corner, where patrons ordered food to go and often ate on the sidewalk. Customers were mostly workers and some youngsters wanting to experience the nightlife, whatever was left of it. They were only serving chickpea and falafel sandwiches, which was kind of redundant considering both were made from the same ingredients. The chickpeas were hot and served inside a small loaf of french bread alongside a cup of chickpea soup. Falafels came with vegetables and sauce compressed into the bread, which had been decreasing in size as flour prices skyrocketed.

Baba Faisal ordered three chickpea sandwiches, and as he inspected the remaining money, he realized he didn't have enough for even one more sandwich to take home for Sami or the girls, so he asked his grandson to keep their adventure a secret. Mustafa went through his sandwich and the soup before his son even had a chance to take a bite.

"Are you going to drink your soup?" Mustafa asked his son.

"No. I don't like soup." The cup was already in Mustafa's hand.

Little Faisal often asked Baba Faisal to walk around the neighborhood with him, sometimes even going as far as the riverbank deep in the marshy land behind their house. They stared at the calm Tigris, and Baba Faisal told his grandson stories about his childhood in the village of Sudah upstream. He showed the boy old newspaper clips and photos. Little Faisal asked if he could keep the photo taken in front of the National Museum some fifty years past. Sometimes he sneaked into his grandfather's room and took his Baghdadi hat.

Baba Faisal could tell that his grandson yearned to live in the village. The boy came to life every time they visited. With the same facial features, he was such a striking imitation of a little version of his grandfather. The two were attached at the hip. Faisal only wished he could remain in his grandson's life forever, but good things were never meant to last.

27

The Haifa neighborhood took a nosedive in the decade following its expansion in the mideighties. Victory Street in particular, where Mustafa and Huda's house was located, had mostly attracted well-off young couples on their way up, many of whom owned more than one car. Mustafa was one of the last men on the street to own one in the 1980s and also the first to sell it when the postwar sanctions pressed their merciless grip. Few families managed to maintain their previously luxurious lifestyles. By 1996, most of the neighborhood seemed to dress in the same worn-out clothes lacking spirit and will. The previously soft, spoiled, and well-mannered boys on the streets now appeared rough and poorly dressed, and they were out and about at all hours of the day and night with complete disregard for the previous informal rules about noise control.

Faisal and Sami had shared the same wooden seat at school for the past three years. They'd been forced to share books as well. Sami was the bad student. He rarely opened his books and often resorted to cheating from his twin brother's schoolwork and exams. They were only in third grade, but Sami had already been in more fights than Faisal could count. He had a scar on his left cheek from when an older boy squared off against him over comments Sami had made about his sister. The larger boy hit Sami's face with the edge of a wooden ruler, slitting it open.

"Please don't tell Mother," Sami begged his brother. "She'll kill me."

"He tripped and fell on his face outside the school," Faisal later said at home.

As unconvincing as that story was, their mother let it go when the bleeding stopped that night and didn't require stitches. In return, Sami promised Faisal that he would give him his next month's allowance. That was a joke, of course. They only got allowances during Eid, and it was barely enough for a small plastic toy. Faisal, in reality, benefited from Sami's rough image in the neighborhood and at school because he was the shield from bullies and little gangster groups that preyed on quiet boys and nerds.

Their class was dismissed early. The main home class teacher, Ms. Suham, was out. Her two-year-old infant son had just passed away in the hospital after a bout of illness that started with fever then diarrhea and uncontrolled dehydration. They knew all about Ms. Suham. She was their mother's friend and had often come to their house to cry and relieve her stress. It had been weird for Faisal to see a supposedly strong and untouchable teacher at school melt down in the living room like ice cream left on their street during the summer. Her two other children had stayed at their house for a few days while she and her husband were attending to their son at the hospital and desperately searching the city for the fluids he needed. Faisal's mother visited the child one time to relieve the mother for a few hours, and when she returned, she couldn't stop crying that night. He heard her in the other room describing to their father how pale the baby was and how he had turned to skin over bone.

With her son dead, Ms. Suham was expected to be out for at least a few weeks. Faisal and Sami were in the afternoon school, which started at twelve and ended at four-thirty. Most of the backup female teachers had already left the school to attend to funeral arrangements, so the students slowly dispersed into the hallways and eventually made their way outside.

They were just outside the main entrance when Sami pulled Faisal's arm and flashed something from the edge of his pocket. A few feet away from there, a few boys were fighting over something, and Sami hit Faisal in the back of his head to get his attention back.

"What's that?" Faisal asked.

"What do you think, stupid?" Sami pulled his hand out a little bit more and Faisal's eyes widened.

"A cigarette?" Faisal was whispering, although he could have yelled with all the commotion nearby.

Sami pulled his arm and led him to where a concrete wall separated the building from an empty lot the kids often used to play in. Sami sat on a concrete block and motioned for Faisal to join, but Faisal remained standing.

"It's a cigarette, you coward. When will you grow up and show some manhood?"

"Where did you get it?" Faisal nervously took a few steps toward his brother, eyeballing the cigarette.

Sami placed it between his lips and lit it with a match. He took a few puffs, coughed, then pulled the cigarette out of his mouth. Sami looked around, and Faisal got even more anxious.

"The other boys will come over here," Sami said, "and

when they see the cigarette, they'll realize they're dealing with men who are not to be messed with." Sami offered the cigarette, but Faisal just watched, the wisp of blue-gray smoke rising from the tip. Sami took another draw, this time deeper and without coughing. Then he got up and wrapped one arm around Faisal's back, holding him in place, and put the cigarette in front of his face.

Okay. Faisal could do this. It was the opportunity of a life-time. That magical puff was going to push him up the ladder of manhood. He couldn't make himself touch the cigarette with his hand, and he barely let his lips touch it as Sami placed it in his mouth and said, "Take it slow!"

Faisal's eyes were focused on the tip of the cigarette as it turned orange-red while he nervously took a deep breath. Then he coughed violently. The other boys were nowhere in sight, nor could he make out what Sami was trying to tell him to do. His throat was tight, his eyes were tearful, and he could barely see Sami frantically pull the cigarette away and throw it against the wall.

With his head still spinning and his breath still shallow, Faisal felt a violent slap on the back of his head. He slowly turned, and there he was: the principal, looming over the twin brothers. They'd been caught. Reality was sinking in. Some twenty feet away, a few boys were giggling. Sami yelled some-thing at them, but the principal shut him up with a slap on the back.

They were suspended until the principal had a chance to meet with their parents to discuss the gravity of their crime. With their mother busy at the funeral for at least a few more days, the boys would have to take a time out and await their fate.

On their way home, Faisal shoved his brother. "Who's the idiot now?"

"Shut up, OK? Without me, you'd forever be a soft boy with the heart of a cockroach."

For the next two days, Faisal and Sami had to fake their school attendance. It was obvious that their parents still hadn't found out about their suspension or they'd already be dead. They took their books in the afternoon and pretended to walk to school, only to turn at the corner, where they wandered around distant streets so as not to be seen until school was dismissed.

Their judgment day came earlier than expected. The funeral crowd down the street was dispersing when Faisal and Sami were walking back home with their books under their arms. The street was wet from an earlier rain shower, and night was on its way. A patch of darkness surrounded the pathway leading up to their house. The streetlight above had been broken a few days earlier, and no one was claiming responsibility. Faisal was certain that Sami had thrown a rock at a bird sitting on the light pole, but no one else was monitoring Sami's mischief. When Faisal saw the principal coming out of their house in his black suit and tie, he nearly fainted. Sami pulled him aside so they could hide in the darkness.

"I hope your parents teach you a lesson," the principal said when he saw them. "A teacher's kids smoking on school premises is only the latest misfortune in our society." His voice was firm, but it slowly faded with his hurried steps. He had done his job snitching, and now they had to walk into the lion's den.

Their father waited for them in his wheelchair in the living room. Fatima and Hadeel were in the corner working on their schoolwork, and their mother was somewhere else in the house. As soon as the boys entered the room, their father spat a barrage of insults at them. Their mother soon appeared and stood there with her hands on her hips, repeatedly shaking her head. The only thing between them and their father's physical wrath were two missing legs.

Sami seemed unfazed. He stood there, took the verbal abuse in silence, then walked into the kitchen, but his father yelled at him to return. The screaming was loud enough now that Faisal was certain the neighbors across the street could hear. His father demanded a shoe to throw at the boys, but Baba Faisal appeared just in time.

He took a seat on the couch. With a smile, he motioned for Sami and Faisal to come over. No one but Baba Faisal could quiet their father's yelling.

Faisal and Sami sat on either side of their grandfather on the couch. He gently wrapped his arms around their necks. His hands were warm and shaking with gentle tremors. Faisal's eyes were fixated on his grandfather's hand. Grandfather was so old! And his skin appeared sunken.

He gently pulled the boys to him. "If you're going to be stupid enough to smoke, at least make sure you don't get caught." He chuckled. "Now. Both of you. Go kiss your parents' hands and apologize. Then we can bury this issue."

Years later, Faisal reflected on that moment, the touch of his grandfather's hands, the calmness of his words, long after Baba Faisal was gone.

28

Baghdad
1996

B aba Faisal decided to reward Fatima by taking her out with him around the city. It was his pension day, and he would treat her to a warm meal on one of Baghdad's busy streets.

She couldn't be happier. It was the first time she had been to the city center for anything other than an urgent matter with her mother. Al Rasheed Street was swamped with pedestrians competing with cars for space and access. The smell of roasted chicken filled her nostrils, and she nearly lost her breath when her grandfather asked her, "Do you like chicken or kebab?"

The last time she had tasted meat was two or three months ago. The few times her mother managed to bring some home, Fatima took after her mother by choosing to sacrifice her share so everyone else could have enough. Her mother said she got severe heartburn the last time she ate meat, but Fatima was certain that was not true. As for Fatima, she had observed her father skillfully separating every small bit of meat from the bone on his plate, and she vowed to leave her share of the meat for him. So she got up to turn the stove off where the teapot was boiling, took her plate with her, and left her small piece of meat behind a large stack of plates on the counter. Later, when everyone had finished their meal, she returned to her father and said a small piece of meat had been left behind. He devoured it like it had come from a golden plate in the sky.

They were now inside a small restaurant, where Baba Faisal pulled out a chair for Fatima and one for him. The table was covered with a worn-out plastic cover with a rose design. Music from Kadim Al Sahir, the Caesar of Arabic Song, blared from a speaker mounted in the corner above their heads.

"Restaurants are places where people should sit down and eat in peace, not have to deal with the loud music," Baba Faisal said.

Fatima looked around hesitantly, desperately trying to fit in. She was the only girl in the restaurant. She felt like she was betraying her siblings just by being there and taking in the smell of food let alone tasting it. Her grandfather placed the order, and soon two plates of kebabs with grilled tomatoes and onions were placed between the two along with a plate of warm, fresh bread.

Baba Faisal took a few bites, then leaned back in his chair. "Go on, you will have to finish both plates. I'm not allowed to eat this type of food because of my blood pressure."

She wanted to ask him why he ordered so much food then, but she let it go. Kebab hadn't tasted this good since she was eight, right before the Kuwait invasion when her father invited a bunch of friends over and served some to-go plates of kebabs from a restaurant to supplement the food her mother had made.

"Enjoy it, and give abundant thanks to Allah for his blessings. This is only possible on the day I receive my pension." He chuckled.

While Fatima was still working through the second plate, he ordered a glass of hot tea.

When they were finished, he said "We'll make a quick stop at my doctor's office. Just right off the street from here."

Fatima sat in the waiting area overcrowded with patients and their caregivers. Her grandfather had insisted on going inside alone, but after fifteen minutes, she knocked on the door and opened it. Regular visits were usually quick in-and-out affairs. Fatima found Baba Faisal lying on the bed with wires attached to his chest. The young doctor looked decades older than he actually was thanks to his male pattern baldness and the yellow mustache that screamed years, if not decades, of cigarette smoking. He looked less like a doctor and more like anyone else that Fatima might have randomly spotted on the streets, but little made sense to her anymore.

He gave Fatima a questioning look, but Baba Faisal said, "That is my granddaughter. Have a seat, Fatima!"

She took a seat on a small, torn, black leather chair and anxiously observed the doctor as he removed the wires from Baba Faisal's chest.

"Hajji," the doctor said, "your heart is very weak, and that's why you keep having chest pain and difficulty breathing. You need a procedure to open your clogged heart vessels."

Baba Faisal slowly sat up and shrugged.

Fatima had so many questions. Why was she only just now learning about her grandfather's bad heart? She got up from her seat and approached him but remained silent as the doctor continued.

"I've done my best to secure the procedure for you at one of our government hospitals, but as you know, and thanks to the devil that is George Bush, the sanctions have crippled us, and we have no supplies."

"So what's the solution?" Fatima asked.

"Don't worry about it, my beloved," Baba Faisal said.

The doctor sat in his wide leather chair, pushed it back against the wall, and sighed. "I've asked one of my friends who knows someone at one of the private hospitals, and they promised to give you priority for the next round of supplies, and I'll do the procedure myself."

The discussion about price lasted all but a minute. The discounted rate, which the doctor said was a special favor, amounted to the combined salaries of everyone in the household for more than six months.

Baba Faisal immediately said no, already dressed and standing as close to the door as possible. "Just give me a refill prescription and let me go."

The doctor shook his head. "You definitely need this procedure."

Five minutes later, Fatima and Baba Faisal were back on the street and headed toward the bus station. She still had many unanswered questions "Where will the money come from?"

"The doctors are exaggerating," he said. "They're corrupt and only want to make extra money by pushing unnecessary procedures." When they took their seats on the bus, he told her, "Keep this visit between us. I don't want your parents to get worried."

"But, Baba, this is your health. The doctor said—"

"The doctor has been saying this for the longest time. I will be fine." He waved his medicine bag at her.

The bus left the station with as many passengers standing as sitting.

The driver up front was unhappy that the last person who

got on, a frail elderly woman who could barely stand, wasn't willing to make enough room for someone else. "We could have made a fortune if we took one more passenger," he said.

"Shut your wicked mouth and keep driving," the woman said.

Sunset was settling in, turning the Tigris dark gray, but it would soon glow under the stars of the clear sky. The bus reached the intersection where Fatima expected a left turn toward Bab Al-Moatham Bridge and Haifa Street, but the driver instead turned right. Baba Faisal tapped her on the shoulder. "We have another stop to make before we go home. This is not our usual bus route."

Still shocked by what the doctor had said, she wondered what other surprise Baba Faisal had in store for her.

Their destination neighborhood was unkempt. The streets appeared as if they hadn't been paved in decades. They walked into a small grocery shop, where Baba Faisal collected some simple supplies, including rice, flour, sugar, and a dozen eggs. He handed the plastic bags to his granddaughter, paid the shop owner, and stepped out. Fatima nervously maintained a close distance with her grandfather as he walked down the street, which then sharply turned to the right onto a narrow dirt road. On either side were houses built of clay, pieces of brick, and other leftover construction scraps. A small stream of dirty water was running on the edge of the road, and Fatima nearly stepped in it, but her grandfather grabbed her shoulder to help her stabilize her steps. At the third house on the left, Baba Faisal stopped. Fatima observed the half-closed makeshift door made from a metal plate and a wooden frame that only covered a third of the plate. Whoever lived there didn't worry much about safety. Or perhaps they had bigger worries. Baba Faisal took the plastic bags from Fatima and walked to the door.

Two women appeared, and in the dim overhead light, Fatima could only guess their ages. One was definitely as old as Baba Faisal and barely able to walk with a cane. The other was younger and carried an infant in her arms. They recognized Baba Faisal. After some pleasantries, he apologized for not being able to visit them for so long, then handed the bags to the young woman.

"You didn't have to do this, my brother," the older woman said, tapping her cane against the ground.

"It's nothing. I consider you family. That's my granddaughter over there, Fatima." He pointed in her direction, then started to walk toward her while still addressing the two women. "I must get going because her family will get worried about us."

"Why don't you stay for dinner? My son will be home soon."

"Thank you for the kind invitation, but we have to go. Please relay my salams to him."

"Thank you for not forgetting the old friendship."

"Not just an old friendship. A forever brotherhood." Baba Faisal took Fatima's hand as they crossed the stream of water and headed back the way they came.

"Who are they?" said Fatima, pressing her grandfather's warm hand as his labored breathing was becoming more audible.

They stopped at the edge of the street, and Baba Faisal had to lean against a wall to catch his breath.

"That's the wife of my best friend from our early days in military training. He was like a brother to me. His name was Suhail. He was executed, but that's something we should never discuss. But look at his family and what happened to them. It pains me."

Fatima wondered if her family would ever end up in a

house like that if their mother wasn't able to work anymore. The thought terrified her, and she pulled her grandfather's hand. "Let's get out of here."

Over the next two weeks, Baba Faisal stressed to Fatima how important it was that she not share any information about his heart. He said it was nothing to worry about, but she knew it was serious. As had been the case for most of her life, she had to remain silent and pretend everything was fine. She kept wondering to herself how her parents could possibly come up with the money for the procedure if they found out. She'd once heard her father mention to Baba Faisal that they could sell their land in the village, but her grandfather insisted that the land was worthless in the devastated economy. Most of the palm trees were dying, and certain government officials had their eyes on the area for residential projects.

Mostly she kept in mind her grandfather's warning: Certain things were not to be discussed outside the house. Other things were never to be even brought up even inside the house.

~

One Friday in late December, Baba Faisal asked Huda to cook a plate of her famous dolma, a stuffed Iraqi dish. "We can take it out and eat near the river bank. The weather is surprisingly nice, and the kids and Mustafa would enjoy it."

Meat was out of the question, but she made a quick grocery run for some grape leaves, eggplant, and potatoes. That wasn't going to break the bank.

But first, Baba Faisal took the twin boys with him to the Friday afternoon jummah prayer at the nearby mosque. As usual, Mustafa declined the invitation but said he'd be shaved and ready when they returned.

The challenging part was getting the wheelchair down
near the riverbank. The shortest way to get there was along a
narrow path behind their house, but that was impossible with
a wheelchair. So they walked past the school and crossed two
more streets, then turned right and went toward the river
along a dirt road. For three hundred feet, they took turns lift-
ing, pushing, pulling, and carrying the wheelchair with
Mustafa in it. Baba Faisal wondered why a country sitting on
an ocean of oil couldn't afford two prosthetic legs for a war
veteran, but saying it out loud would ruin the picnic, so he
chose silence. He clung to the hope that Iraq's negotiations
with the United Nations to sell oil in return for food and medicine would somehow provide prosthetic limbs.

When they got set up along the magnificent riverbank,
Huda handed Mustafa a hot plate of dolma. At least he could
still use his hands.

Baba Faisal walked along the Tigris, holding hands with
his granddaughters, while the twin boys kicked an old soccer
ball around. He stood on a rock next to a large palm tree with a
body as curved as his own back. The tree chose to curve in the
direction of the Tigris, as if it wanted to fall into the water if its
day ever came. Baba Faisal admired its dark-brown trunk, its
forever-green leaves in defiance of age and time. In the tree's
reflection in the river, it appeared pale, almost colorless, and as
if it were melting in the flow.

Baba Faisal closed his eyes and journeyed backward in
time to his childhood days in Sudah, where the palm trees
were alive, colorful, upright. The village had been youthful
and alive back then. When he opened his eyes, his grandchil-
dren had dispersed, perhaps bored with his long silences. He
took a deep breath and was interrupted by a cough and a bout
of wheezing, which he tried hard to hide. He'd need to rest
against the rock to regain his breath before he could return to

his family. They were waiting for him to drink tea and enjoy a simple desert.

~

The next morning, Huda didn't see Baba Faisal getting ready for morning prayer, nor was he up for breakfast. She called him repeatedly from downstairs, but he didn't answer. She sent Fatima to check on him while she rounded up the twin boys from the street.

Fatima screamed, and Huda ran barefoot up the stairs. Baba Faisal was lying in his bed peacefully, pale faced, his lips dark purple, and his left arm dangling over the edge. He had been dead for hours.

29

Baghdad
1996

The neighbors turned out en masse to pay their final tributes to Baba Faisal. He was the father of the street's war hero and a paternal figure to everyone he had crossed paths with. His body was washed at the local mosque, and hundreds lined up to participate in the janazah, the funeral prayer. Word quickly reached his relatives in Fallujah, and they arrived with dozens of men in multiple cars and pickup trucks.

Mustafa watched from his wheelchair as multiple men picked up his father's body wrapped in a clean, white sheet. They seemed to be competing with each other for the right to hold the body. They were in such a hurry to take it underground and send his father on his way to the next world. Mustafa wanted to protest the rush, but what good would that do? When death arrived, the body was no longer part of this world. The soul slipped away, and it was only fitting that the body disappear beneath the surface of the earth.

Mustafa desperately tried to push his way through the crowd, but someone shoved his wheelchair to the side and nearly flipped it over. The twins, Faisal and Sami, were behind him, determined to get their father to the front of the crowd, where he so much belonged.

Someone shouted, "Where will the burial be?"

Mustafa pushed people aside with his hands and yelled, "Sudah. The village."

Why was that even a question? There was no other place where Baba Faisal's body belonged. It was where he was born. Where he was raised. Sudah is probably where his soul went when it left his body. It would be urgently awaiting his body.

The ground in the village cemetery was muddy. It had rained the previous night, which made digging more difficult. Two hours later, the site was prepared next to Haj Mohammad's grave.

Sudah had died long before its son Faisal. It was down to only a few homes now. The others had been abandoned when government officials claimed it for a private farming project that failed miserably and was also left for dead. The palm trees still stood, whatever was left of them, but they'd stopped producing dates, as if pausing their fertility until someone cared for them properly again.

The house was as still as it had been when Baba Faisal's family left. There was a lock on the door, and once or twice a year Baba Faisal or someone else from the family would visit and check on the house, but Mustafa never wanted to return, nor could he understand what was so important in the house that anyone would need to check up on.

The funeral itself was held back in Baghdad. The same family members, friends, and neighbors appeared several times a day to visit, pay their respects, and bring groceries. Faisal and Sami spent most of their time outside, steering clear of the serious and sad adults. The other kids seemed to avoid them, as if they didn't know what to say or how to respond.

Sami took Faisal's hand and walked to the vacant lot often used as a playing field and as an epicenter for mischief. The evening was dark and chilly. There were still a few cars parked in front of their house, and a group of men had just left through the front door to make room for others to visit.

Sami sat on the large rock they had often sat on to rest in between soccer games. Faisal stood above him and said, "What? What did you bring us here for?"

Sami carefully reached into his pocket and produced a cigarette. It had bent at the edge of the butt and was half cut, but he managed to straighten it and with his finger, and he pulled it to his mouth.

Faisal's jaw dropped, and he dropped his head to come face to face with Sami.

Sami took a deep draw on the cigarette. "We're celebrating Baba Faisal. This is for his legacy."

"Have you lost your mind? What are you talking about?"

Sami offered the cigarette to Faisal, but Faisal pushed it away. "Keep these stupid games away from me."

Sami inhaled more of the smoke and rose. He brought his mouth to Faisal's ear and said, "Remember when Baba Faisal saved us from a beating by our parents after we got busted for smoking?"

"Yes? And you're going to celebrate that moment by taking another chance? How foolish!"

"No, Faisal," Sami said. "We're smoking one more time to let the memory of Baba Faisal and his kindness seep into our chests and lungs, where he will forever be remembered."

Faisal was not impressed, but he found himself grabbing the cigarette and taking a slow and careful puff followed by a mild cough. That was it for him. He was not going to miss an opportunity to honor Baba Faisal, but he wasn't going to get himself in trouble either, especially not when their father was mourning. He asked Sami to hurry up and finish the cigarette while looking around for spying eyes. When the cigarette was down to the dregs, Sami threw it on the ground and stepped on it like a real man would, and the two walked back home, Sami looking boastful and Faisal with a sense of anxiety and loss. Baba Faisal was gone, and he had been Faisal's biggest ally in the house.

A few days after the relatives and close friends had gone home, the family was sitting in front of the TV after dinner had been served, although no one was actually watching it. Baba Faisal's favorite place to sit in the family room had gone unoccupied since his death. Who felt big enough to take his place? The wind blew the rain hard against the windows, unusual for mid-March.

"Stop wasting your time playing cards," Hadeel yelled at Sami and Faisal. "You have a test tomorrow."

Fatima took in the scene without saying anything.

Faisal started flipping through his book, while Sami remained consumed with his cards. Their mother served another cup of tea to their father, then sat between the boys. "If you fail this math test again, you aren't playing outside until the end of the school year. And I am not messing around."

Mustafa gulped down the entire glass of tea. "If they fail again, I'm going to kill them. Even if I have to fly to reach them."

The ten o'clock news was on. A special report highlighted the recent victory of the government and people of Iraq in defeating the will of the evil powers of the world, which had colluded with Satan and his allies to weaken the Iraqi people and force them to bow down. Neither hunger nor sanctions could break the will of the Iraqis!

A short and heavy military official stood in front of the camera with a cargo ship behind him. "The first shipment of food has arrived at the port of Basra as part of the oil-for-food program. Under the leadership and direct supervision of our beloved President Saddam Hussein, this shipment and many more to come will be delivered to the deepest places in Iraqi society for our strong and patriotic citizens."

The camera then returned to the central broadcast room, where the female anchor resumed the report. "And on that victorious note, the minister of health has indicated that the oil-for-food program will also include necessary medical supplies, which will start arriving as soon as the logistics are worked out."

Fatima was the only one looking at the TV. She walked up to the set, turned it off, and went upstairs. She stood in front of her grandfather's room, ran her palms against the door, and closed her tearful eyes. She could almost hear him inside getting dressed and putting his Baghdadi hat on. Surely he would open the door soon and ask her to go with him to the doctor's office to find out when the medical supplies would arrive so he could finally get the heart procedure he needed. When Baba Faisal didn't come out, she slowly turned the knob and gently pushed the door with her knee, her vision blurry from the flood of tears, and stuck her head inside. The bed was empty, its sheets straight and neatly made, the brown Baghdadi hat no longer on the pillow. She took a few steps inside and stared more. The scene was dim, colorless, and haunting. The scent and aroma of the past were gone. The air felt heavy and unbreathable. She turned around, stepped out of the room, and quickly closed the door. She sat on the top stair and cried, then cried some more.

More food supplies hit the markets, and prices went down. Since salaries remained mostly the same, families were able to buy more with what they were earning. Huda couldn't remember the last time her refrigerator contained both chicken and red meat. The same stack of cash from her monthly salary felt heavier in her hand. It was still nowhere near as good as the old days, when she shopped at all sorts of expensive stores in Baghdad, but being able to buy new clothes for her kids was a long-lost luxury reclaimed from the claws of poverty.

One thing that Huda could not reclaim, however, was her husband's spirit. Mustafa had slipped into an even deeper state of depression since his father's passing. He stopped going out and spent most of his time in bed, often staring at the ceiling, oblivious to everything around him.

School had ended, and summer came early with a heat wave uncommon in its ferocity even for Baghdad. Huda leaned over Mustafa in bed and said, "I'm going out to pick up your pension. Do you want to come with me? It will be a nice opportunity for some fresh air and a change of scenery."

Mustafa chuckled. "In a wheelchair? So I can be a laughing stock on the streets with my wife pushing me around?"

"What's wrong with that? The office is across the river, and it won't take but half an hour to cross the bridge. Why do you always have to be so negative?"

Faisal ran inside, breathing heavily from a soccer game, and headed into the kitchen. Huda shouted, "Tell your brother to come back in and get ready. You're both coming with me to the market."

"Pick me up a bottle of alcohol on your way," Mustafa said without looking Huda in the eye.

"I am sorry?" Huda said, unsure of what she'd just heard.

Mustafa repeated the same request in the same tone with the same words, only this time looking her straight in the eye.

Fatima and Hadeel were cleaning the dishes, arguing about who would wash and who would rinse.

Sami barged in angry and cursing. "The crybaby decided to take his ball and go home because I wouldn't let him take the penalty kick. I'm going to rip that ball the next time I see it in the street." He walked into the kitchen as well in pursuit of water.

Huda returned Mustafa's sharp look with a fierce one of her own. "No one's drinking alcohol in this house. Such trashy habits are beneath us."

Mustafa slapped her face so hard and with such precision that Huda nearly fell over. "Nobody gets to *order* me in *my house*. No one!"

The rest of the house fell utterly silent.

30

Baghdad
1997

When Huda returned home with the kids that evening, the house was silent again. Mustafa was asleep, or he was pretending to be. Huda had bought the kids their favorite sweets and some roasted nuts, but everyone quietly dispersed into various corners of the house. Huda moved about in silence, still feeling the ringing in her ear from her husband's slap. She didn't know what to think or how to absorb it. He had never hit her before. What had just happened may have been an impulse, a reaction, a moment of anger, a misunderstanding, or anything else. But she wasn't thinking about the past or the present. What mattered was tomorrow. She was not going to get slapped again. That was for sure.

Nobody mentioned it. Huda expected her husband to eventually say something, and she was not going to talk to him again until he did. But Mustafa slipped ever deeper into silence himself. He refused to leave the room except to use the bathroom, and he ate little of whatever food anyone brought him. The wheelchair remained parked in the same place in the living room for days.

As the days passed, Huda was willing to let it go as long as her husband found a way to emerge from his silence, depression, and withdrawal. But she knew him all too well, and it terrified her. He was stubborn. Military-minded. A man who refused to talk, to ask for help, or to admit that he needed anything. Baba Faisal's absence had created a void that no one and nothing could fill.

One evening after the kids went to bed, Huda returned to their bedroom and found Mustafa sitting on the edge of the bed and holding a framed picture of himself receiving the Medal of Honor from President Saddam Hussein. She sat next to him and looked at the image of her husband from the waist up. He was facing the president, but his eyes stared at the distance. No one could look Saddam in the eye, and no one did. In the photo, the medal had already been pinned above Mustafa's left chest pocket, and Saddam's right hand was resting on his left shoulder. Huda gently took the picture. "Look at how proud he is of you for your bravery." She squeezed his hand gently. "And I'm even more proud."

Mustafa took the frame back from her and threw it to the side of the bed. "He destroyed us, our country, and our lives, and he cost me my legs."

Huda frantically glanced from side to side and over her shoulder. It was after midnight, and they were in their bedroom, in their own house, but anyone might be listening.

"Don't say that. You did it for your people, your nation, for us, not for any one person." She held his hand against her chest and listened to his soft crying. The wounded, tough military man she knew so well was in a dark corner of the past.

"We had a good life," he said through tears. "We won

against Iran. We were happy. We had it all. We didn't need to go into Kuwait. So, no, I didn't lose my legs for my country. It was all for one man."

Huda's heart was racing faster, and she put Mustafa's hand back to his side and repositioned herself next to him. It was quiet outside. No rain. No wind. No dogs barking. No children crying. No cars passing by. It was only her, the shadow of her husband's past, and the dreadful silence she desperately wanted to escape.

Mustafa picked up the framed picture again, and Huda braced herself for him to hurl it against the wall, but he didn't. Instead, he slowly slid the frame under the edge of the bed and laid down.

Huda brushed her fingers through his hair as she had so often done in another life. The touch felt foreign and distant. "I know how much losing Baba Faisal has hurt you, but it's the will of Allah, and we have to accept it. He was the foundation and backbone of this house, and if we want to carry on his legacy, it must be through strength and patience."

The next day, as soon as the kids were all back from school, Huda said they were going out together for a family trip. It was Thursday, which meant no school the following day. After much insistence, they convinced Mustafa to leave the house. It would be an ordeal to carry the wheelchair onto a crowded bus, but the family was going to do whatever it took to get some quality time. The kids wanted to eat outside, and Huda agreed to sandwiches at Mustafa's favorite place on Haifa Street.

She had her own plans, though. After dinner, when they all looked happy and satisfied, she dropped her plan on them. They were going to visit the shrine of Imam Al Khadhim, a descendant of Prophet Mohammad. More than anything, Huda wanted it for her husband.

Maybe a visit to a blessed spot would bring him peace of mind.

Huda had been there many times. Thousands visited each year seeking a way to realize their dreams, to rid themselves of illness, to obtain blessings for a child, and for a variety of other things. For once, Mustafa chose not to resist.

They arrived after sunset. Evening lights had just come on, illuminating the four golden minarets with a dark green patch in the center. Embedded within the minarets were two large domes atop of the base of the shrine. The front walkway was surrounded by street vendors hawking candy, cookies, religious books, framed photos, and clothing. Mustafa pushed his wheelchair as slowly as he could, as if he wanted to fall behind everyone else. Huda made sure everyone was accounted for as they reached the main double doors into the shrine.

"Do we have to do this, Mama?" Sami protested.

"Get in, and not a single word," Huda hissed.

They slowly zigzagged their way inside as hundreds of visitors, old and young, men and women, scattered inside the walls. Some were praying out aloud, others were mumbling their thoughts and wishes, and a few chose violence by stepping on others' feet or shoving them to get as close to the metal bar frames as possible. Someone bumped against Mustafa's shoulder, nearly knocking him out of the wheelchair. There were no special considerations for the disabled. Everyone was on a desperate mission.

Huda turned and motioned for Mustafa, but he shrugged and smiled dismissively. Huda pulled Hadeel closer, instructing her and Sami to start praying. She closed her eyes and prayed in silence. A peaceful life. That's all she was asking for. And since she didn't know what constituted a peaceful life, her prayer was mostly a silent one.

When they finally exited the building, Huda shot a sharp

look at Mustafa, who returned it with a smile and slouched himself deeper in his wheelchair. When they were waiting at the bus station, she said, "If you didn't like this place, we can visit the shrine of Sheikh Abdul Qadir Gilani and seek blessings there."

"I don't care if the shrine is Sunni or Shia," Mustafa said. "I don't believe in any of this stuff."

"Why would you say that?"

Fatima and Hadeel were arguing over something, while Sami and Faisal took turns jumping over the concrete seats at the bus stop.

Mustafa chuckled. "I'd much rather have a drink. Even if it's mixed with urine or feces. Anything."

"Alcohol?" Huda spoke too loudly and hoped the kids didn't hear. Sami and Faisal looked over with interest, but Huda yelled at them to step off the concrete seats and get ready. The bus was approaching.

Mustafa's brooding silence grew heavier at home. He said little and yelled even less. He stopped asking the boys where they were going or if they were up to no good. It was as if he had checked out of the world. Huda brought him a glass of hot tea, and before he took a sip, he picked up the framed photo of him receiving the medal of bravery from the president and asked Huda to hang it on the wall again above his head.

She did so without asking any questions.

The next day, he asked her to iron his navy-colored military top jacket. She obeyed. Then he placed the medal back over the left pocket and wore his uniform in sullen silence. He wore it every day as he sat in his wheelchair for hours near the front door.

Mustafa dug through the large wooden box they had brought from Baba Faisal's house in the village. With help from Fatima and Hadeel, he cleaned the dust off every book in that box and asked one of his neighbors to make a bookshelf, which Mustafa placed against the wall across from the TV. He spent hours reading the books, curiously flipping through pages as he observed passersby on the street from his wheelchair. People passed by him and greeted the hero, some out of pride, others of pity. To Mustafa, none of them mattered.

◦∼◦

The days were becoming longer, but even at the end of April, it still got dark before seven. Sami and Faisal had been searching for a bike to buy with their allowance, which they'd been saving for over six months, including their Eid allowance. Faisal didn't know how to ride a bike yet, but Sami promised to teach him.

"I found a kid who's selling his bike," Sami said. "Let's go check it out."

Faisal followed Sami down the street. They turned left near the school and walked over to Haifa Street. After walking five more blocks, Sami turned right into an alley, which opened up onto a narrow street that had little to no lighting. They stopped in front of an old house. After a few knocks on the door, a person around their age appeared, and as soon as he saw Sami, he disappeared behind the door and returned with a bike, which he pushed outside onto the street. He and Sami engaged in discussions about its features, one of which was the front wheel brake, something the boy claimed was rare in that neighborhood. Sami took it for a ride, and when he returned, he told Faisal to try it. Faisal protested, but Sami insisted he get on it, and when Faisal hesitantly sat on the seat, Sami held one side of the steering bar and instructed Faisal to pedal.

"Come on. Press and push. Don't be a girl. Pedal."

The wheels shifted right and left, seemingly as nervous as Faisal was, as the bike wobbled down the narrow street. The bike's owner yelled for them to return, but Sami kept pushing.

"Stop," Faisal pleaded. "That's enough." His breathing became faster as the bike was picking up speed.

Sami shoved the back of the seat, and Faisal screamed in horror as he flew down the dark street. He suddenly lost control of the steering and sharply turned left into someone's front door. Faisal was thrown to the side, and the front wheel came off and spun next to Faisal until it finally came to a stop.

Sami rushed to the scene of the accident with the bike's owner following and yelling obscenities. No one opened their doors to yell at them, and Faisal was happy about that, but his right hand was scratched badly, and he had a bump on his head.

The bike's owner picked up the wheel. "You broke my bike. You'll have to pay for the damages."

Sami helped Faisal up to his feet. "Not our problem if your bike is trash. You should compensate my brother for his injuries." He was pointing at the scratch, which was bleeding now.

Sami and the boy squared off and were about to throw punches before someone yelled at the boy to get back inside.

"Look. We'll buy it from you if you fix it and give us a discount."

The boy seemed shocked at Sami's blunt demand, but then he said, "Fine. Deal. But if you don't come to take it, I know where you live, and I'll bring my father to your house."

They agreed on a price, and Sami took Faisal's arm as the two walked back toward the main street.

"What a way to get a good discount on the bike!" Sami said. "The idiot doesn't realize that all he has to do is slide the wheel in and tighten the bolts again. We're the winners here."

Faisal was still cleaning the blood on his arm with his shirt when they got back to Haifa Street. Sami stopped in front of the liquor store on the corner. He told Faisal to sit down on the curb while he inspected the store as customers sporadically went in and out. Even in a more liberal city like Baghdad, not all neighborhoods thought visible liquor stores were acceptable. Haifa Street, however, was home to a huge variety of stores and restaurants. This liquor store, the only one for ten blocks in any direction, tried to maintain a lower profile by placing the sign on the wall overlooking the side street instead of the main road. Customers knew where the store was, and little advertisement was needed. If anything, having a more visible sign would bring unwanted attention in a neighborhood that tended to be more conservative.

A middle-aged man with thick hair and a mustache stepped out of the store carrying a bottle wrapped in a paper bag. He shrugged his shoulders to pull his jacket tighter over his neck and turned left on the sidewalk. Sami slapped Faisal's head and whispered, "Let's go."

Faisal hurried to catch up with Sami, who was now following the man attentively, trying to maintain a close distance behind him. After two blocks, the man turned onto a street where Sami and Faisal had played many games of cards with other kids.

"What are we doing?" Faisal whispered. When he didn't get an answer, he asked again. "Where are we going?"

Sami turned to him and stopped momentarily. "We are going to get our father the alcohol he's been craving."

A streetlight was mounted overhead every hundred or so steps. The first two lights were working, but the area below the third one was dark. At the end of the street, the man turned left, and the road became a dark alley.

Faisal was still hurting from the bicycle fall, and while his arm had stopped bleeding, he felt a tearing pain at the slightest movement. He was panting and desperately trying to catch up with Sami, who was now closing the gap between him and the man. The alley was dark and deserted. At some point, the man stopped, and that made both Sami and Faisal freeze. Moving the paper bag from one hand to the other, the man's gait became wobbly as he was starting to appear visibly drunk. Sami observed carefully, trying to stay as focused as he could on the shadow of the man as he resumed walking again, his steps now smaller and less balanced. In a quick move, Sami ran and stood right behind the man, and before he allowed him to turn, Sami gave the man a hard shove from the back, forcing him to fall forward on his face, letting out a heavy grunt. The paper bag flew from his hand and landed a few steps away, causing the glass inside it to break. With the man barely moving but visibly in pain, Sami quickly grabbed the bag, turned around, and ran back in Faisal's direction.

"Let's go, fool!" Sami shouted. "Don't just stand there. Come on."

Faisal ran behind Sami as they disappeared into the streets and alleys.

31

Baghdad
Mid-1990s–2001

S ami and Faisal reached their doorstep after running and zigzagging through the neighborhood in the dark. Faisal was panting and wheezing, and Sami leaned against the wall and tried to catch his breath.

He brought the brown paper bag to his face and immediately pulled his face back in disgust and said, "People drink this nasty shit?"

The bag was wrinkled from his firm grip, and a piece of broken glass was sticking out of the side. He gently grabbed the bottle and slowly pulled it out of the bag. The top half was gone, and the rest had a mosaic pattern of broken edges. He raised it under the streetlight and saw a line of liquid in the bottom third of the bottle. The rest had spilled. When Faisal finally caught his breath, he said in a terrified voice, "We just assaulted a man and stole his belongings."

Faisal protested in a begging voice "We—we didn't drink it. It was for Father."

She turned to Faisal, her eyes narrow and scarier than ever. "What?"

"We brought it for Father." He sighed heavily. "We thought it would lighten his mood. We would never touch the stuff, I swear."

She took a step back and leaned against the door.

Fatima pushed against the door, and their mother stepped out of the way. Once inside, Fatima shook her head. She turned to her mother, who had her hands on her hips, still visibly upset but more peaceful now.

"Let it go, Mama!" Fatima said. "They're stupid kids. They made a mistake."

With that, Sami attempted to get up and leave, but Fatima took his arm. "You two better be thankful she didn't kill you this time. If you ever do something like this again, I will not get in her way."

The boys left the room, defeated and in shock. At the bottom of the stairs, Sami turned to Hadeel and said, "Traitor. Spy!"

"Make me stop!" she said back.

"Everyone be quiet and get ready for school," Fatima shouted from upstairs.

Faisal looked into the living room again and was relieved when he realized their father was still outside.

September in Baghdad was usually hotter than other parts of the country, especially up north. Early afternoons were off limits for pleasant outings. But when it came to boys, the need for play time always trumped a desire for comfortable weather.

The city suffered an extended heat wave during the entire summer of 2001, one that showed little sign of abating even as autumn approached.

School would start soon, and Fatima was glad she was finished with high school, although her final score was not as high as she'd hoped. Seventy-seven would be a stretch for her to get into the College of Education at the University of Baghdad, and she was worried that she may be forced to go to a lesser school if she wanted to stay in Baghdad or, worse, that she would have to move to another city for college.

She pulled the garden hose over the flower bed and into the garage. Thick layers of dust had built up, and small bits of trash and dirt from the street had blown onto it during a dust storm the previous week. She turned the water on and splashed it over the floor. She was fascinated by the scent that came from clean water washing away dirt and dust. She took a deep breath in, let it out, and hosed down the floor, pushing the dirt out. Her hair fell over her face, and she pushed it aside, in the process rubbing the hose against her face, accidentally splashing it with water. She threw the hose on the floor. When the tip hit the garage door, it made an astonishingly loud noise.

She leaned down to grab the hose, but another loud sound came from the other side of the door. Someone was actually knocking. Their doorbell had been broken for as long as she could remember. With the water still running, Fatima opened the door. A white pickup truck was parked in front of the house, and standing between her and the car were two women wearing black abayas. One turned to the driver, a young man wearing a dishdasha and a red scarf and said, "Come back in two hours."

Fatima vaguely recognized the older of the two women. "Hello my love," the woman said. "Is your mother home?"

Fatima rubbed her palm against her wet forehead and slicked her hair to the back. "Yes. She is."

Now she realized who the woman was, and she felt embarrassed. The woman was Karima, a relative from Fallujah, and Fatima remembered her from Baba Faisal's funeral. She was a guest, and it was unfortunate that she had to see Fatima in such a messy state. "I'm sorry. Come on in. My apologies. I've been cleaning the floor. Please be careful not to slip."

She led the two women toward the interior door and heard one of them whisper, "She's so pretty. *Mashallah*."

The other whispered back, a bit loudly, "And she's a natural queen of the house. I told you."

They had come to ask for Fatima's hand for Karima's son Yasir. "Give us the girl, and let's keep the kinship running deep between the two families."

Fatima served orange juice and ran back upstairs, embarrassed and in shock. Her mother briefly took over serving duties but soon demanded that Fatima come back downstairs. But first she had to change and look more presentable now that she was the center of attention. The two ladies, however, had already seen Fatima and seemed impressed by her housework, and the two families already knew each other. All that was left was the final OK so the men could come to officially ask for her hand.

"You know I have to ask her father," her mother said. "The final word is his. Of course, that is after we sit down and talk to the girl to make sure she agrees."

"Of course, my sweetheart," said Karima. "We want to do things the proper way as it suits your family. "My son is handsome, religious, and very respectful."

The other woman, Salma, added, "Yes. My nephew is such

a fine young man. He is his father's right hand. Your daughter will live like a queen."

The two ladies left and promised to return in a few days with the potential groom and his father so the girl could meet their son face to face and then make the final decision.

Fatima realized that Yasir was the man who had been driving the pickup truck. She was desperately trying to recall his face while the ladies were telling her about his family and how great this marriage would be for her. The young man had dark-blue eyes. She remembered that much. And Fatima was embarrassed when she thought about how captivating they were. Such a rare commodity!

In the room she shared with Hadeel, she sat across from her mother, who gently rubbed her hands and asked for her final answer. It was a yes. It had been a yes before she even knew who the groom was. Fatima was ready to travel and explore new frontiers. She wanted a life where she didn't have to endure everything in silence.

Her father's only condition was that Fatima must be able to pursue college.

~

A week later, Mustafa watched as a caravan of nine cars took over their street. He received more than a dozen men, all eloquently dressed, while an equal number of women followed with loud ululations. Boxes of fruits and expensive sweets were hauled in and placed on the kitchen floor. Two large lambs over massive plates of rice were delivered from one of the most popular restaurants in the city, courtesy of the father of the groom.

Mustafa and Huda protested, insisting that dinner was their responsibility.

"We are one family," the groom's father said. "There are no formalities between us."

After dinner, a religious man from the groom's family formalized the marriage. Word was sent to the other room where the women sat, and the ladies cheered.

The TV was on in the background. Through the thick cloud of cigarette smoke, Mustafa caught a glimpse of the news and instructed Faisal to turn the volume up.

Two of the largest skyscrapers in America had been brought down by hijacked airplanes. The other men were paying attention to the groom-to-be, but Mustafa could not take his eyes off the television, images of his military convoy attacked by American jets never far from his mind.

32

Belarus-Poland Border
Winter 2021

Apparently, a group of migrants pushed the fence down a week or so prior to our arrival. They got to the gap between the two fences before the Belarusian soldiers rebuilt the broken part of their fence. Thinking they could create pressure on the Polish side to allow them to enter, the migrants stood against the Polish fence for days but were ignored. When their peaceful appeal didn't get any attention, they tried to physically bring the fence down, but the Polish soldiers brutally struck back, injuring many. Since then, those people have been stuck in the no-man's-land. Initially, they refused to return to the Belarus side, but they got desperate, and the Belarusian soldiers blocked them. The strategy is obvious. A human tragedy would put more pressure on Poland. So far, however, there's no indication that the Poles will blink.

Gulistan refuses to let go of the fence. A boy rushes up to the fence from the other side and runs toward us. When he reaches the fence, Gulistan shudders and cries as the two hold hands through the barbed wire fence.

"Come to me, my grandson. Oh, how much I have missed you."

Shortly after, a young woman stands up far away and yells at the boy to return. He runs back, and Gulistan's crying turns into defeated sobs. Before it gets dark, I head back to our camp spot and move all our stuff to where Gulistan is.

It proves to be a night from hell. The temperature falls drastically, and without a nearby fire, I'm forced to curl up against the fence inside my coat while Gulistan enjoys the luxury of the sleeping bag. Sleep refuses to come, and I am finally forced to get up and walk around just to stay warm.

Two days pass before the boy returns. This time, I talk to him and he says, "My mom told me not to come here, but I miss my grandmother."

It rains sporadically, so I enlist some help from other men, and we set up a makeshift tent.

Food has now become a major problem, even more so on the other side of the fence where Gulistan's family remains trapped. Today we heard about an older man who died from hunger and exhaustion. All I can think of is how his family will have to bury him out in the open and in a foreign land that has refused to embrace him in any possible way. Even the cold weather feels more brutal than it should. The rain feels heavier and more punishing than ever. The snow falls and refuses to melt. The sky looks darker, and the clouds appear heavier. The ground, even when wet, pushes back against our feet, refusing to allow us to make the slightest bit of mark in this land.

During a moment when Gulistan walks away with some women, her daughter-in-law approaches the fence to speak with me. This is my first encounter with her. I'm expecting a devilish tone and a rough voice. The image I have of her in my mind is exclusively nasty. But she greets me with class. Her tone is respectful and calm. She shows no signs of wanting to explain anything, prove a point, or attack.

"Just tell her to leave me and my children alone." Her voice is full of pain, and she's obviously hurt.

I ask her what the problem is. Why won't she even talk to Gulistan?

She lowers her head and goes quiet.

When Gulistan appears from far away, the young woman turns around and leaves. "Just tell her to leave me alone. After what she said to me, we have no connection anymore."

Over the next few days, I am able to have two more conversations with the exhausted, young mother. She's seriously concerned about her children. She tells me about the lack of food and water. I take this as an indirect plea for help. But I'm out of money. Some people have been going to a few nearby villages to buy food and water. It's an hour away on foot and sometimes longer, depending on the weather. Gulistan hands me two hundred dollars and asks me to go with a few other men, to buy whatever we can with the money, and to prioritize things kids can eat. And also, please don't forget some blankets and a few extra jackets.

This time, the trip takes two days.

When I throw food, water bottles, blankets, and jackets over the fence and call for Gulistan's daughter-in-law, she walks over, followed by her three children. She picks up her stuff and thanks me for it. Gulistan greets her, and this time, the daughter-in-law mumbles an answer and walks back.

Gulistan turns to me and says, "Can you believe her? You'd think I killed her parents."

I want to remind Gulistan that she accused her daughter-in-law of adultery to secure her ticket out of Iraq, but I bite my tongue. With a few other men, we throw more supplies for the people trapped on the opposite side. Chaos ensues. We make a few more trips, and soon we run out of whatever money Gulistan had on her.

A media van has been here for two days, the longest-lasting journalist crew we've seen in a while. They've taken statements from people along with videos and a handful of live reports. We're told they work for a Russian satellite agency.

The next morning, I notice the young mother walking toward us carrying one of her children. I turn around and don't see Gulistan nearby. Moments later, the young mother is desperately leaning against the fence with the child still in her weak grip.

"Please help me. My daughter is ill. She will die in my hands." Her eyes are tired, tearful, scared, and refusing to blink. Her beautiful face can't be older than thirty, but it screams trauma and tragedy.

Her child's head is dangling from her left shoulder. This is the palest face I have ever seen. How is it possible for a human to be so white and drained? One of her boys holds on to his mother's dress, pulling on it and at times hitting her legs with his head. Dried boogers cover the child's face, which is streaked with dirt and campfire soot. The mother slowly sets her daughter on the ground, but her weak legs fold, and she collapses on the muddy ground. She picks the child up again and this time pushes her daughter's face against the fence. She looks scared and lost.

"Look at her. My daughter will die. Her blood must be very low." She bursts out crying.

A heavy male voice comes from behind her, apparently addressing me. "Do you know her? This lady will lose her child. We must help her."

"I know her mother-in-law. I helped her get here." I'm

unable to break eye contact with the mother. I can't bear to look at the sick child again.

"Yes, that old lady. She's a witch. I've seen how she treats this poor young woman."

I hear Gulistan's voice behind me. When she is by my side, and before anyone can say anything else, I take charge. "Can someone tell me what's wrong with this child? I don't care who said what or when."

"She has a blood disorder," Gulistan says. "Anemia. Her blood level must be very low now. It will kill her if she doesn't get a transfusion."

I look at the mother for confirmation. She nods, tears running down her cheeks and onto her daughter's dirty hair.

By now, dozens of people have gathered on both sides of the fence, adding to the already-high level of anxiety in both the mother and grandmother. One of the men takes the girl from her mother and rushes to the opposite side of the fence, where the Polish soldiers are wandering around haphazardly. The crowd follows the man while he anxiously sprints from one corner of the fence to another, totally ignored by the Polish soldiers, while the rest of us watch in horror.

33

Hundreds of onlookers gather around while Gulistan's cries fill the sky. We concentrate our focus on one corner of the fence and start kicking, pushing, and shaking it. Finally, we rip a hole in it, and the man carrying the child rushes in our direction. We receive the child through the hole, and her mother passes through with several scratches and bleeding shoulders. When her other two kids are also handed to her, I carry the sick girl and rush in the direction of the Russian media van.

It doesn't take a genius to understand the gravity of the situation, with the girl appearing lifeless in my arms, but the media team pretends to be oblivious, continuing to ask using hand signals what's going on. When the message is finally clear, the driver throws his cigarette through the half-opened window and steps out of the van. He icily walks away, and a cameraman emerges from the other side and raises his palm, telling us to stay back, and starts recording with the camera on his shoulder.

The driver returns and tries to push us away, but the crowd

grows larger and shoves me against the van. A man behind me shouts something in Kurdish and jumps into the driver's seat, threatening to drive away. Another slides the side door and pushes me into the back seat with the girl. At this point, the Russian driver accepts reality. There are no Belarusian soldiers nearby who can come to their rescue. Before I know it, the van is bouncing up and down on the muddy road, the young mother quietly sobbing and rubbing her daughter's head.

We reach a small, single-floor, concrete building at the end of a narrow road on the outskirts of the city. There is little foot or car traffic, and the nearest residential area is at least a five-minute drive away. It's some kind of community clinic, but it appears surprisingly sophisticated inside. I've already prepared myself for the worst news. I've run through all the scenarios in my head. I'm already expecting the doctors pronouncing the child dead after failed efforts at resuscitation. What I have not prepared for, though, is how to handle the mother's emotions if she loses her child. This is not something I can be taught, not even after seeing trauma, death, and destruction that an entire population of rich entitled Europeans can even imagine.

But the child is resilient and proves me wrong. After a short period of resuscitation and some IV fluids, the doctor nods and smiles. Within a few hours, the girl receives three pints of blood, and by the morning her color has returned. Her eyes are wide open and curiously fixed on me. I find myself leaning down and kissing her on the forehead as if she is my child or niece whom I've shared years of memories with.

Her mother says, "I don't know how to thank you. I pray that God repays you from his kingdom of wealth, health, and blessings."

I want to tell the young mother that nothing justifies a family separation during such dire circumstances, but my thoughts are interrupted when two soldiers approach and motion for us to get up and get out. At the door, a cute young nurse hands a small bag of candies and toys to the mother plus two bottles of water.

When we return, a mass of people gathers as the van approaches the center of the camp. Gulistan rushes in front of the truck, forcing it to come to a stop. As soon as the side door opens, she jumps at her granddaughter and embraces her with a long hug, bringing tears to many eyes. I take the first opportunity I can get to pull Gulistan and her daughter-in-law aside. "We have two issues to address and right now." They both fix their eyes on me, full of attention. "First, if you two don't settle your differences *right now*, I'm walking away and will have nothing to do with you."

Gulistan attempts to say something, but I interrupt. "Wait. I'm not finished. My word is final and not open to discussion. You two hug each other right now and forgive or I'm done. The second issue is over there." I point to the area between the two fences. There are more people sitting there than there were when we left. The torn part of the fence remains down, but it's only a matter of time before it's repaired.

Gulistan takes her daughter-in-law in her arms and starts kissing her head while apologizing repeatedly for accusing her of things. She didn't mean them, and it was in moments of frustration and anger, and damn be the devil Shaitan for putting such terrible thoughts in her head.

With tearful eyes, the young mother removes herself from Gulistan's arms and says, "I forgive you as you are in the same position as my mother, but I want you to know that I'll never forget the pain you caused me. How dare you accuse me of being unfaithful in my love for your son, for my love, for the father of my children."

Gulistan is an emotional wreck now, and she drops to her

knees. The young mother pulls her up gently and kisses her hand, and to my satisfaction, they both start walking away from me and toward the children.

The second matter is not settled, but I have a feeling that I'm going to be the one making a decision.

As expected, by the end of the day, a military truck arrives, and the Belarusians patch up the fence. But our decision has already been made. We are not going to risk getting trapped between the two fences.

At night, we gather around a large fire, and under the clear sky, an elderly Kurdish man starts singing a traditional folk song. I don't understand most of the words, but it's about a girl whose lover dies of sorrow when she is forced to marry somebody else.

I turn to the young mother and say, "*Alhamdulillah*, all thanks to God, your daughter seems to be doing much better."

She smiles and says, "Yes, indeed. Until the next time she needs a transfusion."

34

Baghdad
October 2001

Fatima's wedding to Yasir Hamdan took place in October of 2001, a little over a month after the engagement. His family threw the kind of party in Fallujah that Fatima and her family had never seen. He was the only son after four girls, and everything about his wedding was bound to be memorable. He was four years Fatima's senior and had already finished college. Now he mostly managed his father's businesses: furniture stores, car parts, fabric export and import, you name it. Their main residence in Fallujah was a mansion with nine bedrooms. The family had another house in the city of Ramadi along with a farm, which a hired family watched over and cared for.

Yasir's parents quickly met their end of the deal regarding Fatima's education. Her comprehensive score was good enough for the biology department at the college of sciences at the University of Anbar. The couple settled in the house in

Ramadi, which was a short drive from the university. As Yasir moved back and forth between Ramadi and Fallujah, so did his parents in order to maximize family time and give the new bride the attention she deserved.

Fatima tiptoed into her new life, unsure if it was a dream or reality. To go from a world of poverty to one of luxury and fortune. To move from a world where she was the punching bag, intentionally and unintentionally, to one of status and respect. She wanted to believe it, but she was also was afraid to accept it for fear of losing it.

"Why me?" she asked her husband one night in bed.

"What do you mean?" asked Yasir, his blue eyes staring deep into hers.

"Why did you choose to marry me? Why me?"

Yasir grinned. "Because you are the prettiest girl in all of Iraq."

Fatima, still looking for her answer, pushed herself against the bed's headboard and persisted. "Please be serious."

"I am serious. You are so pretty. *Mashallah.*"

"Okay, but your family could have found you a pretty girl and from a rich family with little trouble. Why us?"

Yasir wrapped his arm around her and pulled her to him. "Because our families know each other, and my mother has a godly ability to know a great person when she sees one. I trust her instincts more than I trust my mind and eyes."

"So she chose me for you?"

"She picked you from all the apples in this world, and I chose you the first time I saw you."

"But you'd never seen me before."

"I did. In front of your house when I dropped off my mother and aunt."

Fatima pushed his hand away teasingly. "What? You saw me at my worst, sweaty and covered in water."

Yasir chuckled. "I once heard that if a man likes a woman's beauty in its most spontaneous form and without makeup, then he knows she's the most beautiful woman on earth."

"Did you hear that from your mother?"

"Actually, my grandmother." He grinned.

They were both silent after Fatima turned off the light.

"What are you thinking about?" Yasir finally said.

Fatima sighed deeply and said, "I'm scared!"

Yasir moved closer to her. "Of what, my love? What's bothering you?"

Fatima turned on her left side, facing Yasir. "Scared of this world. Scared of losing the happiness I have now."

Yasir remained silent.

"I'm used to seeing good things appear then quickly disappear," she said. "I'm worried that I'm going to lose you. I'm scared of another war. America is burning now, and what if we square off again and all the men are drafted into the army? I don't know. I'm just scared."

The moon had disappeared behind a dark cloud. Yasir ran his gentle hands through her hair and over her face made her feel safe.

"Have you always worried this much?" Yasir asked. "And this deeply?"

"My thoughts can take me deeper than the bottom of the ocean."

"There will be no war. And if there was one, you better believe I'd rather die than serve in the military for another meaningless show."

Fatima was glad the moon was gone. Darkness was a better keeper of secrets. "You want to get on the government's blacklist?" she teased.

"Well, who would spy on me in this room other than you?" he joked.

"You never know. What if I'm actually an informant?"

"I guess we'll find out in the morning if I'm still here or in a cell." He laughed.

Fatima didn't want the silence of the night to claim her again. She whispered in Yasir's ear, "So you mean to say I'm the prettiest woman on earth?"

"Yes, indeed."

"Then give me love like no other woman on earth gets."

Weeks later, Fatima and Yasir returned to Fallujah to spend the middle of the school break at the family's main residence. It was Fatima's first time getting a tour of the city. Looking through the passenger window, she saw people moving about in a laid-back and calm manner. From the main roads and onto the smaller streets, it seemed like everyone knew each other. At every other corner, there seemed to be a mosque, and minarets soared above homes in every direction. Fatima counted seventeen mosques when Yasir said, "Fallujah is nick-named the city of mosques."

"I can see that," she said.

When they passed a strip of sweet stores, Fatima asked Yasir to stop. He pulled in front of a busy store with a massive front glass window. Layers of baklawa were stacked against the glass, and on both sides were dozens of cups of custard. A few men were standing outside and sipping on hot Nescafé. They turned and greeted Yasir as soon as he approached and invited him to join them for coffee, but he kindly declined and said he was in a rush to visit his parents.

Fatima watched from inside the car as Yasir walked back with a box of baklawa. He set it on the back seat and got back behind the wheel. Two more men stopped him as he pulled out of the parking spot and said they would be sure to visit him and his father in the coming days to catch up.

"Thank you for suggesting that we take something with us," Yasir said to Fatima and stepped on the pedal.

"Of course," she said. "We don't want to walk in there like we're checking into a hotel." Her eyes were fixated on the road as she continued counting the mosques.

"Speaking of hotels," Yasir said. "Another thing Fallujah is known for is that there are no hotels."

"What do you mean?"

"I think there's an element of exaggeration here, but in general, the people of Fallujah are known for their hospitality. If you stop anyone on the street or knock on a door and ask where to find a hotel, they will insist that you stay with them."

Fatima was impressed.

That night, in their bedroom upstairs in the large house, Fatima again asked Yasir, "Do you love me?"

"Is that even a question? Why do you keep asking me that?"

"Just answer me," she insisted.

"Of course I love you. You are my wife, my bride, my queen."

"And you will never leave me or marry someone else? Because I am going to give you a big gift. A gift of a lifetime."

Yasir's eyes widened. His face was as puzzled as ever.

"You're going to be a father."

The following year was one of anxiety. Everyone in the country braced as American rhetoric escalated in the wake of the September 11 attacks. Americans were already in Afghanistan pursuing terrorists and hunting for the perpetrators of the worst-ever attack on American soil. International inspectors were visiting Iraq, looking for weapons of mass destruction.

Iraqis were talking about it, more in fear of another war than anything else. Many were unconvinced that the country had the infrastructure to build nuclear weapons. Many also fretted in silence that Saddam may be prepared to carry out any plan he wanted, even if it meant the entire country would be wiped out.

Even so, the Hamdan household swooned with happiness when baby Sumaya arrived in August 2002, just as Fatima was about to start her second year of college.

In February of 2003, Fatima visited her parents in Baghdad, carrying her first child in her arms and the second in her womb. When her mother saw her bulging belly, she shook her head and sighed. "Are you in a race against time? What's the rush? Why can't you focus on your education before making more kids?"

Things had changed around the house. Hadeel scored ninety-eight on her final comprehensive exams, and she was set to start medical school at the University of Baghdad. Meanwhile, Faisal and Sami barely passed their middle school comprehensive exams and showed no interest in pursuing advanced studies in high school. Sami, especially, made it clear that he was not cut out for college. Much to the dislike of their parents, both boys registered for vocational schools with an emphasis on mechanics. It would just take a few years to finish their studies, and they'd be experts at fixing cars and other machinery.

Their mother was disappointed, but their father blew it off. "Just let them do what their minds can handle and their hearts want. They'll quit in the middle if they study something they don't like."

He had certainly changed. The strict military man whose

word was always one and never two had become nonchalant about things, engaging in conversation peacefully and concomitantly. The angry spirit that once exploded in anger and threats had mentally, verbally, and physically withdrawn. His once-strong body first gradually turned into fat in the wrong parts of his body, then later evaporated along with the muscles. He was mostly skin and bones now, his cheekbones like those of a cancer patient. Even his hair had followed suit by turning gray.

Fatima invited her mother to go shopping with her. The family needed some housewares and supplies, and Fatima pretended she needed some too. She knew how proud her mother was.

The American war was heating up in Afghanistan, and Fatima was terrified that the octopus of war would find a way into their lives. People went about their business at work, at home, and in the markets, having gotten used to a difficult life. They had just enough life and spirit left not to break.

Every time she visited her family over the next year, the stench of war was stronger, and she finally asked her parents to move to Fallujah, away from the capital and whatever hell might be unleashed there. Each time, though, her parents yelled at her for even daring to suggest such a thing. She was overcome with a feeling of doom each time she returned to Fallujah or Ramadi, but she stopped talking to her husband about it. She didn't want him to think she was psychologically unbalanced or damaged. But she knew something dark was coming, and she wanted to run as far away from it as possible.

35

It was a cold February night in 2003, and the family had just finished eating dinner. Mustafa was glued to the TV set, watching with interest the national Iraqi TV station praising the bravery of Iraq's citizens and the patience of their leaders in the face of the evil, war-hungry, and power-thirsty Americans. Two inches below his right ear and right against his shoulder rested a small black radio with its narrow antenna pulled out and touching the wall behind his head. Voice of America Arabic was running a report, for the hundredth time it seemed, about the convictions of the American president and his close aides that Saddam owned weapons of mass destruction and further capabilities that posed serious threats to the world. Threats that called for serious action. Serious action meant removing Saddam from power. Efforts for a resolution to support the war through the United Nations had failed, but the United States was persistent and had the British prime minister on its side.

The radio report concluded with two short interviews. The first was with a prominent Iraqi opposition leader in the

United States who echoed those calling for action to over-throw Saddam. Mustafa listened, blocking out the TV, and shook his head in displeasure.

"Traitors! Dogs! Hungry dogs looking for any bone thrown at them by their masters!" He spit at the radio speaker, but the voice continued to draw his attention as the interview shifted to a senior American military leader whose words were being translated into Arabic. "We will do whatever it takes to achieve our goal, which is to remove Saddam from power. Iraqis deserve better."

Mustafa threw the radio on the floor, drawing silent stares from the rest of the family. Huda shook her head, and Hadeel got up, carrying her book, and headed upstairs to her room. She spent almost her entire life now in medical school or her room.

"I wish I still had my legs. I'd volunteer to fight if I had to. It would be an insult to all of us and to our history if we allow foreigners to step on our land."

Huda turned off the TV.

Faisal brought another cup of tea to Mustafa, who waved his hand in the air, uninterested.

"The army was the reason you lost your legs in the first place," Sami said.

Mustafa glared at him. "What do you mean, boy? This is our land, our country. It's bigger than a leader or person."

"All this chaos is just a game," Sami said. "It's all stupid."

Mustafa had not been this angry in a long time. "You are foolish and ignorant. Shut your mouth before I do it for you. Your generation is lost and knows nothing about pride."

Sami rolled his eyes, and before things further escalated, Huda stood between them, blocking their view of each other. She motioned for Sami to leave the room. He shrugged, then

headed out the front door. Faisal went in the opposite direction to the second floor.

Baba Faisal's room had been Faisal's sanctuary whenever
there was tension in the air. He'd already gone through
more than half the books left behind by his legend of a grandfather. Though he didn't understand everything he read, he
was actively connecting with Baba Faisal through the books.
He often fell asleep in the room, even using the pillow Baba
Faisal's head rested on for so many nights. He wondered what
that pillow had absorbed from Baba Faisal. His thoughts? His
whispers to himself? Tears? Worries? Smiles? All of them? Any
of them?

He left the cold room and headed to his and Sami's room
next door, which was also cold and dry. He took the framed
photo of Baba Faisal and returned to where history was kept.
He passed his mother in the hallway. She was carrying a cup of
water and a plate of biscuits to Hadeel's room, which was on
the opposite corner. Faisal stopped, turned around, and
followed her.

Through the half-opened door and over his mother's
shoulder, Faisal shouted in Hadeel's direction. "It must be nice
to get all the attention and to have one of only two heaters in
this house."

"Shush," his mother said. "Don't talk to your sister like
that. She is our future doctor and the pride of this household."

The second oil heater was downstairs in the living room
where his father's nerves were heating up a lot faster than his
skin was.

Faisal sat back on Baba Faisal's bed, surrounded by a pile
of his grandfather's old books. He set the framed picture on his

knee, took an open book, and set it on his other knee. Inside was an old note. The paper had aged, thinned, hardened, and threatened to break if anyone touched it. Faisal carefully placed it over the framed photo.

He had finally put the two pieces together. The note was only one paragraph long, and it was not dated: "Today I had the opportunity to get a picture of me in front of the National Museum, my place of work. It's the most memorable moment in life so far, one I will forever cherish. How much I love you, Baghdad."

Faisal read those words, then gazed back at the photo. Even in the black-and-white colors, he saw vibrancy and happiness. In the small figure of his grandfather in front of the large structure of the museum, Faisal saw satisfaction and belonging. The younger version of his grandfather clearly felt pride, responsibility, and attachment to the land and its values. These feelings were foreign to Faisal. They were foreign to many young Iraqis in 2003. The nation was like a drowning man lost at sea, desperately trying to stay afloat but not knowing how. Iraq was the birthplace of civilization! How could it have fallen so far?

Faisal held the photo in his hand and stood in front of the mirror. He looked back and forth between his own face in the mirror and his grandfather's face in the photo and was struck by the similarities. Medium height, wide shoulders, darker skin, thick eyebrows and hair, and sharp eyes. He wondered if he might be imagining the similarities, but he was not going to burst his bubble by asking anyone else. He'd always been told that he took after his grandfather, something he often felt that Sami was jealous about. There was one thing, however, that grandfather and grandson did not have in common: the military uniform. Faisal would never wear one.

He returned to his own bedroom and placed his grandfa-

ther's brown Baghdadi hat over his head. He returned to the
mirror and looked himself up and down, this time feeling even
closer to Baba Faisal.

March 19 arrived, and Saddam Hussein was out of time.
US President George W. Bush's deadline to surrender
power or be forcibly removed had passed.

Fatima and her husband, Yasir, arrived in Baghdad just
before noon without their daughter. Huda frowned when she
saw her pregnant belly and pale face.

"Things are not looking good," Yasir said, taking a seat
across from her father. "My father is inviting you to join us at
our place in Fallujah. It's more stable there and far from the
capital in case an attack happens."

Her father narrowed his eyes in the direction of the TV set.
The news was on, showing the president meeting with high-
ranking military leaders. Fatima couldn't tell if the clip was
new or from an older meeting.

"Son, we are safe here," her father said. "Nothing is going
to happen. They're bluffing. No one dares invade our country
and mess with our army."

Yasir smiled awkwardly. Fatima could tell he was trying to
stop himself. "Sir, we both know the reality on the ground.
Aerial attacks would be the biggest concern, and there's
nothing Iraq can do to defend against it. Please come with us.
If things remain stable, I'll bring you back whenever you
wish."

"Why are you all so stubborn?" Fatima said. "Did you
forget what happened in 1991?"

The TV camera was now focused on Minister of Information Mohammed Saeed al-Sahhaf as he stood outside one of

the fancy hotels in Baghdad known to house foreign journalists. In his military uniform and his black cap bent sideways over his head, al-Sahhaf was waving his hands in the air in an animated manner and pointing to the calm and quiet background. "We are not afraid. Our sky is ready to give them hell. We won't back down, and the donkeys will be defeated, and miserably."

Fatima's father had cut the phone line in the house years ago, when Baba Faisal returned to Baghdad from home confinement in Sudah. The government was monitoring all the phones, and the last thing the family needed was Baba Faisal or anyone else saying anything critical over the phone. But after Baba Faisal passed, the landline was restored. Fatima had demanded it. And when her parents adamantly refused to accept her and her husband's pleas to go with them to Fallujah, Fatima motioned at the phone with her head.

Yasir put the receiver to his ear, then dialed the house in Fallujah and handed the phone to Fatima's father.

For a few minutes, the conversation seemed to be going nowhere, with her father shaking his head and thanking Hamdan for his generosity but insisting they were going to stay put. Baghdad was their home, and they were not going anywhere. He handed the phone back to Yasir, who made one last appeal.

"My father has men around him, all armed and ready in case unrest hits the streets."

"Your father is a kind man, and we appreciate this gesture. But I'm not leaving Baghdad."

Before heading out, Fatima took Hadeel to her room and placed a stack of cash in her hand. "Promise me you won't say anything about this until after we leave. Give it to Mama, or use it for whatever the family needs." She hugged Hadeel, a stream of tears on her cheeks, then headed downstairs and out of the house.

~

The TV had been on all day, and Huda couldn't take it anymore. She angrily turned it off despite Mustafa's protests. The living room was finally quiet. Hadeel was doing her best to study even though war was brewing outside. Faisal and Sami had strict orders to stay inside and not even go out to the garden.

Mustafa fell asleep on the couch. Huda lay down on a small mattress next to the couch, while Sami and Faisal shared another mattress by the window overlooking the garden. The only sound in the room was that of Hadeel slowly flipping through the pages of her human anatomy textbook.

Hadeel threw her book at the wall when the sound of the first explosion blasted through the room.

36

Baghdad
2003, Zero Hour

E veryone in the house was wide awake now, and the
sound of explosions and rockets grew louder and more
successive. Hadeel ran to her mother, who hurried to close the
curtains—as if that could possibly do any good.

Mustafa was used to war, as much as anyone could get
used to it. The truth was that it was impossible to get used to
the sounds of bombs, bullets, and wailing sirens. He parted
the curtains just enough to glimpse the green, yellow, white,
and red lights streaking across the sky over Baghdad as air raid
sirens sounded alarms from multiple corners of the city.
Memories from the past surged into his mind. Destroyed
buildings. Civilians walking around in a daze. His convoy
fleeing Kuwait set afire by American planes. The shell-shocked
and injured picking their way through rubble. Himself lying in
a hospital bed, drenched in pain medicine and both legs
removed below the knee.

A loud explosion shook the house. "The bastards did it," he said. "They actually did it."

"What did you expect, Baba?" said Sami.

"Do you not know how to keep your mouth shut, boy? When are you going to learn to keep your thoughts to yourself? Talking like that will only make us feel worse."

"The boy didn't say anything wrong," Huda said gently. "Let him express his feelings. This is not the time to yell at each other. Not while hell is breaking loose out there."

"The commotion might be our ground defense forces fighting off enemy planes," Mustafa said. "Let's wait for daylight to break so we can figure out what's happening. Until then, no one leaves this room except for the bathroom."

The commotion was not caused by Iraq's ground forces but by the explosions from the sky, which settled down a bit over the following week. They were replaced with skyrocketing nerves. The streets were almost entirely empty, and nearly all the stores were closed. Schools had shut down weeks prior when students stopped showing up. Conflicting news came from various parts of the south, but it seemed that American and British armies were advancing toward the capital.

Mustafa had banned the kids from going outside, but Sami and Faisal found opportunities to sneak out and talk to the neighborhood kinds once in a while. Neighbors popped in for quick chats before heading back out again. Mustafa went out to the garden a few times during daytime and mostly sat in silence.

"Baghdad will never fall," he kept saying. "It's a red line." But he wasn't sure he believed that himself. When he watched Saddam's speeches on TV from undisclosed corners of the unknown, Mustafa couldn't tell if the president himself believed what he was saying.

During the afternoon of April 8, Mustafa asked Hadeel to

push his wheelchair to the garden so he could drink a glass of tea and take a break from the charged atmosphere inside the house. The sky was cloudy and suffocating. He heard indistinct chatter from somewhere and tried hard to focus, but his thoughts were interrupted by the front door bursting open.

Faisal was returning from outside.

"Why did you go out?" Mustafa yelled. "Didn't I tell you and your brother to stay in the house?"

Faisal nervously approached. "American tanks are on the other side of the city. Someone spotted one on one of the bridges."

Mustafa looked up at Faisal. The boy's thick hair, brown eyes, and heavy eyebrows spreading above the eyes like wings. He looked so much like Baba Faisal. And he had facial hair now. How could that even be possible? Where had Mustafa been during the time his son—both of his sons—leaped from childhood to early adulthood? It was as if his entire life had been on pause since he returned from the front lines in Kuwait. Would his life pause again now that war was bearing down on their own backyard?

Where did childhood go? Was it stored on a shelf while adults fought among themselves for so long that they forgot children even existed?

"Baba," Faisal said. "Are you okay?"

He opened his eyes. "Yes, son. I'm OK. Just lost in thought. So it seems that things are starting to fold."

"Or unfold." Faisal said, cracking his knuckles as a few explosions shook the ground again. "Let's go inside."

Mustafa nodded, and Faisal pushed the wheelchair.

"We'll be fine, son. We've seen and survived worse."

Again, and for the millionth time, Mustafa wasn't sure he believed his own words. There was no good or bad in war.

Everything was dark. The worst part was how people got used to it.

F aisal sat by the window in his grandfather's room and watched the quiet waters of the Tigris River from afar. He couldn't see any action from this angle, so he focused on the river. Wide in form and slow in flow. A mixture of blue and light brown with a touch of gray at the surface. He felt a great urge to go outside and walk across the river and visit the National Museum. He wanted to stand at the spot where his grandfather had his picture taken, and maybe, just maybe, time might somehow reverse course. He still hadn't seen the inside of the museum, and he made a mental note for himself to visit once the war ended.

A rocket hit a corner of the city in the far distance, shaking the opposite side of the river. The war had only just started. With that somber feeling, he walked downstairs to join his family.

The next morning, his father slept in. Hadeel had withdrawn to her room to catch up on studying, as crazy as that was. His mother was in the kitchen preparing breakfast and speaking with Fatima on the phone. They were reassuring each other of their safety and well-being. His father got up from the couch and slowly wheeled himself to the TV and turned it on.

Breakfast was ready: plates of scrambled eggs and fried potato strips and glasses of hot tea.

The news on the TV was not good.

"They've entered the city!" Sami said. "The Americans are in Baghdad."

"American tanks are roaming the city!" Faisal shouted.

"Our Baghdad has fallen," his mother said and sat on the couch, her hands pressed against her knees.

Baghdad had fallen but not fallen. The Americans had entered but not entered. Some people were rumored to have seen their tanks at the edge of the Tigris on the eastern side of the city, but no one could locate these people. Foreign news outlets spoke of major advancements by the American, British, and Australian armies in various parts of the south and middle of the country, but Saddam was seen on the street somewhere in Baghdad with masses of people cheering him on and dancing around his car.

Iraq without Saddam was unthinkable. He was part of their lives. He lived in everyone's head. He was the very air they breathed, but they couldn't exhale. The mere thought of life without him inspired fear and uncertainty. Faisal couldn't remember anything else.

His father was skeptical of everything. He refused to accept any hearsay. And despite his strict instructions, Faisal and Sami left home every day, scavenging for scraps of information on the streets of the neighborhood, at times daring to go as far as the al-Shuhada Bridge.

On that day, however, April 9, Sami convinced Faisal to overcome their fear and cross the bridge to the eastern side of the riverbank. People were wandering around with no clear direction or destination. During the previous weeks, scattered units of the local Ba'ath Party were seen at various corners of the neighborhoods, attempting to fill the void created by the absence of the army. They were intimidating with their guns strapped over their shoulders. That day, however, there were no armed men and no signs of power or law enforcement.

A breeze was flowing over the river and through the metal frames of the bridge, caressing Faisal's face. There was not a single beam of sun above, for thick clouds dominated the sky.

A group of young men and a few elders were sprinting in the direction of Al Rasheed Street, heading along the southern banks of the Tigris.

"Something happening at Tahrir Square?" Faisal asked.

Sami shook his head, narrowed his eyes, and said, "Only one way to find out!"

37

F aisal and Sami walked fast, trying hard to shrink the distance between them and the men ahead in order to hear what they were saying. Soon they found more people behind them, around them, and in front. Those up front passed Tahrir Square and kept walking. Sami turned to someone to their left, close to their age, and asked, "Do you know what's happening? Where is everyone headed?"

The young man took a deep breath, maintaining his pace, and said, "Firdos Square!"

"What about it?" Faisal asked, nearly tripping over two men in front of them.

"They're saying American tanks are there, and people are trying to bring down Saddam's statue."

"That is at least another hour of walking," Faisal said, turning to Sami.

The crowd was growing larger and more animated by the minute.

"We're like everyone else," Sami said, his breathing more

labored. Faisal wanted to ask the young man if anyone had verified that information, but the guy was gone.

The wind was picking up in speed, matching the intensity of the moment. Eventually, Faisal could see it from afar: the large, dark statue, surrounded by tall white columns. It was surrounded by men, boys, and some women, some looking on with interest, others trying to climb up to the body of Saddam atop the cylindrical base, his right arm extended and his hand waving a greeting to everybody. That seemed to be a thing of the past. Now, with an American tank parked a few hundred feet away, Saddam looked like he was extending his hand in a plea for mercy.

When they drew closer, Faisal turned to Sami, who had his hands in his pocket and watched with passive interest. "What are we going to do?"

A man climbed up the base of the statue and wrapped a rope around it. With assistance, he pushed it up higher to the middle and then to the top of the statue.

"We're going to make our way to the front," Sami said. "We didn't walk two hours to miss the action."

Someone was finally able to wrap the heavy-duty rope around Saddam's neck, and when it dangled down, an American tank made its way to the base of the statue. A soldier tied it to the tank, and the tank gently pulled. Everyone stared with anticipation. Faisal looked around repeatedly, expecting Saddam's secret service men to arrive any time and sweep the entire square off its feet. He squeezed his eyes, then opened them as wide as he could in case this was all some sort of stunt or a stretch of his imagination.

The crowd cheered. The statue was starting to bend. The extended arm moved forward, still attached and clinging to its body. The tank drove off farther while people hesitantly dispersed out of its way. What happened next seemed to unfold in slow motion. A hush fell over the crowd as the body of Saddam detached from the base and toppled. It reached the ground when the tip of his hand hit.

American soldiers blocked the front row. The impact of the statue reverberated through the ground, but it was more emotional than physical. The hand was reaching down to the ground, as if still hoping that someone, something, might grab it and lift it up again. Instead the crowd erupted in joy, the gentle wind carrying the sound of applause away from Firdos Square.

"*Allahu Akbar!*"

"Down, down with the criminal!"

"Finally, it happened!"

"Good riddance!"

"Oh my God. This actually happened."

Faisal was drowning in the crowd. He didn't know how to react. An American soldier climbed up the base of the statue and attached an American flag over it, which was soon replaced by an Iraqi flag by a random Iraqi man, unleashing a wave of proud whistles and cheers. A middle-aged man with wide shoulders in a worn-out suit cut through the crowd and bumped his shoulders against Faisal and Sami, nearly knocking them to the ground. Then he advanced to the front of the crowd, which by now had overwhelmed the Americans. The man took off his shoe, and with it firmly in hand, he smacked Saddam's head while shouting a string of expletives. More people followed suit, taking off their shoes, flip-flops, and slippers.

"I think we should leave." Faisal said nervously. He was starting to feel light-headed. The sounds around him seemed more distant and faded.

"Not until I get a piece of it too," Sami said, then ran toward the statue. People were hitting it hard with hammers, rocks, and pieces of metal. He grabbed a small piece that had broken off Saddam's hand, then he and Faisal headed toward home.

They didn't arrive until early evening, and Faisal didn't think about food or water even once. He went inside first. Sami followed with the small metal piece of the statue in his hand. Faisal was worried about how his father would react to their latest adventure. To his surprise, he embraced them both, his eyes red and tearful, a broad smile on his face.

He'd already heard the news. And he was happy? It was as puzzling as the expression of joy at Firdos Square. Who actually liked Saddam and who didn't? Faisal had no idea now. Where was the nation that until very recently belonged entirely to Saddam? Where did the truth lie, or hide, or pretend to be?

His mother was upset, though. "Don't you dare cross that bridge again!"

The next morning, it was Faisal who pushed Sami to go out again. To appease their mother, they decided to remain on this side of the river.

Down their street, Faisal saw a man carrying a fancy chair painted in golden yellow and dark gray with fancy fabric. Hardly typical furniture in their area. He knew the guy, a neighbor who wouldn't have been able to afford that chair if he'd saved his entire salary for a year. They greeted him, but he passed right on by, grunting from the weight of the chair.

A few minutes later, Faisal spotted a woman on the opposite sidewalk carrying a floor fan. Sami turned to Faisal with a puzzled look on his face, and Faisal shrugged.

The scene on Haifa Street was even more puzzling. People were walking around in every direction carrying all kinds of furniture and goods.

They took a stroll down Haifa, going southwest and in the direction of Shuhada Bridge.

"We're not crossing to the other side," Faisal said.

"No, we're not. Stop being a wuss. I just want to see what's going on with all these people!"

Faisal scoffed. "They're looting. What's so hard to understand about that?"

The more they walked, the more densely populated the street became. Dozens of people were coming out of various government buildings carrying all sorts of things. Faisal and Sami stopped by a three-story building that housed various municipal offices, and Sami was determined to go inside and check things out.

Two men in tattered dishdashas were struggling with a long wooden desk. They couldn't get it through the front door. After a few maneuvers, one of the legs broke, and the men threw the desk aside and ran upstairs again.

Sami and Faisal followed them to the second floor. It had been entirely stripped of furniture and office supplies. Papers and files were scattered all over the floor. At first Faisal didn't want to step on anything, but tiptoeing around felt pointless after a few minutes, so he and Sami went ahead and walked over everything.

"Hurry up," Sami said and headed toward the stairs to the third floor.

"Wait, Sami. Wait." Another group of looters arrived and scavenged the rooms Faisal and his brother had already checked out.

Sami ran up to the third floor, but Faisal stood at the bottom of the stairs and looked up in horror. People were bumping their shoulders against him and rushing up the stairs, their faces hungry for whatever they could get their hands on. Other people were forcing their way downstairs, having already secured their share of the spoils.

Minutes passed. Faisal anxiously shifted his weight from one leg to another, determined not to follow the mob to the third floor. Then Sami emerged from upstairs, carrying a metal office chair. He meticulously shifted the chair around the curves to protect the brown leather, which seemed almost brand new. Faisal followed him outside, still shell-shocked.

Sami rolled the chair and its five legs with the tiny wheels over the curb. "Are you going to help me carry this or keep watching like a retard? The wheels will break over the concrete. Come on. We need to get this home."

Faisal shook his head.

Sami sighed and lifted the chair in the air, nearly dropping it twice before he balanced the leather seat over his head. He walked toward home spitting obscenities from the side of his mouth.

Their father was outside in front of the house in his wheel-chair when they got back. His eyes widened when he saw Sami with the chair. "This is what you two have been up to today? You're both cowards and sorry examples of young men."

Sami took the chair into the house, hitting the edge of the door with one of the wheels. Faisal followed him in.

"You come back here!" their father yelled. "Right now!"

Their mother stood in the living room with her hands on her hips. She grabbed Sami by the collar. "What is this? We've turned into mobsters now? Looting public property? Are you robbing your own school?"

Their father made his way inside and slapped both boys on their backs. That was as high as he could reach from his wheelchair.

"It's ..." Sami mumbled. "It's not from the school. We got it from a building nearby."

"It's the same thing," their father said. "It's wrong and barbaric." He grabbed one arm of the chair and shoved it aside. "Take it away. Throw it outside."

Faisal wanted to plead his case, but he wasn't going to sell his twin brother out, especially not when they were both already so deep in trouble.

Their parents knew they couldn't keep the twins in the house. That was obvious. But they drew a red line on looting or any other lawless activity.

Later that day, one of the neighbors from a few houses down came over to discuss events.

"The Americans created a power vacuum," their father said. "What's next? Where are we headed?"

His friend lit a cigarette and placed it between his lips. "At least protect the important buildings. Animals. The banks? The banks have been looted and emptied. What a shame!"

Faisal suddenly had a thought. He ran upstairs, where Sami was arguing with Hadeel and accusing her of using studying as an excuse to get out of housework.

Faisal took Sami's arm and said, "We have to go!"

Halfway down the stairs, Sami forced Faisal to stop. "What's going on? Where are you going?"

Faisal brought his index finger to his mouth. "We have to check something out. It's urgent. Just follow me and make sure Baba doesn't see us."

They disappeared down the stairs. Once outside, Sami said, "You know Baba and Mama will kill us. We can't get near anything."

"We are not going to loot. I have to check on a place. It's very important. Follow me!"

38

F aisal led Sami for a good twenty minutes as he turned from one street to another, through alleys, and between stores and houses. Every time Sami asked where they were going, Faisal said, "Just come and I'll show you."

It was one of the few times, if not very first time, that the tables had turned, where Faisal was finally leading the way on an adventure.

Pickup trucks and cars were driving past carrying all sorts of looted material.

Faisal finally slowed down and pointed at a building far away on the opposite side of the river.

"The National Museum?" Sami asked.

"Yes. I want to check it out."

"You mean take stuff from it?"

"No, idiot. Do you only think stupid thoughts?"

Faisal always wanted to visit and look at the thousands of historical and archaeological pieces, many of which dated back more than three thousand years, but he'd never gotten past the front gate, precisely where his grandfather had taken that photo. An American tank was parked across the street, and two soldiers stood there nonchalantly with their guns strapped to their shoulders.

Faisal and Sami reached the outer gate and stopped when a white pickup truck left at full speed. Three men were holding onto large objects covered with blankets loosely situated in the truck bed. Their faces were covered with red-and-white checkered scarves.

The gate was wide open. No guards. No ticket office. No signs of order. Faisal led Sami through the gate. They ran into two masked men, each carrying a Sumerian artifact. The two men slowed down, and Sami and Faisal paused. After a few moments of staring at each other, the two men took off running.

Faisal and Sami resumed walking toward the main doors. For at least fifty feet in front of the door, torn papers and notebooks lay scattered on the concrete. They tiptoed forward as another man came outside carrying a small wooden table. He noticed Sami and Faisal's careful steps, so he anxiously watched his feet until he passed the pile of papers, then took off. At the door, Faisal heard a woman crying inside.

Neither he nor Sami had been inside the museum, but it was obvious with a quick glance around the hallway and the first showroom that the place was doomed. The looters had left behind horrific scenes of destruction. The crying woman appeared at the end of the hallway. She looked distraught. Her hands were trembling, and her eyes twitched as she said in a broken voice, "Why are you stealing? This is our national treasure. Please stop."

Faisal and his brother froze. He felt his stomach's urge to purge, and his eyes widened in embarrassment. An elderly man appeared from a room on the left side of the hallway, carrying torn notebooks, and barraged them with a lecture as he approached them.

"We're not here to rob," Sami said.

Unconvinced, the woman answered, "So what are you doing here?"

Sami pointed toward Faisal with his chin.

"Our grandfather used to be a guard at the gate outside, many years ago," Faisal said. "He has since passed away. We wanted to come and see if this place was safe."

The woman started crying again, but the man shook Faisal's hand.

"This is my wife." He gestured toward the woman with his head. "We've been working here for twenty-seven years."

For nearly ten minutes, Faisal and Sami followed the man from one room to another as he showed them looted galleries, broken artifacts, scattered books, and empty shelves. There was nothing to say. The scene spoke louder than words.

They finally reached the main gallery, the beautifully illuminated high ceiling. But the floor was mostly empty, with only a few fragments of broken pieces scattered about and a few large pieces that were too heavy to carry away. Faisal's soul felt like it was being compressed in a vise.

The woman stood before Faisal, her eyes still moist. "What's your name, son?"

Faisal swallowed hard. He wondered what his grandfather would say if he were alive and standing there now.

Sami helped a few museum employees move a few objects that hadn't been looted yet into a side gallery. "Faisal. Help us secure these pieces."

So Faisal joined him, and together the men and boys moved piles of broken pieces, which had survived thousands of years and dozens of kingdoms and rulers only to be smashed by unknown hands.

"This is not the work of random people," the man said, panting as he carried a heavy piece with as much care as a mother would her newborn. "They were organized mobs. This was all planned."

"What about the Americans outside?" Faisal said.

"What about them?" the woman said. "They didn't come inside."

"I mean, did they try to stop the looting?"

"The Americans just sat there and watched," the man said. "They could have easily parked the tank at the entrance. But—"

"They allowed this looting to happen," his wife said.

Sami appeared from the other end of the hallway with a metal lock in his hand. "I found this in one of the broken cabinets. We could lock the remaining pieces in the gallery for now."

At that moment, a young woman and two young men appeared with TV cameras and a microphone.

The crew followed the couple around as they told the world of the vandalism and thievery inflicted upon the museum. Faisal quietly led Sami toward the exist. On their way, they passed by a cast of Lamassu, the protective Sumerian deity that looked like a winged bull, attached to the wall on the right, its face deformed by looters and vandals. It had survived thousands of years of upheaval, but it could not survive this. Faisal imagined that it wanted to fly away from all this with its wings to wherever the Sumerian souls had departed.

The twin brothers were back on the main street, where some American soldiers were finally enforcing some order. The crowds comfortably strolling the streets earlier were now being dispersed. From inside a Humvee, someone shouted orders in Arabic that everyone was to be inside their homes by sundown. Faisal and Sami hurried along, looking forward to overturning the reputation of their adventures in their house-hold. They had done good.

~

For the following month, life seemed to move slowly as Iraqis tried to make sense of fast-moving events. More US military units appeared by the day and around every corner. Saddam had disappeared, and although the Americans were said to be actively looking for him and with a hefty prize on his head, many Iraqis struggled to understand life without the name Saddam hanging over their heads. But they slowly came to understand that Coalition Provisional Authority head Paul Bremer was the new leader of the country.

"An American ruling Iraq!" Faisal's father said one morning when Bremer appeared on TV. "What kind of world do we live in?"

"They're targeting former Ba'ath members and anyone else who poses a threat," Faisal's mother said.

Faisal wished they'd turn off the news, but it wasn't really an option anymore. The entire nation was the news now.

A heat wave was building. In the past, the streets would empty in the early afternoons as people withdrew to cooler air at home, from fans and air conditioners and anything else that provided relief from the inferno outside, But since the fall of Baghdad, that urge for coolness also collapsed. Iraq felt like a foreign country. Iraqis were misfits in their own land. Staying home meant staring at the walls, arguing with family members, raising their blood pressure from watching the news. Strolling the streets in no particular direction and for hours upon hours brought on physical discomfort, but it was easier to handle.

One day when Faisal and Sami crossed the river, they had an opportunity to come within a few feet of an American Humvee and even exchange high fives with a soldier without getting shot at. Faisal liked how that felt and how it looked.

"I wish I knew English," Sami said. "I would have asked that soldier to give me a piece of chocolate from Texas."

"And you've been to Texas before?" Faisal said. "Or tasted their chocolate?"

Sami scoffed. "Why do you always have to ruin my moment."

"Because you're stupid. What do we know about Texas?"

"I've seen my share of cowboy movies." Sami chuckled and kicked an empty bottle of cooking oil against the sidewalk, then froze in place as he turned the corner onto their street. There was some kind of commotion in front of the house.

They ran home.

39

Baghdad
2003

An American Humvee had parked in the middle of the road, blocking both sides. Two American soldiers were standing behind it, one in front, and two more by Faisal and Sami's front door. Dozens of men, women, and children were swarming the area as the soldiers continuously tried to push them away, at times pointing guns. When Faisal got closer, he noticed another Humvee parked a hundred or so meters ahead but with no people around it.

He and Sami pushed their way through the crowd and reached the front after repeatedly emphasizing that this was their house. On the driveway, two soldiers stood above their father, who looked up in distress from his wheelchair as the Americans took turns asking questions through an Iraqi interpreter.

"How long did you serve in the military?"

"I have to think. Between the military college, mandatory service, and follow-up appointments, over ten years."

"Do you have any weapons on you?"

"Do you see anything on me?"

"Answer questions the way we ask and without an attitude."

Faisal's father was visibly upset, and Faisal wondered if the interpreter was adding some spice to the translation.

Faisal and Sami stood near their mother and sister at the end of the driveway as the questions kept coming.

"Were you ever a member of the Ba'ath?"

"What does that mean? Half of the country was in the Ba'ath Party. It was required."

The American soldier's facial expression stiffened as the interpreter relayed the response. He then frisked Faisal's father, who was caught off guard and attempted to resist. In the process, a second soldier joined in, pulled Faisal's father from his wheelchair, and pushed him onto his stomach. Faisal's mother and sister screamed, and Sami took a step forward, but a soldier pointed a gun at them.

"I only signed on with the Ba'ath Party because I had to. There was no way around it in my line of work."

The Americans tied his hands behind his back and pressed his cheek against the concrete.

More neighbors gathered to witness the action. When some tried to intervene, the soldiers aggressively dispersed them, only for the crowd to turn around and form again. Two shots in the air were all it took to get everyone as far back as the soldiers wanted them to be.

One of the soldiers took Faisal, Sami, and their mother inside the house with an Iraqi interpreter in tow. "*Khala*, please do what they say so there aren't any more problems," the interpreter said.

"What have we done?" she said. "Why are they doing this to us?"

The soldier used the tip of his gun to move stuff around in the kitchen, living room, and bedrooms upstairs. Soon he was joined by another who came from outside, and minutes later the house was ransacked.

When the soldiers finally exited the house, the interpreter had a brief opportunity to speak freely. "Someone from your neighborhood told the Americans that your husband prevented him from joining the military years ago because he refused to join the Ba'ath."

With that, he disappeared before anyone could respond.

Everyone was in shock. That night, they spent hours trying to figure out which neighbor would have said that. They had no enemies in the neighborhood, and Faisal's father insisted that he had no authority to prevent someone from joining the army anyway.

Two days later, Faisal heard screaming and some kind of crash outside in their private courtyard. He heard his mother downstairs shouting at his sister: "Go get your brothers. Hurry!"

Outside in the courtyard, his father was face down on the ground, his wheelchair thrown sideways against the wall. He groaned in pain as Hadeel and one of the neighbors were struggling to get him up.

"What happened?" Faisal shouted.

"I came outside and saw your dad getting assaulted," the neighbor said, panting. "They were young men and some teenagers. All had their faces covered. They ran away when I approached them."

Hadeel returned with some medical supplies and started cleaning blood off her father's face. Faisal's mother was crying.

"I heard them repeatedly say '*Rafeeq*, Ba'athi, criminal'

while punching him." The neighbor was calm now, but his voice was heavy as lead.

Faisal's father could only open his right eye. The left one was quickly swelling up and had a circular, dark line around it. The slightest touch from Hadeel made him wince in pain.

Sami ran outside barefoot into the street. "Come outside, you cowards! Face me. You think you're tough, attacking a disabled man? I'll rip your faces off. My father is cleaner than your mother's dignity."

Sami walked down the street and continued his taunts.

"I'll go get him," the neighbor said. "It's better if this doesn't escalate."

They returned minutes later, the neighbor pulling Sami by his arms.

"Let me go! I'll find them and drag them into the streets. Whoever they are, they're cowards hiding behind their whore wives. Let me go!"

Sometime after midnight, the family was still licking its wounds, physical and emotional, when something hit the window of Hadeel's room, instantly shattering it. She was downstairs when it happened and therefore unhurt, but Faisal rushed into her room and found it: a fist-sized rock in a bed of broken glass on the floor.

He took it downstairs and slipped on his shoes.

"Please, son," his mother pleaded. "Please. We don't want trouble."

"No one is going outside," Hadeel said. "No one. Understand?"

Faisal sighed and sat on the couch, bracing for another attack. But the street outside was as quiet as inside the house. Nothing else happened that night. Nothing that Faisal or anyone else heard, anyway.

But in the morning they discovered something worse than

a broken window: someone had written all over the front wall and door with paint. "Ba'ath criminal. *"Rafeeq."* "Get out of our neighborhood." "Saddam's man." *"Ba'athi."*

The words may as well have been painted in the family's own blood, sucked out of their bodies and splashed onto the wall. Faisal understood the words perfectly well. They promised a new life, a terrible life where the family would be strangers in their own land. The words may as well have been written in an alien language. Everything imaginable and unimaginable was happening at the same time.

Faisal and Sami bought a bucket of paint and covered the hateful writing outside. Since their father was still bedridden, Sami rolled the unused wheelchair outside and sat in it for hours at a time, guarding the house and watching for any suspicious behavior. But he couldn't sit there and watch twenty-four hours a day, and only a few days passed before the next attack. This time, rocks and empty bottles were thrown onto their garden over the concrete wall, and their front door was brought down after being violently rammed by a heavy object.

Faisal and Sami ran outside together. It was a dark night with the moon hidden by clouds. Not a single star was visible. There was no new writing on any walls or doors, but there was trash all over the ground.

Sami produced a pistol from his pocket.

"Where did you get that?" Faisal said, shocked.

"I got it after the first attack."

"Why didn't you tell me?"

"Because you would tell mother."

"I—"

"Where are you, cowards?" Sami fired into the air, first once and then again twice. "Come out. Face me like men." Bang. Bang. Bang. Three more shots. Then silence.

Faisal braced himself for hell, but no attack came.

Lights in one house after another came on, but no one came out.

Next came a military raid. Just as dawn was breaking, three American soldiers barged into the house in full combat gear, pointing guns at anything that moved or even breathed. An interpreter followed them in, a scarred slash across his face and dark glasses over his eyes.

Faisal stood on the stairs with his hands in the air.

The soldiers wanted to know who had fired the gunshots. Sami admitted that it was him, that he wasn't shooting at anybody, that he was guarding the house against an attack. He told them where he'd hidden the gun, and they tied his hands after they confiscated it.

His mother wiped away tears with her scarf as Hadeel emerged screaming from the kitchen. "Where are you taking him? Stop. He didn't do anything wrong."

One of the soldiers shut her up with a brief point of his gun. Faisal, however, refused to be silenced, and he followed his brother outside just moments before more gunshots rang out.

40

Belarus-Poland Border
Winter 2021

There's an old Arabic saying: sever someone's neck rather than their access to food. Food! The most difficult challenge for us thus far.

Hunger is creeping into our bones, into the soles of our feet, and threatening to break our backs right when we're playing the game of who-blinks-first against the Polish government. Even the strongest minds buckle inside a starving body. Two more people have died since yesterday, unleashing an uproar in our camp. Last night, a dozen or so journalists arrived at the Polish side of the fence and have been taking pictures and videos since early morning. They seem to be concentrated in one area a few hundred feet from where we are. Some people who still have internet connections on their phones have been reaching out to their relatives and friends back home and all over the world, trying to bring attention to our humanitarian crisis. Some have been lucky enough to garner interviews with journalists through WhatsApp and Viber.

Tragedy and disaster bring people together. While languishing in this open prison, we've developed small communities of twenty or so people apiece. Each group has claimed an area to pitch tents and build fires, and they work together to secure food and water, whatever they can find using every means possible.

One of the men in our group shows me the screen on his smartphone and says, "Look. You're famous."

It's a short video with Russian commentary. I can see myself carrying Gulistan's sick granddaughter as we rush from the media van to the small hospital. A few short clips of the child attached to IV lines follow, then the camera focuses on the mother's exhausted face before it returns to me, this time when I'm dozing off next to the child's hospital bed.

I never even noticed the Russian journalists filming us, but I'm not surprised that they did. They were using us to push their point of view, of course, but it works for us too. We'll take anything that leads to sympathy and support.

The Poles have finally lightened after the international outcry even though the hated fence is still standing tall in our faces. There's more media presence along with intermittent supplies of food and clothes from some relief agencies. Gulistan and her family have been sharing a small tent with the women and children of another family while we, the men, continue to sleep outside next to the fire. We eat our small breakfast of boiled eggs and bread, which we received from a truck belonging to a relief organization.

Gulistan adds water to the kettle, further diluting whatever is left of the tea. She pours me a cup, and I sip it down without looking at the contents in fear of forever losing interest in the traditional dark Baghdadi chai.

Things have been quite peaceful in our little neighbor-hood with Gulistan and her daughter-in-law seemingly at ease with each other. Gulistan's granddaughter steps out of the tent with a smile. Gulistan says something in Kurdish, after which the girl approaches me and in a shy posture says, "*Shukran.*" Thank you.

"Look at Naza," Gulistan says. "Isn't she beautiful? She's a flower that's blossomed again. All thanks to our Lord for bringing good people our way to save her life."

Naza can't be older than nine. Her beautiful, dark hair stands in such contrast to her chronically pale face. She and her siblings walk away with their mother to get cleaned up.

Gulistan shakes her head and sighs deeply. "Faisal. See that pretty girl? She'll die in our hands if we stay here. We may not get lucky again."

A few men swing by and invite me to go with them to search for any new relief trucks that may have brought food, but I motion for them to go. I will catch up with them later.

"So, what exactly is wrong with Naza?"

She pours me the last few drops of the tea.

"My little grandchild was four when she got typhoid. At the time, we lived in a small town between Erbil and Kirkuk, where my son used to work before we moved back to Erbil. We took Naza to many doctors, and she had round after round of treatment. Two years later, she started getting pale and tired. We first thought she was seeking attention because it had been less than a year since her father was killed and her twin brothers were infants. One day, she collapsed on the doorstep. A month later, they diagnosed her with an abnormality in her bone marrow at one of the hospitals in Erbil. They told us we had to move to the city and be close to the hospital because she'd need regular blood transfusions."

A few boys nearby are tossing a torn soccer ball, and it

lands near the fire between me and Gulistan, flipping the empty tea kettle over. I turn and cuss them away while one of the boys rushes and grabs the ball without an apology.

Gulistan chuckles, then turns serious again. "I lost count of how many times we admitted her to the hospital. We were finally told she would eventually die if she didn't get a bone marrow transplant."

I listen attentively, blocking out the noise from the boys fighting over who will kick the game-determining penalty shot. Gulistan's ever-ready tears flow down her cheeks all over again. "They said medicine may have caused her disease, or maybe it just developed on its own, but I'm convinced it happened because her father died. I think it's the curse of ISIS following us everywhere."

Naza returns and hands me a small piece of chocolate. Her mother appears behind her and says, "She wanted to give you a gift for being such a kind uncle and for everything you have done for us. May God bless you and protect your family."

Whatever is left of them, I whisper in my mind without looking at anyone in particular, but I reach out to take the chocolate from her hand with a smile. Before I can take it, Naza's brothers rush and stand right in front of me, their eyes on the piece of chocolate. I let go of the candy and say, "How about you go and share it with your brothers?"

The children run away with the chocolate. The two ladies are sitting across from me now, with the daughter-in-law warming another bowl of water.

Gulistan says, "Tell us about your folks back home, Faisal. I want to know all about your family."

"Whatever is left of them," I say again, this time out loud so they can hear.

41

Baghdad 2003

Faisal watched as soldiers shoved Sami into the back of a military truck next to two other young men who were blindfolded and motionless. When Faisal attempted to stop them, a soldier shot twice in the air, freezing Faisal and everyone else where they stood. Before he could do anything else, another soldier grabbed him by the arm and pulled him back to the front of the house and motioned for him to be quiet and still.

The truck drove Sami off into the unknown.

Faisal's father lay on the floor, his head tilted to the left against the wall, his eyes half open and rolled back. Hadeel knelt over him. His hands rested at his sides, and as soon as she touched him, his body rolled sideways without any resistance. She cried aloud, drawing her mother into the room. Both of them screamed, and Faisal placed his hands over his head. He just lost his brother to the Americans only to be slammed with the reality of having lost his father too, this time to another world.

Faisal's life and his family's had been turned upside down, their souls twisted and hurled from the window onto a street of death. Neighbors rushed into the house, and one of the men suggested taking Faisal's father to the hospital, but Hadeel mumbled that he had long since passed and that there was no good subjecting his body to discomfort more than what it had endured while alive. She picked up the phone and dialed her sister in Fallujah. Poor Fatima was pregnant and easily rattled these days, but what she'd experienced so far was nothing compared to the tragedy Hadeel was about to unload on her.

The family had been shattered, Sami lost out there in captivity, their father descended upward to freedom from the prison that was their homeland. The rest were left with sadness and uncertainty, the worst of both worlds.

Faisal listened to the women and families consoling his mother downstairs for the loss of her husband. "*Al baqiya fe hayatikum.*" May the rest of his unfinished life be added to yours. But did they really need more years of misery? Faisal reflected back on his memories of his father and didn't see many colorful moments. Instead, he found blank, gray pages. The neighbors wanted these kinds of pages to be added to his family's history?

Fatima arrived two days later carrying a very pregnant belly and a gloomy face. Her husband was held at a security checkpoint and turned back, forcing her to travel by bus and on foot.

Just as the Mustafa household had suddenly been swept off their feet, the streets outside experienced another wave of uncertainty and anxiety, even a touch of the military terror from the past. American soldiers were picking up men all over the city, and many of the faces that even recently had smiled at the foreign soldiers were starting to frown.

With emotional support available to his mother now that Fatima was home, it was time for Faisal to search for his twin brother. He tried the local police stations, whatever was left of them, and knocked on the doors of neighborhood personnel and clergymen. No one had much to offer beyond pointing out the fact that the Americans were rounding up thousands of men in a random and paranoid fashion, often including people who had never been part of any organizations or even knew how to hold a weapon.

Faisal sat on the curb near the small restaurant where he once ate along with his father and Baba Faisal. People were gathered out front, but there was no food being offered. He hid his head between his knees and tried to block out a conversation a few men were having nearby.

"They fired me from my military post. How am I going to feed my family now?"

"I guess I'll be next. I also serve in the national reserve forces."

"I am not going to hand them my weapon. I've hidden my gun. In times like this, we need protection."

But Sami wouldn't have been taken away if he hadn't fired a weapon.

"Look. Look at them. Passing by on our streets like they own our country!"

Faisal looked up. A Humvee flying the American flag was slowly driving by, taking up most of the road by driving right in the middle. A small sedan covered in dust and mud approached the Humvee from behind, slowing before coming to a complete stop. The driver stuck his head out and said a few inaudible words before starting to drive again. The space was cramped, and the Humvee wouldn't move. The sun was scalding, making the street seem as if it was about to melt and swallow everything on it.

Faisal remembered the first time he and Sami walked by a Humvee. On that day, a little girl had a flower in her hand and was handing it to an American soldier, who gently took it with a careful smile, drawing applause from onlookers and observers. That, however, was a memory of times long past. Today, no one approached the Humvee or tried to take a picture with the soldiers.

The sedan's driver slowly maneuvered his vehicle to go past the Humvee, moving even slower as he drew alongside the truck. Two soldiers quickly got out of the Humvee and with anxious-looking faces stepped in front of the sedan and pointed their guns right at the windshield.

Anyone who hadn't been paying attention before was now joining the spectacle. The soldiers shouted, and the driver slowly and stepped out of the car, his hands raised in the air, confused and horrified. The soldiers pointed their guns right at him as he stood on the side of the road, shaking and unable to say anything. They approached the vehicle and looked through the windows. They didn't seem to see anything that drew their attention, but one of them turned to the driver again and started yelling. Soon, the driver of the Humvee motioned for the two soldiers to get out of the way and drove his truck to the left, forcing the sedan sideways against the concrete median in the middle of the street.

"Pigs!" someone yelled from the sidewalk behind Faisal. "Donkeys! Get out of our land!"

"Stop harassing our men and children," a woman said. "He didn't do anything wrong. You don't own our streets."

The scene quickly erupted in chaos, with shouts, chants, and objects thrown at the Humvee. Tomatoes, shoes, slippers, flip-flops, and even plastic toys struck the vehicle from all directions. The two soldiers outside turned around anxiously, contemplated their next move, then quickly jumped in the Humvee, which sped away from the scene, leaving behind a mass of people who were now approaching the driver of the sedan and checking on him while he said in a trembling voice, "I just needed to pass them to get to the pharmacy. My wife needs medicine."

Faisal couldn't find Sami, but Fatima's husband was able to gather some information. Yasir came home later that day after finally clearing the checkpoints outside Baghdad. "Sami is in Abu Ghraib prison."

"What crime did my son commit?" Faisal's mother said. "Who does that?"

"It's not just Sami, *khala*," Yasir said. "They've taken thousands of people there. Their crimes range from priors to possession of weapons to calling for an insurgency." Yasir's tone conveyed his lack of conviction in the accusations.

The TV was on, and a short clip showed a meeting of Paul Bremer with a few senior Iraqi opposition leaders who had just returned from abroad to help build a transition government.

"You see, *khala*?" Yasir said as he pointed at the screen. "These are the thugs and scum the Americans rely on. Instead of turning to us, the Iraqis who actually have a connection to this land, they bring over the so-called opposition, mostly spies for foreign governments."

For over four months, the family heard only scraps of information about Sami. He was still in Abu Ghraib, but at least he was alive. The prison, a horror show during the Ba'ath Party days, was just as fearsome today under new management. No one could visit Sami in person, and every time Faisal and his mother went to the prison, there were hundreds of other women dressed in all black, desperately looking for answers about their husbands, sons, and fathers. His mother would beg through the barbed wire, and her pleas and cries passed right over the heads of the guards.

Then the stories started to come out. Stories about torture, rape, and psychological manipulation.

Faisal didn't know what to believe, but he took a small measure of comfort in the fact that his mother didn't entirely believe what she heard. "Iraqis always exaggerate things," she said. But the looks on everyone's faces suggested that anything and everything was possible.

"It's not enough that Baba is gone," Hadeel said. "Now we have to sit and pray that nothing happens to Sami."

"Is that going to disturb your studying?" Faisal said drily. "That seems to be all that you care about."

"What? Is that what you think of me? That I'm a robot with no heart or emotions? What do you know about what I'm going through?" Hadeel barged out of the room, stormed up the stairs, and slammed the door to her room.

"Why did you say that, son?" Faisal's mother said without looking at him.

"I'm sorry," Faisal said and wrapped his arm around his mother's head and kissed her hair. He could swear that there was little to no gray hair before, but now it looked all pale and aged. She cried with his embrace, and he said "I didn't mean to attack Hadeel. I'll go and apologize to her."

He went upstairs and knocked on his sister's door, but she shouted at him to leave.

One evening, Sami randomly reappeared, his eyes looking like he hadn't slept in months. His hair was long, dirty, and unkempt. His face lacked expression, his gaze distant. His mother threw herself at him and hugged him hard.

With cracked lips and two missing teeth, he tried to say something, but all he could do was mumble. He motioned with his head in the direction of the couch where his father used to lie down, and Hadeel broke down crying while his mother held him to her again.

He smelled like he hadn't showered or bathed in months, perhaps since he had been taken away. Faisal held his hand and helped him sit down as the tough task of breaking the news was the responsibility of none other than him.

Sami spent the following two weeks searching for the name of the person or persons who gave the Americans false information about their father, leading to the attacks. Faisal pleaded for him to stop looking for trouble, but Sami was defiant. The most he got was the name of a man who had had a beef with their father many years ago over money. That man had mysteriously disappeared at the onset of the invasion, so the rest remained a puzzle, and Sami finally and reluctantly decided to put it to rest. For the time being.

Sami was more distant now, choosing to spend more time outside alone. He barely spoke to Faisal anymore, not even about what had happened to him in Abu Ghraib. Faisal suspected what might be going on but was terrified to confirm it.

42

It was the evening of December 13, 2003, and one of the rare times since Sami's return that the entire family got to share tea over dinner. Faisal's mother had banned television during dinner or any other sit-down because it always led to an argument, heartbreak, or both. That day, however, was an exception, even by the standards of the daily chaos in 2003. The ex-president, Saddam Hussein, was finally arrested after a months-long manhunt. There he was, right on the screen, being yanked out of a hole by American soldiers. The same clip played over and over again, presumably around the entire world.

Faisal sat on the couch with his arm against the wooden armrest and his feet coiled under him, trying to maintain as much space as possible from where his father used to sit, his way of keeping his presence alive. "Who would've thought he'd end up like this!"

"Nothing even makes sense anymore," Hadeel added.

Their lives had become one massive nightmare with so many moving pieces that they could no longer keep up. All they could muster was drawing imaginary lines like the one separating Faisal from his father's place on the couch. The standard of happiness was so low now that it was nearly worthless. The boundaries between happiness and sadness, safety and danger, belonging and loss, right and wrong, freedom and oppression had been shattered over generations of coups, wars, uprisings, and now a foreign invasion. It was as if the land itself was searching for a lost identity in the minds of its confused citizens rather than people building their identities on its rich soil and deep roots. Iraqis felt like apples that had turned rotten because the tree had been watered with toxic water for so long.

Saddam's face leered on the small TV screen, with his thick, unkempt hair and long, filthy beard. He'd been taken to an undisclosed location for processing, where an American officer wearing plastic gloves was giving him a physical examination. Without resistance, Saddam opened his mouth, then raised and tilted his head when asked to do so. They inspected his teeth and oral cavity, ran their hands over his beard and thoroughly checked his hair as if looking for weapons.

The cameras continued clicking. Faisal's mind flashed back to when Saddam had straddled Iraq as a nationalistic leader, a dictator who lived off the lives and hopelessness of others, and a world leader whose ambition and war aims knew no limits.

Faisal pulled his legs from underneath him. "Imagine how much $30 million will get the person who led the Americans to Saddam's hiding hole!"

"No amount of money is enough for traitors," Sami shot from the other side of the room. "Whoever told on him deserves death."

"He was hiding," Faisal said. "Shouldn't he have come out and led armies against the invaders?" Sami looked like he was about to say something, but Faisal steamrolled him. "Considering his rhetoric, one would've expected him to go out like Hitler, who'd rather kill himself than be captured by his enemies."

His mother turned the TV off, sat between the two boys, and took a deep breath. "Whether we agreed with Saddam or not, the way things are unfolding is a black spot in the history of our nation. It's an insult to our sovereignty."

Sami stared at Faisal, as if declaring that their mother's words were directed at him.

"I can't be the only one in the country who feels that while the Americans are true invaders, Saddam was in no way a saint," Faisal said. "He started a fire, then went into hiding."

"He was our leader and still is!" Sami said. "We must rid the country of these infidels. Their true aim is to convert us to Christianity."

Faisal chuckled and rolled his eyes.

"Did you not hear what Bush said?" Sami's deep eyes were fixed on Faisal. "He said this war is another crusade."

Faisal turned to his mother. "Mama, tell Sami about how the Ba'ath Party sidelined Baba Faisal and forced him into home confinement."

"How do you know about that?" she said.

"I overheard you talking about it once."

She went silent. The room boiled with emotions.

Sami still hadn't talked about his experience in Abu Ghraib, whether he was tortured or not, and Faisal wondered what kind of people he was exposed to there. What could cause such a drastic transformation?

"I think we need to stay out of trouble as much as possible," Faisal said, "and not get involved in whatever's going on out there."

His mother nodded.

"And let these people just roll all over us and rape this country as they wish?" Sami said, yelling now.

"Why are you taking this so seriously?" Faisal said. "It's beyond you and me. Our country has leaders who—"

"Don't say leaders. They're traitors, parasites, and the scum of earth."

Faisal inhaled deeply and tried to put his words together carefully to avoid widening the divide between him and his brother. He exhaled, stretched his legs out, and said, "Whatever they are, this is our reality now, and we must abide by the rules until Allah opens the next door."

His mother smiled and nodded, but Sami was not having any of it. "Allah has given us minds, hands, and the ability to fight back. Patience is for cowards."

Hadeel put down her half-empty cup of tea. "One can't enjoy a cup of tea in peace in this house. There's hell outside and inside. I'm sick of it." Then she walked out and headed upstairs to her room.

Their mother broke the awkward, heated silence in a soft and appealing tone. "Why don't we talk about our financials and living situation. Things are turning bad for us, and we barely have money for food. You two are not kids anymore. We need to tackle this issue."

Gunshots rang out on the street. Faisal went to the window but couldn't see anything. There were more successive shots, and he headed for the door, but his mother pleaded, "Please, no one goes outside. I don't want to lose any of you. Please!"

Faisal returned to his seat as more shots were fired, from farther down the street this time. Minutes later, it all went silent again.

"Those must be some proud and brave sons of this country who actually care about dignity," Sami said.

Faisal shook his head at him. "About our financial situation," he said. "I talked to one of the mechanic shop owners on Haifa Street, and he may have part-time jobs for both of us, depending on how their business is going." He was looking at Sami now, who avoided his eyes.

"Brother, you go ahead with that job. I'll make my own arrangements." Sami then turned to his mother. "Mama, we will take care of it. Don't worry."

"May Allah protect you both for me and never deprive me from seeing you together, as one family, just as your father would have wanted."

Fatima and Yasir visited the family from Fallujah at the end of April 2004. It was her first time back in Baghdad since her father's funeral. She now had two girls. The first was born in August 2002, and the second hadn't turned six months yet. She came against her mother's wishes, arguing that concerns about safety, insurgency, American checkpoints, and random searches had become part of their daily routine.

On the day they arrived, news broke about an incident in Fallujah where several American military contractors were captured, burned alive, and strung up from a bridge.

"It's chaotic and concerning there now," Yasir said as he ended a phone conversation over the landline. "That's what my father is telling me."

"I'm proud of Fallujah's people," Sami said. "The invaders got what they deserved."

Fatima and her mother both shook their heads in disbelief.

"Things have been escalating lately," Yasir said, "with growing distrust for the Americans, especially those serving as go-betweens, the interpreters, the civilian officials, and others who are calling themselves consultants. They're supposed to be the ones facilitating communication and transition."

The living room fell silent. All eyes were on the TV footage of riots in Fallujah.

Yasir ran his hand in his hair and sighed. "My father has armed men, and they'd never compromise the dignity of our people, but ..." He seemed to be searching for words. "Only God can understand how such a horrific thing could take place. This is going to escalate quickly."

He turned to Fatima with a concerned look, as if silently telling her they'd have to return to Fallujah soon.

Two days later, things were indeed taking a turn for the worse. American soldiers were mobilized to the outskirts of Fallujah. In response, more riots took place inside the city, some targeting the city's own infrastructure. The anger seemed pulsatile. Fatima couldn't understand it without seeing it in person and feeling it.

On the third day, Yasir's father called to inform him that he must return at any cost. There was a side road into the city from the farthest western point, which meant an extra hour of driving, but that was his best chance. There were no American units there yet, and his father knew someone at the checkpoint and left word to allow Yasir and his family to pass.

Fatima's mother embraced her granddaughters and then embraced Fatima. "*Binti*"—my daughter—"we didn't see enough of them or you."

Fatima wrapped her arms around her mother's neck, trying to hide her tears, and whispered, "*Inshallah*, it will all be fine, Mama. I'll be back, and next time we'll stay so long that you'll have to kick us out."

Her mother forced a chuckle as Fatima withdrew from her embrace. "This is your home and forever will be, *binti*. No one will ever kick you out."

They packed their belongings into the car, and Fatima placed the children in the back seat. They were already getting cranky. Yasir climbed in and rolled his window down. Fatima did the same as they bid farewell to the family. Hadeel blew kisses in the air for the infant daughter, who was struggling to get out of Fatima's grip.

"I think she is trying to tell you she wants to stay with us," her mother said with a smile.

"I don't mind," Fatima said. "You can keep her for me. Two is a handful."

"No way!" Hadeel said jokingly. "I'll fail medical school if she stays here. Nope!"

There was some reserved laughter as the family somehow managed to slip into a few moments of distraction. Fatima waved at her family and forced out a smile.

It was the last time they saw Fatima smile.

43

E motions built up in Fallujah, including in Fatima's household, to match the American military mobilization building up outside the city. Men of status and influence came and left, attending meetings until the late hours of the night. They discussed weapons. A defense strategy. The mood was one of anxiety, uncertainty, but also charged with a readiness to die for one's dignity and family, fighting against anything that threatened their existence.

But despite the image of confidence projected by the community and tribal leaders, deep down was an element of exhaustion and despair. Disappointed in the way things had so quickly turned south since the fall of Baghdad, and contrary to the popular belief at the very beginning, so many people felt as though they'd lost the reins of their own lives to chaos. It had become a matter of survival, and survival meant fighting anything new, anything foreign, anything that posed a threat to their simple, daily lives.

Fatima looked from the rooftop of her in-law's mansion as she collected the dry laundry. The streets and homes in her neighborhood were eerily quiet, disconnected from their usual vibrant nature. Below her, three pickup trucks were leaving the house after a long meeting and heated discussions. Her husband was standing next to his father, Hamdan, at the door.

One man stuck his head out the passenger side of one of the trucks and said to Yasir and his father, "Let's watch and see what happens next."

"Hopefully no one makes a move without consensus," Hamdan shouted as the truck sped away.

War? Again? Fatima clenched with anxiety. She looked into the distance, behind the mosques, houses, schools, trees, and neighborhoods in search of the enemy. The threat was foreign, unknown. Faces that once seemed friendly had somehow become hostile. But were the Americans really enemies? Were they out to kill Iraqis? Or were they just trying to find the people who'd murdered Americans and strung them up from a bridge? What were they really *doing* in their land? How long were they going to stay? Who was going to rule Iraq, its cities, and their daily lives?

She felt her husband's hand on her shoulder and jolted in fear. She knew his touch and was used to it, but nevertheless she felt scared. She turned, horrified, and saw Yasir smiling.

"It's me, *habibti*. Not an alien down from above."

Fatima looked away and faced the city again. "There are enough terrors on earth that we don't need aliens to scare us."

Yasir stood alongside Fatimah. "What's bothering you, my love?"

She sighed deeply and exhaled. The sound of an explosion came from far away, and she jumped and screamed, "*Ya Allah!*"

He stepped closer to her. "What's wrong, Fatima?"

She leaned against the low concrete wall around the roof. "Everything out there. The whole world we're living in now."

"I didn't know you were a philosopher," Yasir said with a chuckle.

Fatima turned around and faced Yasir. "Something bad is coming. I heard you talking to your dad about the American military building up outside the city. And all these people coming and going. I don't like it."

Yasir took a deep breath. "We're just getting ready to defend our city in case they decide to invade us."

If he was trying to make her feel better, it wasn't working. "And you have an army that can stand against the Americans? This is an invasion now? A full-blown war?"

"Listen, Fatima. We're not the only ones. As a matter of fact, in Baghdad and other cities around it, road bombs and random attacks against the Americans have become a daily routine. At least we're not doing that."

"But you burned some of their workers!"

"Who did? Me? I ... ... we had no involvement in that. I was with you in Baghdad when that happened. My father has no idea who did it."

"I didn't mean you or your father personally. But those men were brutally attacked and killed inside Fallujah. How do you expect the Americans to react?"

"Well, Fatima, they forcibly entered our country. Now it's their job to secure it and maintain order. Everything is their doing and therefore their problem. We're not going to allow any foreigner to enter our city and threaten our families, women, and children. Fallujah does not bow." He gathered his breath. "And don't forget that down south, the Shia forces of the Mahdi Army have also been clashing with the Americans. It's not only Fallujah. We will be viewed as cowards if we step back and watch."

Fatima said nothing.

Yasir gently took her hand. "Let's go downstairs. My parents are waiting for us for dinner."

The sun was sinking below the horizon. Its orange glow had become denser, and not a single cloud was anywhere on Fallujah's skyline. Fatima wondered if the sun looked this beautiful in Baghdad and what her mother was doing at that moment.

On the steps of the stairway, Fatima stopped and held Yasir's arm. "Promise me you will be safe. Promise me you won't leave me alone in this world. Please promise me everything will be fine."

Yasir gave her a wide smile. "I promise, I promise, and I promise."

But do promises have a place in war? War is the monster that makes people run from the beautiful view on the rooftop for the safety of a dark basement. It's the wind that violently uproots people from the foundations of their dreams and throws them into the claws of terror, the fire of fear, and the smoke of hate. War is darkness, and there is no beauty in darkness.

Seventy kilometers to the east, Baghdad's sky was anything but clear. Dark clouds hung above the city, blocking the sun and its beauty. The waters of the Tigris seemed to reflect not sunlight but fear, hate, insurgency, paranoia, anger, and the rest of war's vocabulary. Baghdad was slowly losing its day and living a constant night. Random bombs, street fighting, and militant clashes were daily occurrence during the summer of 2004. Clouds of smoke from roadside bombs and explosions rose up during the day to join the clouds in the sky, covering the city like a sinister lid.

Sami returned home late one evening and found his mother sitting on the living floor by the front door. Her back was curved, and her head was hidden between her knees. The April breeze attempted to pull Sami back into his childhood days when he and Faisal ran back and forth in the front garden, but those memories paused at the screech of the aged metal door. When he closed it behind him, his mother slowly raised her head and gazed at him with tired and twitchy eyes. "Where have you been, *ibni*?"

He was tired too, and his face must have showed it. He stood above her, inspected his wristwatch, and sighed deeply. He attempted to walk past her, but she grabbed his ankle and said in a pleading voice, "I've been worried sick about you. Allah will punish you for torturing me like this!"

He sat next to her. As soon as he wrapped his arm around her, she let out a flood of emotions and cried.

Sami didn't know what to say or how to respond.

In her choking voice, she said "You will break my heart too. I just know it."

What had he done to deserve this? "Mama, why are you saying this?"

She pulled herself from his grip and stared at him. "The city is burning, and people are dying from explosions and bombs every hour, and you expect me to sit here until midnight and wait for your return from wherever the hell you went and feel fine? And when you finally come home, you're like a robot. Do you want to give me a stroke?" She slapped his chest with her weak and trembling hands.

"Mama—"

"Your sister in Fallujah is as good as dead. Their city is being leveled, and we haven't heard from them in days. Instead of growing up and taking responsibility, you go out and wander the streets like a loser!"

The sound of explosions came from far away. His mother flinched and twitched while he sat there motionless. Another explosion went off, this one closer, and she twitched again.

He stood up, gently took his mother's hand, and walked her to the couch. Faisal was sitting there and shaking his head. He held the phone in his hand, and he dialed, only to hang up in frustration moments later. "I still can't reach Fatima. The call won't even go through."

Hadeel came into the room. "Of course the phone lines in Fallujah are down with all the fighting going on there," she said to Faisal, then turned to her mother. "Mama, please calm your nerves. This is not good for you. Fatima and her family will be fine, *inshallah*. Stop worrying, please! Come with me to my room. You need to sleep, or you'll get sick."

Sami watched his sister lead their mother out of the room and up the stairs in slow and staggering steps. She looked a hundred years old and walked like it. Their mother had always been a mountain in the face of pain and adversity, but now she was bent like a dying tree.

Sami and Faisal were alone in the living room now.

"I know where you've been," Faisal said. "I know what you've been up to. I have followed you to the house on the other side of the city twice so far."

Sami was stunned. "Okay. What have I been doing?" He desperately hoped his brother would guess wrong.

Faisal quickly got to his feet and got in Sami's face. "Whatever you're up to in that house and with those sketchy people is not good. And you're going to tell me right now what exactly you are getting yourself into."

Sami sighed heavily, dreading the moment, as he attempted to maneuver his way around the subject, but Faisal was not having any of it. Faisal's finger was right in his brother's face as he whispered in anger, "*You* are not going to do anything stupid that would threaten the safety of this family, *understand*?"

Sami pulled Faisal by his collar, sweeping his feet off the ground, and shoved him against the wall. "Where were you when Father was beaten and our dignity was spilled on the street like dog piss? Huh? Where were you when I was led away like a slave and thrown in the dark corners of hell? Tell me!"

Faisal's eyes were twitching, and his face turned pale. Sami then released his grip and resumed in a softer tone. "I'm out there to take revenge for our family and to protect us. Don't you ever question me."

Sami turned and started walking away when Faisal shot back, "And what might you be doing until midnight to bring our family's dignity back?"

Sami stopped and turned around one last time. "I wasn't going to drag you into this, but since you give me no choice, be ready tomorrow at sunrise. I'll take you where we will get our revenge."

44

Faisal got up early and left with Sami in the morning while their mother was still asleep. He knew where they were going since he'd already followed Sami there twice.

They walked the small streets, avoiding crowded areas, and stayed as far away as possible from parked cars since any one of them could explode at any moment. There was no chance of riding in a taxi or taking public transportation. Walking was it, and it took them nearly two hours before they turned into the edge of one of Baghdad's oldest and most exhausted neighborhoods.

Most of the houses seemed to have taken a long journey backward in time and then returned. There were more broken and boarded-up windows than intact pieces of glass. A kid was running on the side of the street naked while a young girl, probably his older sister, chased him with his clothes in her hands and yelling out obscenities Faisal had never heard from the gentle gender before. As poor as the neighborhood looked, there was no shortage of cars and trucks, most very old and broken down. Two young women stood by the door of a house on the corner of the street and followed Faisal and Sami with their eyes until they passed. From there, a boy whistled behind an electric pole and disappeared behind a wall.

Faisal had followed Sami to this street, but Sami skipped the house Faisal had seen him go into the previous day. "What are we doing?" Faisal said, panting. "I thought—"

"Just keep walking, and don't look anywhere other than forward," Sami whispered without turning to Faisal.

Two blocks later, Sami made a sudden turn onto a narrow street where two pickup trucks were parked next to each other, blocking the way for any other vehicles. Three armed men stood in front of a house, and Sami slowed his pace. Faisal studied the three men in his peripheral vision. They looked no older than thirty, and their faces were covered with red-and-white checkered scarves.

Sami turned to the house directly across from the men and motioned for Faisal to follow him. The house was nicer than most of the others, painted in light gray with a small and narrow metal door painted in blue. It had aged well, though layers of paint appeared to have given it an uplift. Once they stepped inside, two armed men greeted Sami and quickly inspected him in a routine motion. When they walked up to Faisal, Sami nodded at them and said, "That's my twin brother. I've told you guys about him." They patted Faisal up and down.

What had Sami told these men about him?

A large portrait of Saddam carrying a handgun in his right hand overlooking a massive crowd of Iraqis hung on the wall leading to the first room on the right, where Sami briefly entered, greeted someone, and returned while Faisal nervously stood, still unsure what to expect.

"Here, my brother, we are going to get our revenge for what happened to our father. Follow me!"

Faisal was about to say something, but another man emerged from a door on the left carrying a walkie-talkie in one hand and a rocket launcher in the other. He passed them quickly while responding to a frantic voice on the other side of the radio.

Sami led Faisal down the stairs and into a basement. He knew his way around the place far too well. On both sides of the wall leading downstairs were numerous photos of Saddam in all sorts of attire and at various functions and occasions. At the bottom of the stairs, Sami greeted another man, who took a handgun strapped to his waist and handed it to him. Then he used a key to open a door. The room was pitch dark. Faisal heard moaning and crying inside.

When Sami turned the lights on, several voices cried at once, begging and pleading. "Please, enough." "Don't hurt us." "We beg you." "By the name of Allah and everything that is dear to you and your families. Please."

Faisal felt light-headed. This already was worse than he had imagined. He closed his eyes, unwilling to see the men's faces. He smelled feces, urine, and blood. He turned and attempted to leave, but Sami grabbed his hand and said, "Right there. Look. Over there in the corner is the son of bitch who opened the gates of hell on our family."

Faisal hesitantly opened his eyes and saw a heavyset man rush halfway across the room toward Sami, halted by the chain attached to his shackles. His pleas poured over Sami, but Sami just stood there, unmoved. The man's face was covered with red wounds and blue-and-black swellings. Two of his front teeth were missing. Faisal could swear he only saw half of the man's fingers on each hand, but he refused to look again. He whispered to Sami to leave, but his brother was just getting started. He pulled Faisal further inside until they were both looming over the chained man's head.

"Go ahead, son of a whore," Sami said. "Tell him how many people's lives you ruined. Tell him!" He kicked the man on the side of his neck, knocking him down.

Faisal's hands were shaking now.

Moments later, the man got up again and said, "I'm sorry. I'm really sorry. I already told you. I had no choice. They—"

Sami slapped the man's face.

"The Americans issued the de-Baathification rule, and one of the men on our street told me they were giving out a hundred dollars for each name of a former Ba'ath official or leader. I really needed the money. I am so sorry!"

Faisal tried to place the man's face and voice in his memory, but nothing registered.

Sami must have read his thoughts. "Remember the kid we bought a bike from? This donkey is his uncle. He lives two streets down. I had to go through a spiderweb of a network to confirm it was him. He's the one who gave our father's name to the Americans."

Sami slapped the man repeatedly as Faisal desperately tried to stop him, but a man behind him said, "Leave your brother alone. He needs to get it out of his system. If you knew what this guy has done, you would do worse." Faisal heard the man behind him spit.

Sami was now kicking the man repeatedly on the head, face, and back. "You told on my father when he was nothing but a disabled military man and a patriot who saved lives! You falsely reported him, and he died! *You* are the reason he died. *You* are why I was taken away!"

The man was now unresponsive and quite possibly dead, and none of Faisal's attempts to stop Sami were successful. "I was tortured and raped and nearly killed because of you! Now take it! Take it! Take it!"

There was silence in the room as the other prisoners

recoiled against each other in horror while Sami panted and groaned like a wounded animal or an angry beast that had just finished killing its prey. The armed man standing at the door gently grabbed Sami's arm and said, "Let's go, comrade. It's enough. He took his punishment." Sami took a few steps toward the door, then rapidly turned around, ran back to the corpse, violently kicked its head with full force and screamed, *"I was raped because of you!"*

For a long time on their walk home, neither Faisal nor Sami said anything. Faisal kept visualizing his father surrounded by American forces, the animalistic look on Sami's face when he returned from Abu Ghraib, and the almost certainly dead man in the basement. His heart raced faster with every step and every thought. His breathing tightened at every sound, and he could swear that he could still hear the desperate pleas chasing him from that dark basement.

When they crossed the bridge to the other side of the Tigris, Sami finally broke the silence. "You are not to tell anyone about that place, the people you met, or what happened there." He sounded like a man now. Sami was no longer Faisal's twin childhood brother. He was a wounded animal, a stranger from the wilderness. But who was Faisal to judge his brother?

"You just killed a man," Faisal said, his voice breaking.

"I should have done it last week when we caught him. And don't ask me how we got him or who the other people in the house are."

"I don't want to know, but I do know that I don't want you in that world."

Sami scoffed. "Too late, brother."

A Humvee passed them with an American soldier in dark sunglasses scanning his surroundings and with his machine gun mounted over the top and ready to shoot at any time.

"You see them? It's on now. The real war. We're going to take revenge for every innocent life they ruined, arrested, killed, and destroyed. They are invaders. We will take revenge for the Ba'ath and for Saddam!"

Faisal stopped at the edge of the other side of the bridge and said, "Ba'ath? Now we're fighting for the Ba'ath Party? Father only joined them because he had to!"

"Ba'ath, Saddam, Iraq, Iraqis, nationalism, our oil, our women, our history. Everything!"

Faisal had never felt as much distance between him and his twin as he did on that day. They didn't talk much for the next two weeks. Each time Faisal looked at Sami, he saw the man in the basement. Sami continued his regular outings and made it clear to Faisal that if he were to ever say anything to their mother about it, they'd never see his face again. Faisal wanted to forget about it all, to suppress it, to find a distraction. But how? The only distractions were the bombs, explosions, raids, and the depressing news out of Fallujah and their mother camping by the phone every day, waiting to hear from Fatima.

The phone finally rang a few days later, and Faisal wished that it hadn't. That phone call conveyed an entire city's worth of sorrow, sadness, and hopelessness.

Faisal found Hadeel holding the receiver to her ear, speechless, and tears pouring down her face. He grabbed it from her and pulled it to his ear. Fatima's broken, sobbing voice was on the other side. "What will I do now, Hadeel? My life is over."

45

F aisal frantically yelled through the telephone. "It's me, sister. Are you there? Fatima?"

"I'm here, Faisal." There were no more words after that. It all turned to whimpering on the other side.

His mother and sister were in the kitchen. "Yasir was killed," Hadeel said.

It would be another week before they were finally able to visit Fallujah. The US Army ostensibly withdrew from the city on May 1, 2004, but the handover to the Iraqi Brigade took a few days to finalize. Faisal accompanied his mother on three occasions only to be turned back at various checkpoints. Finally, they were told that the roads to Fallujah were open but under heavy security and scrutiny.

Fallujah was a horror show. Devastation. Rubble. A brutalized city licking its wounds. Faisal's eyes widened each time he saw destroyed buildings. His mother kept shaking her head.

The driver dropped them off at the Hamdan household,

and a short, old woman named Khajja draped in black slowly opened the door.

"Where is my daughter? My Fatima!" Faisal's mother yelled.

The funeral had ended the previous day, nine days after Yasir was killed by a rocket shot from an American helicopter as he fought on the rooftop of a building in downtown Fallujah. Fatima remained in her mother's arms for long moments as the two wept and sobbed.

"Your poor luck, *binti*. Your poor luck. Your husband was the flower of the garden of men. Gone!"

"Stop," Khajja said. "It's haram to say that. Don't make it harder on your daughter."

Yasir's father sat on a thick mattress on the floor, his back against the wall, reading the Quran. He offered nothing more than nods anytime someone tried to talk to him.

Yasir's mother wiped her tears with her scarf. "My son was a good man. He carried no ill feelings or wishes for anyone. Strangers came to our city, some to fight, others to loot. Our men just wanted to defend their city and our people. He was the only one in his group who died that day. Only my son."

A few months later, when the mourning period had wound down, it was time for Fatima to consider her future and discuss it with her family. She was a widow now and able to move on and remarry as far as the law was concerned. For her, though, the law of love took priority, her love for Yasir and for his parents. They also were attached to her and her daughters more than to anyone else in the world.

"All I ask," her father-in-law said, "is that if you move back with your family that you allow us to see the children. If you choose to remarry, and that is your God-given right, then at that time we will discuss the girls and their care. I will never abandon them or you."

She gently pressed on his trembling hands. "You are my family and the world to my daughters. I will not leave this house as long as you allow me to stay here."

He suppressed a tear and said, "You are forever our daughter, and I will never forget this gesture of yours."

"It is not a gesture, *ammo*, it is my duty and the least I can do after the love you surrounded me with since the day I stepped into this house."

Over time, Mr. Hamdan slid out of his long period of depression and mourning, but the house remained empty. The gatherings of the old days had dwindled.

When Fatima delicately asked him about the status of affairs in their household and the community, he answered, "My daughter, things have changed. I lost most of my loyal men, and whatever was left of them are now being chased down and intimidated by the radical new groups associated with Al Qaeda."

"What is this Al Qaeda group everyone is suddenly talking about?"

Mr. Hamdan sighed deeply. "They're a mystery to me and most other people. But some see hope in their slogans, and people are starting to rally around them."

She hadn't left the house since her husband's funeral. Even milk and food for her daughters were being delivered by the family's servants. She had no interest in keeping up with the news. Her phone conversations with her mother and Hadeel were brief and void of substance. They were all exhausted.

"What about these other militant groups? Who are they? And what do they want?"

Hamdan seemed unsure where to start or whether he

should even say anything. "During our battle against the Americans, all sorts of people came to Fallujah to join the fight." He momentarily went silent.

Fatima understood that his silences were fertile soil for sadness and trauma. "And now what's the problem?"

"They're acting as if they have control over the city, our lives, and how we practice our religion. They're attacking some of our own local groups for refusing to comply."

Fatima's mother-in-law stepped into the room. "That's why it's so much better for him to stay home and steer clear of that mess. It's enough that we lost our son."

In the middle of 2006, the streets in Baghdad were boiling without letup. One could not make a trip to the market, to work, or to school without facing the real possibility of witnessing an explosion or some other violent atrocity—or even becoming a victim oneself. The names of faceless enemies and perpetrators kept changing. Observers shifted alliances. The only constant was bloodshed.

Sami stood outside the entrance of the general hospital in the Dijla neighborhood near the Tigris, where Hadeel had recently started her clinical rotations for medical school. He and Faisal had been taking turns accompanying her to and fro to ensure her safety, as their mother had ordered. It wasn't a safe environment for even the strongest of men, let alone a young and single woman in her twenties.

Hadeel was already half an hour late getting off her shift, and Sami was getting restless. An ambulance was approaching with its sirens wailing, cutting through traffic at full speed and all but ignoring pedestrians. It was up to the pedestrians to get out of the way or get run over and become another emergency case.

At the large entrance to the hospital, two soldiers forced the ambulance to stop. "No entry!" they screamed, waving their weapons. The driver exited the vehicle and ran to the back, where he joined the passenger as the two anxiously opened the rear double doors. People swarmed the ambulance as the medic asked for help unloading the wounded.

Sami stepped closer to where he could see inside the ambulance. He counted at least seven people being carried out, all covered in blood, some with unrecognizable faces and body parts. Yelling and screaming grew in intensity as the bodies were carried into the hospital through the main gate. When the space behind the ambulance was clear, Sami stepped closer and looked inside. A pool of blood was dripping onto the street. Bright red-and-black stains covered the sides as well as the doors. Two women in black abayas appeared, wailing as they made their way through the entrance while slapping their faces.

"What happened?" Sami asked one of the men standing on the curbside, stoically sucking a cigarette.

"What else would it be, young man? Another explosion somewhere."

In the far distance, smoke rose behind some old buildings and homes, creating a dark black line that widened as it ascended into the sickly, pale sky of the city, a sky that had seen enough death and witnessed way too much sadness, the sacred land beneath the firmament pierced with so many cries of pain and suffering.

Sami heard Hadeel's voice behind him, snapping him back to awareness.

"I'm sorry, brother. We had new casualties that just arrived. I was forced to help."

"No problem," Sami said and started walking.

He moved quickly, with Hadeel panting and wheezing as she tried to catch up. A few blocks later, she stopped. "I can't keep up with your pace anymore. I've already been on my feet since the morning. I need to catch my breath."

Hadeel had her white coat draped over her left arm, and in her right hand she held her small purse. Her hair was pulled back in a disorganized manner, and Sami could see a few stains of blood on the bottom of her pants and over her shoes. Her white coat, however, looked neat and clean.

"I don't even get to wear the white coat," she said. "As soon as we arrive at the hospital, we're rushed to attend to a fresh round of casualties."

Sami inspected her dry face, shrunken cheeks, and sunken eyes. She stepped back and leaned against the concrete wall of a nearby house and curved forward, her hands resting over her knees and her face pointed between her feet. "I can't keep doing this."

Sami had never been good with emotions. He could only manage to take a few steps in his sister's direction. Was she crying? He couldn't tell.

Another ambulance passed them, followed by two police cars yelling out instructions for everyone to clear the road.

"I can't stand seeing death every day without being able to do anything about it. No!"

Sami hesitantly took her hand and helped her up. "Let's go home, sister. It's not safe out here on the streets."

"This is my point. We keep running away from death, only to run into more dead bodies. What are we made of? We're humans!"

Sami resumed walking, and Hadeel followed.

"I'm twenty-two," she said, "and have already seen more than a hundred dead bodies. That's not including our father.

These are people who'd lost limbs, were run over by military trucks, or were cut in half by rockets. Old people. Kids. Infants."

It was going to get dark soon, and Sami motioned for his sister to pick up the pace.

He'd gotten used to seeing death. Everyone had grown accustomed to crying out loud or deeply within. Time heals everything, he had always heard the adults say, but Iraq's healing powers had atrophied. People didn't even have time to grieve anymore. They had to witness it, feel it, let it rip them apart, spill their bloody emotions, then get up and go—or lie there and die like the rest. Be heartless and keep walking, or lay down and feel and be murdered by monsters.

After they crossed the bridge and walked into the residential area, the streets became more deserted. Faisal, in filthy clothes, was waiting by the front door.

"Did you ask the shop owner if he has a job for me?" Sami said.

"I did. He said there might be some more jobs coming soon. He'll let me know as soon as the need arises, and you will be his first pick."

They headed inside, but Faisal stopped in the doorway. "Did Hadeel tell you?"

"Tell me what?"

"Some people in our neighborhood are harassing her."

Sami felt his face flush hot. "Harassing her how? And why?"

"Relax. It's not serious. Just some idiots asking her why she's choosing to walk kilometers to a Sunni-majority neighborhood to work in a hospital when there's one nearby on Haifa Street."

Sami gripped the doorframe, hard. "They're accusing her of serving the Sunni people over the Shia?"

"I don't know, man. I don't keep track of the census around here. Since when do people care if a hospital is Sunni or Shia? How dumb!"

"I'm not the one saying it. You suggested that, and with the way things have been headed in the city, I think that's exactly what they mean."

Faisal shrugged.

"Who is it? Do you know who's harassing her?"

"I don't know, Sami, and I don't think it is a big deal. Drop it."

Sami nodded. "Leave it up to me. I know how to handle it. They want to harass a young student who doesn't even have the authority to choose when to break for lunch? We'll take care of these sectarian idiots."

Sami went inside.

"We?" Faisal said. "Who's *we*?"

46

Baghdad
2006

Sami pressed his sister to give him the names of the people who were harassing her, but she refused. "They're just upset because Al Qaeda damaged their shrine in Samara," she said.

"These Shia deserve it and more," Sami said. "I wish they'd brought the whole Askari shrine down."

She hissed at him to lower his voice. "Why would you say that? Our parents raised us better than that."

Sami shrugged. "They're killing us. We shouldn't fight back?"

"Who is us and who is them? You're starting to sound like the monsters out there."

It turned out that Faisal couldn't secure a job for Sami. The shop was on the verge of shutting down, and Faisal was barely getting paid anymore. And their mother had slipped into retirement with no will to pursue any more work. She was content with spending long hours glued to the TV and watching the carnage play out on the streets from a relatively safe distance.

She was watching a TV news segment showing heated discussions inside the Iraqi parliament, followed by a short clip where Prime Minister Nouri al-Maliki had strong words for anyone threatening the existing balance of power.

"Nothing good has happened since this man took over," she said.

"He's another American puppet," Hadeel said as she cleaned the dinner plates and carried them back to the kitchen.

"Maliki is a product of Iranian extremism," Sami said. "He reeks of hate and ruthlessness. He needs to go."

Faisal shook his head. "I'll never understand what we gain from dredging up politics. You have no power or say in any of this. Why can't we just enjoy our dinner and tea in peace? Please, turn the TV off."

Sami angrily turned to Faisal. "People like you are the real problem now. Sure, just sit back and let Shia leaders whip up hatred and violence on the streets."

Faisal laughed. "Are you going to tell me Al Qaeda is a bunch of angels carrying toys and giving out hugs?"

"The Shia have the majority in the government, all the important ministries, and massive resources. They can make peace if they want it."

There was a knock on the door, and everyone sat in silence and listened. They turned the TV off and focused. No one showed up at anyone's door after dinner unless it involved an emergency or trouble. The knocks resumed, and everyone looked at the window overlooking the garden and driveway. It seemed quiet and peaceful outside, but that was no longer any guarantee of safety.

There were more repeated knocks, but they were gentle. Sami stood up, but his mother grabbed his hand.

"It's OK, Mama. I'll check it out. What if someone needs help?"

"Let Faisal answer the door," Hadeel said.

Sami was offended, but he complied. Faisal opened the door to the darkness just enough to peek outside and turned on the exterior lights, bracing his foot behind the door just in case, his brother standing not too far behind him in the darkness.

Sami heard an unfamiliar voice. "Good evening, neighbors. We're sorry to disturb your evening."

"No problem," Faisal said. "How can we help you?"

"We're collecting donations for our brave men out there who are fighting Al Qaeda terrorists. They're threatening our existence and killing our women and kids every day. We need to—"

"We're poor as dirt," Sami interrupted, "and have no interest in contributing to anything. Just leave!"

The figure on the other side of the door moved closer, and Sami was now able to make it out more clearly. Only his eyes were showing beneath a scarf wrapped around his head. He held a gun in his right hand. "You have a doctor in this house," he said, still friendly.

But there was another voice, heavier and more confrontational. "Yes, the doctor. I'm sure she could be of financial help to us."

Sami shoved Faisal aside and opened the door wide. He was now standing directly in front of two armed men, who somehow still maintained their composure.

The first man took a step back. "Look, brother. We're not here for trouble. We're just soliciting help for our brothers against Al Qaeda and other forces out there seeking to destroy the blessed path of Imam Hussein."

"We are not Shia. Understand? We want no part of your holy war. Leave us alone."

Faisal coughed a few times, cleared his throat, and spoke in an apologetic tone. "Please don't mind my brother. He's just upset after witnessing a lot of casualties recently. Our father was Sunni, and our mother is Shia. More importantly, we are all brothers and Iraqis. Please accept my apologies."

Hadeel came to the door. "Let's please wrap this up in peace. Look, guys, you apparently think I'm a rich doctor, but I haven't even finished medical school yet. Whoever told you otherwise was mistaken."

Sami's mother was at the door now too, and Faisal took a step back to make room for her. Sami noticed that his hands were shaking. "My sons," his mother said, "let's please handle this like brothers. We are all belong to this land, and we've lived in this neighborhood for so long."

Only a few moments passed in silence, but they were as heavy as the carnage on the streets every day. The two men looked at each other. Then the first strapped his gun to his back and said, "OK, we're sorry to disturb you. Have yourselves a safe evening." They both slowly walked away without turning. Hadeel closed the front door, and Faisal smacked Sami's elbow and returned to the couch without saying anything.

"What is your problem?" Hadeel exclaimed.

Sami's mother grabbed him by the shoulders and started shaking him. "Why do you have to behave so irrationally? Are you my enemy? Do you want to give me a heart attack?"

Sami turned sharply toward Faisal. "Did you want to give them money so they can kill more women and children with their guns? This is what your foolishness will lead to."

Hadeel looked through the window into the darkness. It

was quiet inside and outside. She nervously closed the curtains.

"They'll be back," Faisal said. All eyes were on him now. "They looked like amateurs. When they report this exchange with their higher ups, they'll be back tomorrow or sometime later, and we must prepare for their wrath."

Hadeel let out a long frustrated sigh. "I've seen what they do to people who stand up to them."

Sami's mother wasn't done with him yet. She grabbed his left elbow and forced him to turn around and face her. She looked as terrified as a mother would be if her child were hanging over a fire pit. He braced himself for more screaming and slapping, for any variety of emotional breakdown. Instead, his mother brought her broken face near his, looked at him through her red teary eyes, and in a soft, choked voice said, "Why, *ibni*? Why did you do that? I can't bear any more loss and heartbreak!"

Faisal nervously rubbed his temples and said, "You need to figure out a place to go. Tomorrow morning, without delay."

Hadeel wrung her hands. "Yes, brother, we can't—"

Someone pounded violently on the door.

"They've come to kill you," Faisal said. "You need to run."

F aisal grabbed Sami's arm. "Let's go brother!"

Hadeel peaked through the curtains when a violent blow pushed the front door in, nearly bringing it down.

Sami appeared dazed.

"Go over the rooftops," Faisal said as he pulled his brother upstairs. "Run as far as you can. They'll kill you."

Faisal could hear a commotion in the living room as he carefully peeked over the concrete wall around the roof. And he saw numerous figures moving about in the darkness below near their front door. Multiple cars were parked on the street. He pointed to the house behind theirs. He turned to Sami, who still stood, frozen.

"Jump to the neighbor's rooftop, and from there go to the next one. There's an electric pole next to their wall that you can climb down from and run." Faisal wasn't sure at that moment how much of that survival tip was from his memory and awareness of the neighborhood and how much was from an instinct for survival that his subconscious had already worked out to prepare for a moment like this.

Before Faisal knew it, Sami was already disappearing in the darkness over the rooftops. Faisal then headed inside and started descending the stairs. He could hear Hadeel's and his mother's cries. He hurried down the stairs, taking them two at a time. At the top of the stairs to the main floor, a man pointed a weapon at him and ordered him to stop.

"Get him down," said another man at the bottom of the stairs. "That's him."

Everything happened so fast after that. Faisal was dragged down the stairs by his arms, face down. His knees repeatedly hit against the edges of stairs, sending bolts of pain up his spine. He was thrown on the floor of the hallway leading to the kitchen, and his mother threw herself over him. "This is Faisal. He's not the one you're looking for. Please don't hurt him."

Hadeel joined her, but a masked man pulled her away and shoved her against the wall. Faisal attempted to get up, but his mother forced him down again.

"Please don't hurt him," she said. "My other son is the one who mishandled the situation, and he ran away."

"We've checked on him," one of the men said, "and he's been involved in several attacks against us. So you either find him, or this one pays for it." He placed his boot against Faisal's chest.

Faisal recognized the voice but couldn't match it to a face, not amid this hurricane of emotion and horror.

A heavily built man with wide shoulders that barely fit through the door stepped inside. He was wearing a dishdasha and flip-flops, and his body language was somehow as nonchalant as it was dominant. He was obviously the authority.

Faisal's mother bent over and started kissing his dirty flip-flops. "Please, please don't hurt my son."

The man showed his respect by gently pulling her up while she continued begging for mercy.

Faisal would rather have died than see his mother begging a stranger to spare his life. He wanted to rewind ten minutes so he could jump with Sami over the rooftops. He closed his eyes and pressed hard until the darkness inside his head pulled him deep within himself, away from these displays of power, weakness, domination, and humiliation. In that darkness, he no longer saw their neighborhood, which had always hurried to the rescue at the first cries for help. He searched his mind for the lights of neighborhood homes that always turned on in unison during any trouble as a show of support from the souls inside. But the lights did not come on, not even in his mind. Those homes were as consumed by terror as his own family's.

He felt the sudden and violent impact of something hitting him in his face and pushing him into a deeper and more painful darkness.

47

Baghdad
2006

Faisal slowly opened his eyes to a blurry light that sent shock waves of pain through his head, forcing him to close his eyes again, but he instinctively reopened them. Such is the drive for survival. Pain in the light is better than comfort in darkness. Faisal had no choice but to return and face reality, no matter how bitter and unbearable. Better to be a living human than a memory.

A voice lured him out. Mama's distinct voice. Her face gradually materialized above him. "*Ibni* Faisal. *Ibni!*"

Any time you open eyes and see your mother's face and hear her voice, you can't help but know you're alive, and you have a purpose again no matter how painful.

Despite the excruciating pain in his neck, Faisal lifted his head up and looked around. He was lying on the sofa. In the same place his father had once occupied. He got up and hysterically reached down to his knees and feet, repeatedly touching them and slapping them. He continuously kicked in the air while his mother and sister grabbed his shoulders and desperately tried to calm him down.

"Let me go! I have to get up and walk. Let me go!"

After they finally calmed him, he took a few wobbly steps, nearly falling, and then leaned against his sister as he took in a deep and painful breath. His sharp headache returned, but he didn't mind. He wanted to sit down, lie down, and rest, but he refused to get back on that sofa.

"Please lie down, *ibni*," his mother begged.

"You have a broken nose and bad bruises on your face," Hadeel said. "You can't exert yourself like that."

The pain only got worse as he gained more awareness.

His sister told him that the invader had kicked him in the head before leaving, and they threatened to come back and finish the job if they didn't find Sami.

That afternoon, a neighbor visited them. She was his mother's friend and a fellow teacher at the school. She sat across the room from Faisal as he drifted in and out of aware- ness. He attempted to get up to greet her, but she motioned for him to not exert himself.

"Don't bother, my son. I am not a stranger."

Then it hit Faisal. The voice. The masked guy from the previous night. He was this woman's son. How could he not have realized that at the time? His own mother was withdrawn in sadness, and Hadeel was in the kitchen fixing coffee. Faisal stared at the woman until their eyes met, and he didn't let go. She shifted uncomfortably, and when she looked back at him a few moments later, his piercing gaze was still fixated on her. He fought off the pain and slowly sat up, still not taking his eyes off the woman. Her obvious discomfort made Faisal even more certain that her son was one of the attackers.

"Drink your coffee," his mother told her friend, "or it will get cold." The woman seemed unaware that she even had coffee to drink. She picked up the glass and set it down again without taking a sip.

She cleared her throat. "I feel terrible in my bones and soul, Huda. My son was one of the men who invaded your house last night."

Faisal's mother didn't even change her facial expression. "I know."

But Faisal was shocked. He wanted to ask his mother why she didn't confront the guy at the time, but the neighbor kept saying, "I am so sorry!"

Nobody said anything for a long while.

"What happened to us, Huda?" his mother's friend said.

"The monsters of war snatched our children out of our arms."

Faisal felt like someone had stabbed his brain with an ice pick, and he lay back down.

"I couldn't even stop him from harming our own neighbors. His father is unhappy with him, but he's old and ill. Oh God. What has happened to us?" She pushed her untouched coffee aside. "They will come back. They'll take your house from you. And if your other son returns, they may kill him. Please listen to what I am about to say."

She certainly had their attention. Everyone was staring at her.

"My husband and I will demand they pay you for the house. It will be better for you and safer to get away from here."

Hadeel picked up the untouched coffee. "Maybe you should leave!"

"We are not selling the house, giving it up, or moving out of this neighborhood," Faisal said. "Tell them."

"Both of you shut up," his mother said. She glanced back

and forth between Faisal and Hadeel. "I am in charge in this house."

The neighbor was now staring at Faisal's mother with anticipation.

"If they pay us for the house, we'll move away," his mother said.

The big guy with the flip-flops showed up again, this time accompanied by only one man. He sat across from Faisal in the living room while the other man stood by the front door.

They were not in trouble again, the man said, but they had to face reality. Their son who was missing was part of a terrorist group. They were certain of it. And Sami's group was targeting Shia sites. The neighborhood was increasingly Shia, so having a family that hated the Shia could not be tolerated.

"But I myself am Shia," Faisal's mother said.

Which sounded strange to Faisal's ears. His family never spoke of such things.

"And your husband was Sunni," the man said.

Faisal stared at him. "We don't discuss this sort of thing in our house and don't believe in it. This entire conversation is insulting!"

"We are in a new world, young man," Flip-Flops replied, his cool demeanor somehow more unsettling than shouting or threats.

"You should say that to your brother," the man at the door said.

Silence ensued, and Faisal grew impatient, but the calm composure of the mountain sitting across from him, and the memory of what his men had done before, cautioned Faisal against breaking the silence.

The man took out a small brown envelope and threw it on the floor. "Since you're the man of the house and want to be in charge, I suggest you accept this payment for the house and start preparing to leave."

The money, given in US dollars, was not even enough to furnish a house let alone buy one. Faisal fumed with anger. But even one dollar of payment for their house under the circumstances was a concession. The family was outnumbered and outmaneuvered. They were outlaws in a city that for centuries had been accustomed to foreign invaders, but this time Iraq's own sons and daughters were killing each other, the ultimate violation.

Fatima and her daughters visited from Fallujah when she heard about what was happening. She looked decades older since the passing of her late husband. There was so much to worry about: Sami's disappearance and possible whereabouts, the urgency for the family to move, Hadeel's struggle to finish her studies amid constant cancellations of clinical rotations due to the chaos in her field, and Fatima's current state of affairs.

Faisal listened as the family discussed all this over dinner while one thing, and only one thing, floated in his mind. His twin brother. Faisal had played and replayed the events of their lives since the fall of Baghdad, with each image sliding over to make room for the next. Every one of those images was traumatic, and Faisal's mind couldn't let go.

The lives of every member of the family had paused. Their needs, both emotional and physical, were on hold, their individual existences all but dead so that whatever was left of the family could continue to live.

"What are you thinking about, brother?" Fatima asked him around midnight after she had put her daughters to sleep.

Faisal sighed deeply, with his head resting against the bare concrete wall. "Sami!"

"*Inshallah*, he will return safe, and nothing will happen to him." Her voice was void of emotion. She, too, could do little but survive after losing her husband, just enough so the next generation wasn't also dragged down in the mud.

"Pray he doesn't return," Faisal said. He noticed that, unlike his sister, he sounded sad. "He'll be dead if they spot him anywhere around here."

Fatima rubbed her nose and cracked her knuckles. "How did things get so bad? What did he do to anger these people so much?"

"I don't know, sister. No one knows what's happening. It's hard to make sense of anything nowadays."

"But you're twins. You should be able to keep up with each other more than anyone else."

Faisal felt a wave of embarrassment. Twins!

People always thought twins had a special connection to each other, but Faisal no longer even recognized Sami after he returned from Abu Ghraib. He remembered how Sami had unintentionally confided in him about being tortured and raped in prison.

"No one in our family has suffered more than Sami," he said. He knew how that must have sounded to a woman who became a widow at the age of twenty-three, but it was true. "Things happened to him at an early age that even adults can't handle."

He wanted to tell Fatima that Sami had been raped, but he held back. What good would that do now that he was gone? Sami couldn't discuss it with his family on his own terms, so why drag another family member, a woman, into that dark cell?

Faisal shook his head as he thought and thought and thought of ways he could have helped his brother more, but every corner Faisal turned in his mind led to a dead end.

His mother came into the room with a glass of tea.

"Chai this late?" Fatima said.

"I couldn't sleep. I kept twisting and turning. My tea was on the table from earlier, and when I heard you two talking, I thought I'd come and sit with you."

Join the party, Faisal wanted to say, but he let his mother settle in, hoping she'd get Fatima's attention so he could return to his thoughts.

Then he heard Hadeel scream upstairs.

48

Baghdad
2006–2007

After Hadeel's scream, things went silent momentarily, which made Faisal even more worried. He was the first up the stairs, followed by Fatima and their mother. At the top, they found Sami standing next to Hadeel, who was still in a state of shock. Fatima's girls were now awake too, and the younger one was crying. Sami waved his hands for them to keep quiet. His face looked pale, his clothes were dirty, and he wore a black wool hat rolled up above his forehead.

His mother glared at him. "What are you doing here?"

"I came over the roof. I'm sorry I scared you." He was now nervously looking at Hadeel, who shot a blank look at him.

"You're crazy for taking this risk," Faisal said. "What were you thinking?"

Sami looked away, as if only now realizing the gravity of the situation.

Faisal forestalled any possibility of debate and got in Sami's face. "You can't be here. They'll kill you if they find out you're back."

Sami remained quiet and still.

"What are you going to do, brother?" Hadeel said. "Where are you going to disappear to?"

Fatima turned on the overhead light. "He's not going to disappear. Not from us." She turned to Sami. "I'm going to take you to Fallujah, and you'll hide there, away from here."

Sami took a step back and leaned against the wall. He ran his hand through his dirty hair, then said, "Hide? I'm not hiding from anyone."

Faisal grabbed Sami's hand and gently pulled him closer. "Get off your hero horse and focus, brother. We have a problem that's much bigger than you realize."

"Oh, no. Trust me. I am well aware. Matter of fact, I'm the only person in this family who truly understands what's happening and what's going to happen next. You are the ones in oblivion." He moved his head in a circular fashion, indicating all the family members.

Faisal shook his head, and his mother stepped closer to Sami. "Please, *ibni*," she said, "settle down. I know you've been angry since the passing of your father, but—"

"That's where you're wrong. Again."

"Then grace us with your wisdom," Hadeel hissed.

Sami backed away from his mother, but she followed him with her arms and eyes.

"While you all are looking out for your personal feelings and the well-being of the family," Sami said, "there are sons of this country who are giving up everything so they can put an end to our misery and occupation and bring this nation back under our wings."

Hadeel scoffed. "And you, a twenty-year-old, claim to know how to solve everything?"

"I know people who know," Sami said, his voice colder than ever. Nobody said anything, so he continued. "You all focus on yourselves, and I'll see to revenge."

"What revenge?" Faisal yelled.

"Revenge against everyone who's responsible for where we are now. Revenge against the people who killed our father. Revenge against everyone and anyone who has a hand in the making of our hell."

"What has happened to you, brother?" Fatima said, then turned to Faisal and shoved his shoulders. "How did you let your twin brother change like this? Where were you? Why? Why?"

Their mother looked sharply at Sami. "You're staying with us, and tomorrow Fatima and Faisal will find a way to sneak you into Fallujah. Understand?"

Sami pushed her aside and took a few steps toward the stairway leading up to the rooftop. He turned and said, "And don't think I'm not aware of your plans to give up this house to them. Rest assured, once you're out of here, we'll bring the ceiling down on their heads and burn their bodies."

His mother slapped him. "You are not like them! You are not going to kill anyone. You are not. My sons were not born to be murderers."

She sat on the floor and covered her face with her shaking hands. Faisal, Hadeel, and Fatima turned to attend to her. Both of Fatima's girls were now screaming in their room.

And when Faisal turned back, Sami was gone.

A s was typical of the past four years, there was no time to dwell on losses or crumble into emotional rubble. As ever, the family brushed off the immediate pain, focused on the urgent matter at hand, then handled it. They hoped they'd be able to address everything else later, but they always found themselves facing new challenges.

Faisal promised his mother that he would find Sami and bring him back. That was the only way she'd agree to get out of bed and face the most immediate problem: leaving their house and finding another one before the intruders returned.

A two-week search led them to a rental house once occupied by two of Hadeel's schoolmates who had since graduated and moved away, a two-bedroom home in one of the oldest neighborhoods on the east shore of the river.

Then the intruders came back and ordered the family to leave everything behind except their clothes and immediate personal belongings. After much begging, Faisal was allowed to take the large wooden box containing Baba Faisal's book collection.

Fatima's in-laws came and insisted the family move to Fallujah and live with them. Hadeel was graduating soon, and they could find her a hospital in Anbar for her postgraduate training. Their mother would not take part in that discussion. She kept reminding Faisal she was counting on him to bring his twin brother back.

Fatima returned to Fallujah after she made sure her family had settled in the new rental home. The kitchen was smaller than the main bathroom in the old house. The stove had one burner, and there were no cabinets. The living room only fit one sofa, which they bought at the Friday market. There was no TV for now, but their mother didn't mind. For days Hadeel called the new house a dirt stable and the old house a home of respect. They knew no one in the neighborhood, and no one talked to them or even showed the faintest interest.

Faisal was hammering nails on the broken wooden leg of one of only two chairs in the house.

"How are we going to afford rent?" Hadeel asked.

"Well, Father's pensions plus Mama's retirement payments should cover it." He paused and added, "Barely," then violently hammered in the last nail. "My job, although still part-time, will help cover our other monthly expenses. I'll also try to find another job."

Their mother stood at the entrance to the kitchen, surveying the shrunken home and the shrunken family.

"Next week after I graduate," Hadeel said, "my official placement will start, and I'll get a small stipend that will cover some additional expenses."

Faisal stood and crossed his arms over his chest. "Our sister will finally be a doctor," he said with a wide smile. "*Mashallah*."

"Do you remember when you were ten and freaked out from the warts on your hand?" she said. "You cried every day."

"Your grandfather took you to see a guy who practiced folk medicine," his mother said.

"Yes," Hadeel said. "I went with them too."

Faisal rolled his eyes. "Seven damn warts. They would not go away. I even burned one with a hot piece of metal, but it grew back again. Oh, and the funny thing was, Hadeel kept arguing with Baba Faisal and in front of the guy that a real doctor could treat it better."

Hadeel laughed out loud. "Yes, and the guy got irritated, but Baba Faisal told him that I was going to be a doctor in the future." She caught her breath and resumed. "The guy then told me to keep quiet until I became a doctor. He wasn't happy that I questioned him."

Faisal inspected his fingers and smiled. "The man did heal me. He pricked the warts with small bits of wheat while reading some verses of the Quran, then gave them to Baba Faisal to throw away in certain places. Every Wednesday, for seven weeks. And they were gone!"

H adeel graduated from medical school but without much ceremony. Four of their fellow students had died a few months earlier when a car bomb exploded next to a bus stop in front of the hospital. In less than a year, half a dozen of their well-known professors had either been detained, shot in front of their homes, or forced into hiding due to their beliefs, whatever they were, that the terrorist groups found incompatible with their new order. She received her diploma and left early and celebrated with her siblings.

Fatima was visiting from Fallujah, and Faisal suggested they walk across Bab Al-Moatham Bridge to Falafel Abu Nawara, which had the best falafel in all of Baghdad.

Iraqi security forces seemed to be stationed at nearly every corner and intersection. The American military presence was heavier too as the US was cracking down on both Sunni Al Qaeda and the Shia Mahdi Army.

Falafel Abu Nawara was a tiny aluminum box that barely fit two people and its small kitchen. It sat a hundred feet off the main street, overlooking the Tigris. The structure was embedded with so many layers of paint that it was hard to tell what the final color was. There were more rusty spots and bent corners than Faisal could count while standing in line, which stretched and zigzagged along the curbside for at least two hundred feet.

Abu Nawara, "Father of Nawara," was an elderly man who

was at least seventy and who apparently hated rest. If he really
had named the small hut after his first daughter, as rumor had
it, she must by now have her own family and kids. Yet Abu
Nawara went about preparing sandwiches, one after the other,
as if this were his first day and he had something to prove.

"You two go and find a spot for us near the river," Faisal
said, "and I'll get our food."

"I need my sandwich with extra pickles," Hadeel said with
a smile. "And tell him to not be cheap with the potatoes."

The long line outside every day spoke volumes. Baghdadis
rarely gathered en masse anymore, but they were willing to
put a lot on the line for Abu Nawara's falafel.

Faisal scanned the riverbank. His sisters had found a
concrete slab on the edge of the path overlooking the river and
seemed to be engaged in a serious discussion. He remembered
the last family picnic, when Baba Faisal was still alive and
their father was in the wheelchair. He pictured himself and his
siblings at their current ages gathered around the parents and
Baba Faisal, their only worry having to flip the large dolma pot
without the meat sticking to the bottom. They never worried
about such things anymore. During the tough years of the
economic embargo, whenever one of the kids complained
about food or other missing luxuries, their mother would say,
"Many in this world have it worse than us. Be thankful!"
Faisal's mind flew back to the present riverbank like a balloon
that had been deflated and left to drift to the ground,
shrunken and voided. He wondered to himself if there were
still people out there who had it worse than them. He looked
at where his sisters were sitting. Their grandfather, their
father, Fatima's late husband, and worst of all Sami: all
missing.

An annoyed voice interrupted him. "Young man. Let's go.
What's your order? The line is long!" He anxiously turned

around to face the open window, where a frustrated Abu Nawara stood with his eyebrows raised. How long had he been trying to get Faisal's attention?

"Four sandwiches, one with extra pickles, all with extra potatoes." Four sandwiches for only three people, but he knew he'd go through his second sandwich before his sisters were halfway done with theirs.

Faisal delivered the food and sat between his two sisters.

"I hope this graduation gift doesn't make you go broke," Hadeel said with a smile.

"Don't worry," Faisal said. "My new job pays more, so you can think of this a new employment gift."

Fatima took a bite from her sandwich. "I'm glad you're working in a more respectable place."

Hadeel quickly added, "Yes, fixing radios and TVs is much better than diving into car engines and coming home drenched in oil."

Faisal ignored their commentary and worked on his second sandwich.

When they were finished with their food, he pointed to the other side of the river. "Over there, our old house is some-where behind those trees." The distance seemed to stretch beyond space and time. Although they lived there recently, it felt like an eternity ago.

Fatima stared at the water, slow in motion, calm in move-ment, and dirty in color. "What happened to the Tigris? It looks terrible."

"Everything is dirty nowadays," Hadeel said. "Especially humans."

Faisal scanned the length and breadth of the river. There were no boats and no fishermen.

"Brother," Hadeel said. "I think Fatima has something to

tell you." She giggled, but Fatima shut her up with a slap to the wrist.

Faisal turned to Fatima. "What is it?"

"Go ahead," Fatima said. "Tell him." She looked away, clearly embarrassed.

Hadeel answered for her. "Fatima has a suitor in Fallujah."

49

Baghdad
2008–2009

Fatima's suitor, Mr. Salah, was in his midthirties and had lost his wife due to cancer a few years earlier, leaving behind a daughter, who was turning four. Mr. Hamdan broached the subject with Fatima, but she immediately turned it down. He reminded her that although they appreciated her commitment to them and that they loved her more than she could ever imagine, she had to move on at some point. Since she refused to leave Fallujah, this was her chance to settle down and still be close to them. Fatima was convinced that she was cursed and that another marriage would bring about more heartache, but under persistent pressure from the family, she finally relented.

Fatima was told that Salah was struggling financially and that his income, as an accountant, was limited. She didn't care. What she insisted on was that he never get in her way of visiting her late husband's parents, to which he agreed with a wide smile. Little did Fatima know that those same parents were the ones who had suggested that he propose to Fatima. They adored her and loved her children and wanted Fatima to move on and have a new life of her own. She was deserving of happiness.

The family got to meet him in person at their new small rental house in Baghdad, and Faisal, as the man in the house, approved of him. "He seems nice and has a good demeanor. I'm happy for her.

"I wanted Fatima to live here with us," his mother said.

Faisal scoffed. "Here? In this cave?"

"No, just near us, in Baghdad."

He inspected the dirty window blinds, which probably had not been washed in years, and marveled that his sister, now a medical doctor, ended up in such conditions. He raised the blinds for his mother to see outside. The street was empty. No kids playing. No men standing around and having discussions. No women passing by holding the hands of their children. An empty street and an empty life. "You want Fatima to live this kind of life? No. Let her be happy where she is."

He turned around again and saw his mother's broken face. She placed her hand over her lower abdomen. Faisal knew all too well what his mother was thinking at the moment.

"Allah," she said, "make me happy by seeing my son again. Return him to me safe and sound."

Faisal was the only one who had seen his brother recently. Right before they moved to the new home, Sami had suddenly appeared behind Faisal one night as he was on his way home from work. Sami just wanted to reassure them that he was safe and that he was staying with some friends who were as good to him as any family and siblings would be. He was not coming back. He made that very clear. He promised Faisal that he

would catch up with him again and advised him not to look
for him.

Faisal told his mother a limited version of the story: Sami
was safe and staying with some friends.

He saw his brother again a few months later on a cold
night in 2008. He was walking back from the electronics shop.
He had grown accustomed to repeatedly looking over his
shoulder to see if anyone was following him or if anything
unusual was going on. Mostly he was looking for his twin
brother to appear out of the dark air that seemed to have swallowed him. On countless occasions, he nearly tripped when
looking behind him instead of in front, checking behind cars,
around corners, next to electrical poles, and any other spot
someone might watch another person from afar.

That evening, Faisal was exhausted from a long workday,
which had consisted of fixing seven TV sets and four electric
heaters. He had his hands in his front pants pockets as he
slipped through the narrow streets, his breath piercing
through the cold air like a cloud of smoke.

Sami's voice, calm and monotone as it was, rattled him.
"You keep turning around like that, and you'll fall and get
hurt."

Faisal turned around, and his brother was right there.

"My twin brother and soul," Sami said and extended his
hand. He pulled Faisal aside on the curb, then took him in
with a deep embrace.

Faisal pulled away and studied Sami's face under the overhead streetlight. He had grown a beard, and his mustache was
thick and uneven at the edges. They stood across from each
other, the distance separating them no greater than when
they'd once shared a womb. Yet when Faisal looked into his
twin brother's eyes, he saw a distance separating them the
length of the war.

Sami deflected Faisal's questions about his whereabouts and parried with questions of his own about their mother, Hadeel, Fatima, and their new house.

Some men having a heated discussion approached from the other corner of the street, and both Faisal and Sami silently watched them pass.

"We took care of them," Sami said. "The house."

Faisal narrowed his eyes at Sami.

"I told you I'd bring the house down on their heads," Sami said. "And I did. We bombed it. It's gone. If we couldn't enjoy it, better to ship it and them to hell."

Faisal grabbed Sami by the collar and shoved him against the concrete wall. Faisal's breaths were shallow, and he panted loudly as he pressed Sami's body tighter. "What did you do? Do you even know who you've become or what you are involved with?"

Sami didn't resist Faisal's grip. He only maneuvered himself enough to catch his breath. "Those people kicked you out of your house, threw you, your mother, and your sister onto the street like dogs. They're the very same people who told the Americans your father was with the Ba'ath, and we know how the rest of that story went. Now you're going to teach me about mercy and kindness?"

Faisal withdrew and stepped back, barely able to breathe and unable to string meaningful words together. He wanted to think his brother was bluffing, but Faisal knew Sami all too well. When he spoke in that cold tone of his, he was deadly serious.

Faisal looked around for any traffic or bystanders but saw only darkness. He stomped his foot on the ground and said, "We are not killers. We don't do the barbaric things those other people do. What has gotten into you?"

Sami brought his face close to Faisal's. "Barbarism

appeared on our doorsteps uninvited. Now we are all on its train."

"What train? Have you lost your mind?"

"Our country has been hijacked by the infidels who came here from across the oceans and by those who want to change the identity of this nation with their sectarian Shia beliefs. We have to rescue the country and take it back."

"Rescue?" Faisal whispered in a hoarse voice. His anger had tapered down, or perhaps he had exhausted his emotions.

"Yes. And the only path to reclaiming our land and our dignity is by returning to the foundations of our faith, our beliefs, and the teachings of our religion."

Faisal shook his head in disbelief. He couldn't remember a single time when Sami had ever even read the Quran let alone prayed.

"I know what you're thinking," Sami said. "I've changed. I've found the right path. I'm blessed to have come across sincere brothers and mentors who are willing to sacrifice anything and everything to solidify the word of Allah in this land."

Faisal got himself together and decided to change his approach. They'd been driving away from each other in opposite lanes so far. He put his hand on Sami's shoulder, looked him in the eye, and said "Have you thought about our mother? You're breaking her heart every day. I can't keep lying to her about your whereabouts. You obviously haven't just been in hiding. It's only a matter of time before this blows up on you and on us."

Sami took his brother's hand, held it to his heart, and said, "I'm not coming back, brother. I don't want to even come and see her because I don't want the sight of her to sway me from my path. Tell her I love her. I love you. I love you all. Some of us have to die for the rest to live."

Faisal broke down crying, took Sami in his arms, and brushed his hands over his hair. "Please, Sami. Please, come back. We'll move away. We'll do anything. Don't break our mother's heart. I can't tell her anything. You would have to tell her yourself."

Sami pulled himself from Faisal. "Lie to her. Tell her I'm in prison or ran away. Anything."

Faisal wiped tears from his face. "We are twenty-one years old. What do we know of the world out there?"

"Trust me. The world out there has matured us so fast that we might as well be fifty-one. I can shoot any gun and can easily evade most of the lame security checkpoints." He looked at his wristwatch and tapped the ground with his feet. "I have to get going."

"Please come with me. To your mother's arms."

"Don't. Don't try it. I have to go."

Before he left, Faisal grabbed Sami's arm and pulled him back for another hug. "Promise me you'll be safe and keep in contact with me."

"The first, I can't promise. The second I will do as long as I am alive and around."

Sami kissed his brother's head and disappeared into the darkness of Baghdad.

F aisal couldn't sleep for days, and he spent long hours in deep thought and silence, imagining hundreds of scenarios that included Sami committing acts of terrorism and murder. The dreaded environment at home always pulled him out of it. But his mother kept asking him for news about his twin brother. He melted inside from despair.

Faisal could no longer hold back. He had to share the

burden with someone. Although both Fatima and Hadeel had also been asking about Sami, Faisal confided only in Hadeel. He told her about his latest meeting with Sami and what he'd said and suggested. To his surprise, Hadeel seemed as if she had suspected as much, but she still broke down crying as if she'd just learned that Sami had died. He might as well have.

They agreed that neither Fatima nor their mother should know. So Faisal lied. He told his mother that Sami was still in hiding after having another run-in with those Shia groups. He'd moved out of Baghdad and was not coming back anytime soon because any association with him could put the family in danger. Faisal didn't care if his mother bought it or not just so long as she stopped asking him to go out and check on Sami.

Six months later, Sami made contact with Faisal again, but this time it was through a letter that a child delivered to the shop. After reading the first few lines, he bolted outside, but Sami was nowhere in the area. Soon he'd be nowhere in the world.

In the letter, Sami asked for his brother's forgiveness and said he loved him more than he could ever imagine. Sami hoped to go on a suicide mission so he could finally be able to rest his case against everyone who had been responsible for his and his family's misery. He expected to be one of the few chosen members of the cell to carry out the mission—if he was blessed enough.

Tears had long ago lost their way to Faisal's eyes, the thin thread connecting them to his miserable life, so for Faisal it didn't matter anymore how anyone responded to sad news. Once this kind of news came, the sadness was part of their soul, so deep that it didn't matter what one said, did, or wished.

As the months ticked by, Faisal's mother surrendered to the reality she'd been denying. Sami was almost certainly caught up in trouble with some extremist groups, and he either wasn't willing or wasn't able to come back. Either way, she stopped berating Faisal on a daily and weekly basis about what may or may not have happened to Sami.

In the summer of 2009, Hadeel talked to Faisal and Fatima about a colleague of hers who wanted to propose to her. It was obvious that the two had been in love for a while, and the matter was mostly a formality now. But there was one problem.

50

Belarus
Winter 2021

I t is now past the midpoint of December. More journalists have been pouring into the camp from both sides of the fence, with those on the Belarusian able to conduct interviews with hungry, exhausted migrants. I've done three interviews myself in the last forty-eight hours alone, usually alongside little Naza and her family. On one occasion, Naza's mother scolded her for constantly smiling on camera when the whole point was to show that we're suffering. But a smile can't hide the muddy clothes, torn shoes, dirty faces, and dry lips that rarely touch water or bread. Go on, pretty mountain girl. Go on and smile. Defy the ugly face of the world.

An old woman collapses inside a nearby tent, and a herd of journalists rush to cover the scene. Her body is soon carried out while a few young women, probably directly related to her, wail and scream. Two men carry her over their shoulders toward a media van similar to the one we took Naza in. This time, the crew locks the doors and rolls up the windows as the crowd grows.

I run to the driver's side and bang on the window, but the driver puts his head on the steering wheel, disregarding the chaos on the other side of the glass. The van door soon opens, and a cameraman jumps in, barely making it before the driver cuts through the crowd on the muddy road. A barrage of insults follows them, and moments later the old woman is taken back to the tent when it becomes obvious that she has passed.

I've seen enough death over the years that I vowed to avoid dead or dying people as much as I can in this godforsaken life. I return to our campsite and find Gulistan sitting by the fire. My mother's face flashes before me, and I retreat to the opposite side of the camp, away from the crowd.

I sit by the fence, all by myself. I recoil against the concrete pole, then put my hat over my head and down over my eyes and cry. I cry and cry. I cry for myself, for my mother, for my siblings, and for Baghdad. I cry for the land that gave birth to me and handed me off to this strange land with its war-scented memories. I refuse to close my eyes so as not to be taken back to memories of war and loss back home. I let the tears do their thing with my eyes and face, uncontested and unchallenged. I refuse to be pulled back to the past.

A hand gently rubs my back, and I can't tell if I'm still in the camp or back in Baghdad. My hat slips down over the back of my neck, and Mother's gentle fingers brush my filthy hair and tell me everything I need to hear without words. *Hang in there. Be strong. Keep it together. You are not alone. I'm with you. My heart is carrying you.* It's the voice of Baghdad and the heart of Mama.

I look up, and Gulistan is standing over me, calm yet somehow charged. I sense that she can see into my heart, my soul, and my emotions. She pulls me up and wraps her arm around my head, a touch of Mama that I've so dearly missed. "My son, don't let the tough times bring you down. Let's go back to our campsite. Allah will guide us through this."

Two days after we bury the old woman, chaos crescendos inside the camp. People are seriously doubting their survival in the face of Polish stubbornness. International pressure mounts, but against whom? What we've see in Western media reports so far has focused on criticizing Belarus for misleading migrants into thinking they could cross the Polish border without any trouble. Western leaders are calling out Belarus for being pro-Russia and for all the human rights violations the two regimes have committed.

With their frozen hands against the barbed wire fence, the desperate migrants want to scream into Western Europe and say, "We love your attention to human rights, and this is why we are here. Please allow us to cross into your paradise, and *then* you can settle your issues with Russia and its cub Belarus!"

Iraqi officials have been dragged into this circus as well, some by choice, others against their will. The crisis has caused them a great deal of embarrassment since they are the main reason that we, the migrants, ran away in the first place. Those among us who came from the Kurdistan region, the likes of Gulistan and her family, are getting extra publicity due to the increased media coverage there.

When reports circulate around the camp that Iraqi officials in Belarus and Poland are offering to help the migrants return to Iraq, all sorts of insults are thrown around. No one came this far, physically and emotionally, to pack up and go back to the swamp we couldn't wait to get out of. But when two more people die from hunger and freezing temperatures, things change, and they change quickly. Hundreds of people make phone calls and talk to various representatives and journalists and decide to give up on the European dream and return home. And just like that, within hours, more than a dozen buses arrive and transport the Iraqis who agreed to return. They are so quick to facilitate our return but refuse to help us cross the fence. I refuse to entertain the idea or even discuss it. The subject is off limits during our evening roundups over the firepit.

Three days later, I catch Naza limping behind a tree.

"Are you all right?" I ask.

"My legs are weak," she answers as she lets her body settle into the mud and her head against the tent fabric, still wet from last night's rain. I gently help her up, and we stroll around the camp until I find a familiar group circulating small glasses of hot milk. I manage to get their sympathy to spare Naza a cup, which she quickly gulps down despite the steam coming off it. It's my goal now to eliminate every possible reason for Gulistan and her daughter-in-law to consider returning home.

On our way back to the tent, Naza looks up and asks, "Uncle, do you think I'm going to die here?"

"Why do you say that?" I ask and crouch down to look at her face to face.

Naza immediately answers, as if she'd rehearsed her response. "My mother keeps telling Grandma that I'm going to end up dying here. I've heard them argue about it, and I don't want my death to be a reason for them to fight."

"Where did you learn to speak Arabic?" I ask, desperately trying to change the subject. Her Arabic is impressive.

"In my school, we had many kids who moved from Mosul after ISIS took over their land. I learned from them."

In the evening, the clear sky makes room for the moon to glow with a soothing beauty that is as accessible to us miserable humans here as it is for the fortunate Europeans on the other side of the fence and far into the west and beyond waters and forests. The camp has been quiet, or rather in shock, since the first group of migrants returned. We feel more reassured when we see TV reports showing some of them arriving at the Baghdad airport. Several people from our group have also gone down with COVID, so I start a small fire next to our tent and decide to avoid larger groups. I'm mostly avoiding negative talk and the depressing mood.

Gulistan and her family gather around the fire, and I watch the kids as they shift in their seats, periodically asking their mother for food. I have not had anything to eat since yesterday, and the only loaf of bread I was able to secure from a relief truck today ended up in Gulistan's hands. She made sure her grandkids got every bit of it. They're still hungry, but to distract them, Gulistan invites them to the tent for story time. Naza declines at first but later joins the others when the freezing wind becomes unbearable, leaving me and the young mother alone in front of the shifting flames.

"She's becoming pale again," I say as soon as Naza disappears inside the tent.

Her mother frowns and says, "Let me make one thing clear. If you and Gulistan have a plot to convince me to take my kids back, you can forget about it. I've come this far and will make sure it's worth it … for me, for my kids, for Naza."

A small piece of burning wood breaks and falls between my feet and hers. I slowly kick it away and step on it, putting it out. After a short pause, I say, "There are no plots. I'm not interfering. I'll only help you keep your children safe here. Beyond that, what you want to do is your decision and only yours."

For a good two or three minutes, the only sound is the crackling fire. Then her hesitant voice breaks the silence.

"She's never liked me. I'm not the one who ran after her son. He put his eyes on me while he was serving with the Peshmerga in our neighborhood."

I have no intention to say anything. I poke the fire with a stick and flip some of the wood upside down to give it new life before the wind sucks it away. Why am I still here? How naive am I to still be stuck in this drama? She is not done yet. And she's not even trying to lower her voice so Gulistan can't hear. I can only pray that Gulistan is in deep sleep, or we'll be in deep trouble.

"I had a distant relative who was crazy about me. He proposed to me multiple times. He is the one she accused me of offering sexual favors to in return for his help with our smuggling and travel costs. And I swear by my father's grave and by my children's heads that I have never touched him. I loved her son. I loved my husband and said no to my own relatives for him."

I can hear her sniffling, and I stoke the fire even more aggressively, hoping to cover up the sound of crying that I'm certain is coming.

"I wouldn't be surprised if she comes out and accuses you and me of doing something. She's that crazy."

I want to ask, though, why her mother-in-law disliked her from the beginning as she claims, but she beats me to it.

"She was jealous of me when she saw her son up to his head in my love. Her husband died a long time ago, and if it were up to her, she'd never let her son get married so she could boss him around like a little boy."

I want to remind her that she's talking about her husband, who is now dead, but I decide to break my silence instead by focusing on her sick child.

"Listen. You're like a sister to me, and Gulistan might as well be my mother. I promise you that I'll do everything I can to help you get your kids to safety and for your daughter to get the treatment she needs. I only ask that you drop the animosity, for your sake and for the sake of your kids."

"I'm not a hateful woman. I promise you that. If only you knew what I've had to go through."

"You don't have to tell me. It's all on display. God will reward you for your patience and strength. Just don't—"

"Forgive me. I hate myself for dredging up the past like this. I promised myself that I wouldn't, but I miss my husband. The kids miss him. My boys will keep asking when he'll return from his long trip to help us get through the fence."

The fire has dwindled out, and her crying is more audible. I recoil inside my coat, unable to muster any thoughts or words. A child cries somewhere nearby, and another one follows suit. I check my wristwatch, and it's past two o'clock in the morning.

"I'm sorry if I bore your with all this talk," she says, "but you're like a brother to me now. We're family whether we chose it or not."

"Right now, the world would be better if I could get this fire restarted," I say, hoping the previous subjects get buried for good.

She gets up and starts the fire again, then turns to me and asks, "What about you? Did you leave a wife or fiancée behind? Did you have a girl you were willing to leave the world for?"

My memories open up with her last words and invite me to take a trip back to a rich and heavy time, a trip I'm not sure I want to take. I'm not even sure what to call it.

51

Baghdad
2009–2017

Hadeel's colleague and suitor was Dr. Ziyad Othman, a classmate since their first year of medical school. His family, originally from Tikrit, had fled to Amman, Jordan, during the peak of the insurgency and subsequent civil war two years earlier. He was planning to reunite with them now that he'd graduated and finished his required rotations. Time was of the essence because Dr. Ziyad had to join his family in Amman and register with the United Nations refugee program.

Faisal rejected out of hand the idea of Hadeel getting married to anyone, especially if that meant leaving the family and leaving the country. He didn't even know why he felt so strongly about it.

"You've always been the selfish one," he told his sister, "withdrawn to your world of studying and now your personal life, oblivious of the hell we live in."

This triggered a heated argument, and Faisal's mother and Fatima loudly lambasted Faisal.

"Let the poor girl go and build her life," his mother said.

Fatima was visiting in part to soften the mood, and she agreed with their mother. "What future does she have here among the animals out there? They're killing doctors right and left. If the guy is good like she says and really wants her, I support her decision."

Faisal softened his stance a bit and even apologized to Hadeel, saying he'd been ambushed by the subject. He thought to himself that it was impossible that Hadeel had not pleaded with her sister to take her side, which was of course understandable, but what Faisal feared most was more anguish for their mother if Hadeel were to pack up and go.

Just when he thought Hadeel would be happy with the blessings from her mother and sister and the silent agreement of her brother, she turned to her mother and said, "But I don't want to go and leave you here."

"My dear, this is the fate of every girl. She eventually marries and lands in another nest. It is the natural way of life. I want you to go and be happy."

"I want you to go with me!"

Everyone's eyes turned to Hadeel, but she turned to Faisal and said, "We can all go. You, me, and Mama. We can start another life there. It will be good."

"I am not leaving this city," their mother said. "I'm not going anywhere until my Sami returns. You can burn me, cut me into pieces, and pull out my soul, but I won't leave."

Her voice was cracking now, and Faisal put his arms around her. "Mama, no one will force you to do anything or go anywhere against your will. And I will never leave your side."

Faisal walked to work the next morning, cutting his way through the busy streets and filtering out the noise around him. He wondered how it was possible that he could have grown up and become a young man without feeling love for the opposite gender. It was expected that the boys got crushes on their neighbors' daughters or random girls in school or on the streets. Somehow, he'd missed all that, the feelings that boys and girls naturally feel toward each other when their hormones kick in and they become fascinated with the body, its beauty, and its burning emotions. Faisal, deep down, felt envious of Hadeel, who had stumbled upon love and was refusing to let go of it.

Three months later, Hadeel processed her marriage paperwork with Dr. Ziyad so they could travel to Amman, where the two doctors later had a respectable wedding.

～

Over the next three years, between 2009 and 2012, Faisal's mother slowly seemed to accept Sami's disappearance from their lives. He managed to avoid his mother's questions about any details he knew about what might have happened. Then, the answers started to get old, and his mother became suspicious.

One night she pressed his hand against the cover of a Quran. "Swear by the name of Allah and on this holy book that you are not hiding anything from me."

Her face was pale and shrunken. She could see Faisal's hesitation. That only solidified her suspicion. That was clear. And with his hand still held tightly against the cover of the Quran, Faisal was forced to tell his mother all that he knew about Sami and his previous encounters. And she broke. He wished he could take Sami's place, that Sami would have to deal with their mother's nervous breakdown.

She dragged him with her to government offices and prisons, asking if they had her son's name in any of their records. Most of the time, they looked at her with ridicule in their eyes. At the prisons and police station, they told her there were no records with Sami's name. Faisal was certain they were not even checking given the chaos in the jungle that Baghdad had become. He was just another young man lost in the fire.

When Faisal was not working or desperately looking for an additional part-time job to cover expenses, he was wavering between despair at the thought of his mother still waiting for her son and his own guilt for not jumping his brother on one of the occasions they'd met and for not reporting him to the authorities. But then, where would that have left Sami? Faisal was certain his brother would be underground if not in a cell or even a mass grave.

He refused to believe that his brother would ever blow himself up on a public road in their own city or target innocent civilians. He had to hold on to that conviction. And as the religious militant groups were moving on from Al Qaeda and calling themselves a variety of new names, Faisal had a feeling his brother was still somewhere out there being told where to run and when to hide and when and where to point his gun.

Fatima, for her part, convinced her husband and Mr. Hamdan to search for Sami, but it became more and more obvious that under Iraq's new sky, when someone left or was snatched into the dark world, there was no return.

By 2015, Hadeel and her husband were still stuck in Amman, awaiting the UN refugee process. The rest of the family had already been approved and left for Australia in 2013. The couple was unwilling to have children so as not to complicate their case, and they didn't have formal paperwork that would allow them to practice as doctors in Jordan, so they assisted local doctors in various clinics without a permit for ridiculously low wages to maintain a barely dignified living.

Faisal had bought his mother a cell phone by then, and most of Hadeel's conversations with her mother ended with her saying, "Mama, I wish we had the financial means to help you."

Fatima had managed to get pregnant twice and added two boys to her growing family. For Faisal, it was difficult to comprehend how people, anyone, could move on about their daily lives and get married, make babies, laugh, joke, fight, and pursue anything normal. For him, life was painfully slow and monotonous. He couldn't see color. He saw no point in fighting for survival or hoping for a better day. He just went through the motions so the ship wouldn't sink and pull him and his mother down. He wasn't giving up, but he saw nothing worth making an extra effort for. Not until 2018.

52

Baghdad
2018

By early 2018, life in Baghdad was slowly settling down, with a greatly reduced intensity of street violence and bombs, but the political leaders continued to play their cat and mouse games in the Green Zone, the central part of the city heavily fortified by the Americans and now occupied by various government headquarters and residences. Faisal and his mother lived far from there and were never even curious enough to check it out. Every time he heard the phrase "Green Zone," Faisal felt anything but green. Everything was dim, both outside and at home.

They'd remained in the same rental house despite the owner raising the rent several times. It was still cheaper than anything else Faisal could find. His mother had started to get out more and made a few friends in the neighborhood, two of whom shared the misery of a missing family member or seeing them killed in front of their eyes. A few months earlier, she heard a rumor that many young men from Baghdad who had joined Daesh, the extremist group that had overtaken Al Qaeda and which the West called ISIS, had all moved to Mosul when ISIS took over the city in 2014.

Ever since, she'd obsessively scrolled through all sorts of web pages that covered ISIS fighters, news, and prisoners. She and her friends had hundreds of videos saved on their phones. She watched the video clips that people circulated to show the criminality and barbarism of ISIS fighters, but the mothers of missing young men searched those videos for something else, for the faces they had brought into this world only to see them slip away.

Fatima was absorbed with her new family, taking care of her children from the first marriage, the two children from her second marriage, plus her husband's daughter from his first marriage. She was happy in Fallujah, and despite all efforts from her mother to persuade her to move, she wouldn't budge.

Hadeel and her husband still didn't have their immigration paperwork, but they refused to admit defeat.

Faisal had remained at his job, which had expanded to a warehouse that sold used home electronics. The pay was miserable, and the hours were scattered. At times, the owner would just decide to close for a few days and pursue other opportunities in Istanbul, Erbil, or Beirut and return. He didn't trust Faisal or anyone else with the warehouse while he was away, and that was more insulting to Faisal than the low pay and lack of a raise since he'd started years ago.

His mother set a small breakfast plate on the floor between herself and Faisal with the tea kettle on the side. She'd had gone through the last three eggs in the refrigerator. The kitchen, small as it was, was empty. There were only two new pieces of furniture in the living room: a TV and a small sofa.

"We're barely making ends meet, *ibni*," she said as she

poured a cup of tea for Faisal. She set it in front of him, then poured hers.

The last few months had been difficult. Her retirement money was no longer enough to cover rent, and her husband's pensions were barely covering some of their groceries and daily needs. Plus, in the last two years, she'd been diagnosed with high blood pressure as well as high cholesterol and a severe form of arthritis that required expensive medicine. Hadeel had not been able to send her the medicine lately, and most of her retirement money for the past two months had gone to medicine.

"I have exhausted all means of finding another job," Faisal said. "There just isn't much out there." He tried his best not to sound frustrated or overly concerned.

"It doesn't have to be a career, son."

"Mama, I'm willing to do anything, even construction work," he said, no longer able to hide his frustration.

"Don't worry, *ibni*. Allah will find a way."

"We've been saying that for months now. Allah doesn't just open doors for people. We have to find doors and knock on them."

Faisal's cell phone rang, and he took another sip of his tea before answering it. He pulled it to his ear and only a few seconds later hung up. The warehouse owner was gone for another week and told Faisal not to come. Faisal considered his finances, the loans adding up at local grocery stores, and the next round of medicine for his mother. When he weighed all that with the money he had in his possession, Faisal decided it was time to bite the bullet, swallow his pride, and do what he'd contemplated for some time while hoping and wishing he'd never have to.

Once well-hidden upstairs in the old house, Baba Faisal's

wooden box was now in his bedroom, which itself had a wooden door that seemed to have been broken for longer than even the house could remember. There was no more dust on the box, but it nevertheless looked abandoned, neglected. Faisal lifted the lid, slowly removed the books, and set them on the floor. With the exception of two notebooks that contained diaries and personal information, he placed everything else in a carton box, which he then carried over his shoulders and slowly walked to the front door in defeat. He hauled three generations of memories, wisdom, and knowledge to be sold in exchange for a bare minimum to cover basic needs.

"Allah be with you, *ibni*," his mother said on his way out the door. "May He protect you and keep you around me." Her words stayed in mind all the way to the end of the street as he panted and sighed under the weight of the box.

Mutanabbi Street was less than twenty minutes from the house on foot, but with a box full of books, the journey took Faisal over an hour. He had come to this iconic street countless times in the past, mostly with Baba Faisal and then at times alone when he needed a break from war, hate, and disagreement and to take refuge among the silence of books. Mutanabbi had been the destination for book lovers and literature enthusiasts for generations. Hundreds of thousands of books changed hands on both sides of the street that housed hundreds of bookstores and book stands. This time, however, Faisal felt foreign in this forever-welcoming world. He was getting rid of books in a place where people came eagerly to own them. He passed the Shabandar Coffee and Tea Shop, another icon in Baghdad and one of the oldest destinations for intellectuals and news enthusiasts to have hot drinks and enjoy heated discussions while soothing music played in the background.

His phone rang, and he set the box down on the side of the street to answer. It was his mother.

"I was thinking, *ibni*, maybe bring the books back, and we will try to find something else to sell."

Faisal looked around and watched the scarce foot traffic on this side of the street. In the distant past, there would barely be space for anyone to walk, but today few people wandered about, although Al Mutanabbi was lately starting to feel a little less dead than it had.

He asked a passerby if that particular spot belonged to anyone and was told, "It's public space. Set your box wherever you want as long as a store owner doesn't claim it as theirs."

"No, Mama," he said, returning to his phone call. "Don't worry. *Inshallah*, we will make up for this in the future. Now let me go so I can set up my small stand here, and wish me good luck." He hung up before she said anything.

There were three book stands on the opposite side of the street, two of which extended from bookstores with reasonably busy traffic around them. Feeling amateurish and outlandish, Faisal took the books out of the box, set them on the ground, then flipped the box upside down and started setting some of the books on top and placing the rest of them sideways against the box. He realized he had not even thought of a price for each book. How much were they worth? Was anyone going to show interest? Would this be worth his time and effort? Would he regret it if they sold?

An old man in a wrinkled gray suit stopped by and scanned the books on top of the box. Faisal watched his eyes and saw little interest, or perhaps the man was worried that the price of each book might break the bank. The man leaned over and picked one up. It was a history of Mesopotamia, and Faisal quickly decided he would let the man offer a price and that would be that.

"This book is worth gold for what's between its covers," the man said.

Faisal felt a glimpse of hope for his first sale of the day. The guy, however, slowly put the book down and walked away without saying anything further.

The sky was clear, and the sun was nearly straight overhead. The chilly February day was starting to warm up, and hopefully it wouldn't be as bad as he feared.

He spotted the old man with the gray suit again as he stepped onto the sidewalk behind him. He followed him with his eyes, wondering if he'd come back and purchase the book.

A woman's voice interrupted his thoughts: "How much for everything?" She was standing next to him and pointing at the books in a circular motion, emphasizing her interest in "everything" as she had just inquired.

In his moment of surprise, Faisal followed her hand and without looking at her said, "I don't know. How much are you willing to offer?"

"A hundred thousand dinars," she said firmly. He looked up again and saw her face fixed on the books, but his face was now fixed on her. He wasn't thinking about how a hundred thousand dinars couldn't cover a week's worth of groceries and daily necessities. She was tall, taller than him even when he stood up to face her. Their eyes met, but she still meant business and said, "Ha? What did you say?"

"How much did you say?" Faisal asked, his eyes hesitantly scanning her face. Her hazel eyes glared at him. They were narrow on the edges but wide in the middle, making them impossible to miss in their entirety. Her thin lips were pale but shiny at the same time. She wore no makeup, and when she spoke again, the indentation in the middle of her chin threw Faisal off his feet, his heart, his mind, and everything he owned.

"OK," he said without any thought. "They're yours."

She stepped in front of him, did a quick count of the books while slightly bending her knees, her long dress slightly touching the ground, then got up and handed Faisal the money.

"Can you help me carry them, please?"

"I'm sorry, what?" Faisal slowly slid the money into his front pocket, still trying to recover from a feeling that was foreign to him.

"Just across the street, over there." She pointed to the opposite curbside, some twenty or so feet away.

She had already taken some of the books across and returned when Faisal finally woke up from his thoughts.

"I'm sorry. Yes, let me help you." He grabbed the box from her hand. She had stacked the remaining books in it and hesitantly gave it to him, their eyes meeting again. He carried the box across the street and set it down next to a tall wooden stand where she was pointing.

"There is good," she said. "*Shukran*."

He stood there, still in shock. Shock at having sold all the books at once, and shock at what he had still been feeling or trying to understand how to feel. She, on the other hand, was already down on her knees next to the box, inspecting the books with meticulous care. The street was getting busier, and the crowd jostled him from behind, so he slipped away with his hand in his pocket, tightly holding on to the paper bills, and walked to the opposite end of Mutanabbi Street.

He felt sweat running down his back, his body temperature clashing with the cold winter breeze. Twenty minutes later, he was at the pharmacy to pick up his mother's medicine. He then turned around and walked back in the same direction he had come from. From afar, he watched people emerge from the narrow end of Mutanabbi, and he walked opposite its traffic until he was back in the crowd. Faisal was on a mission of his own, but he didn't fully understand it. He just knew he had to be back there.

53

_____

Baghdad
2018

Faisal stood in the same place he'd taken earlier, minus the box and the books. A middle-aged man had since parked his small cart nearby, selling fresh-baked sesame-coated cakes. Across the street, the woman who had bought his books was now setting up more books on a wide board below the tall wooden stand. People were filling the street after getting off work. It seemed to be the peak time on a short winter day, almost as busy as it was during the summer, when crowds flooded the street in the evenings until the late hours of the night.

So simply dressed yet astonishingly sophisticated, the tall and slender woman stopped briefly, pulled her light-brown scarf back, and adjusted whatever part of her hair swung over her back, then sat on a low chair and leaned against the book stand.

Faisal walked toward her, slowing down as he got nearer.

Her face was down as she read a book, and she didn't look up. Faisal remembered a saying he once read on social media: "Readers don't steal, and robbers don't read." If she really was selling books, as she appeared to be, she wasn't paying attention. Or so he thought.

Faisal noticed that three of the books she had bought from him earlier were now placed neatly next to each other on the top shelf of the rack. As soon as he reached toward one of the books, she folded her book and looked up. She seemed to recognize him after he picked up one of the books he had sold her.

"How much for all of them?" Faisal said with a smile as he placed the small plastic bag of his mother's medicine on the stack of books, then opened the book and pretended to skim through it.

She got up, looked at the cover of the book he was holding, and answered without smiling, "Three hundred thousand."

Faisal narrowed his eyes. "Seriously?"

"Yes. The books are worth more."

Faisal put the book down, nearly dropping it, still nervous. He didn't know if he was supposed to be furious with her or mad at himself or if he should have even returned at all.

"So you cheated me out of my books."

She returned the book to its proper place. "No, my friend. This is business. I offered, you accepted, and I paid in full. You should have known the value of your goods before you set them out for sale." Faisal's eyes were fixed on her chin. "Oh and by the way, that was the worst place to sell books."

"Why is that?"

"Because it's away from the heaviest foot traffic turning onto the street from over there. It's hard to be noticed."

She was sharp, and Faisal had to step up his game. "But you noticed me."

She chuckled. "That's because I was across from you and realized you must be naive."

"And an easy target to exploit."

"Again, it is business. This is a tough market as it is. If I treated everyone with a kind heart, I'd go home broke."

A boy emerged from behind the stand holding a small book and said, "Miss Amani, my father wanted me to ask if you have extra copies of this one."

So her name was Amani.

She disappeared into the store directly behind the stand. Moments later, she returned and shook her head at the boy, who ran back down the sidewalk.

"I feel stupid," Faisal said without looking at her.

She took a step toward him. "Look, if you think I cheated you, give me the money back, and I'll give you all your books, although that's not generally how I do business." The look on her face was more serious than before, and she opened up the book she'd been reading earlier.

"Not at all," Faisal said. "I was just being silly. Plus I spent half of that money on medicine for my mother." He thanked her, not knowing what for, then excused himself and left.

A few moments later, he heard her voice behind him. "Mister, mister."

He turned around and found her behind him holding up the plastic bag of medicine. "You left your bag."

"Thank you so much," Faisal said and took the bag from her. "Oh, and it's Faisal."

"OK," she said without much reaction.

"And you're Amani, right?"

She looked alarmed and took a few steps back. "How do you know my name?"

"I heard the boy call you Amani earlier. Anyway, thanks again."

This time when Faisal walked away, Amani didn't follow. But he spent most of that night replaying his encounter with her, closing his eyes so he could hear her voice again in his head. He felt something new. The young woman's face had color and vibrance in it. Color! Yes, color!

"The ugly face who paid you only a hundred thousand for your entire book collection robbed you," his mother said.

No. Hers was the most beautiful face he had ever seen.

Faisal made three more trips to Mutanabbi Street over the following week with one and only one purpose: to glimpse Amani's face one more time, and then another and then another. From far away, he looked, stared for a few brief moments, and walked away. Without any books to sell her and no money to buy from her, he was intimidated each time he thought about approaching the stand to see her or talk to her. He chickened out each time and walked back home, unsatisfied and defeated. He'd seen her four times so far, with only one of them a close-up, direct encounter. All four times, she somehow looked so well-dressed in such simple and inexpensive clothes. She still wore no makeup and made no attempt at fashion. She didn't need to.

Amani was a book girl, and Faisal found himself agreeing with the popular saying "Don't judge a book by its cover." She looked simple and easy to overlook from outside, but Faisal glimpsed her depth during his short encounters with her. He wanted to know more about her. What if she was already married or engaged or in love with someone? Was this even love? He had no idea what it was supposed to feel like.

He finally gathered the courage to walk up to the stand the following week. This time she was standing right behind it, and she immediately noticed him. He intentionally wore the same clothes he had on during his first encounter with her.

She gave him a dismissive look as he approached, but he smiled anyway.

"I don't see my books here anymore," he said.

"You mean *my books*. I bought them from you. Are you going to keep showing up here attempting to make me feel guilty?"

"Not at all," said Faisal, suddenly feeling rattled. He felt sweat building up on his palms as he nervously rubbed them. He was starting to regret his visit, realizing he had done nothing to learn more about her and had no idea how to start a meaningful conversation. He stood there, awkwardly quiet, and Amani said, "Excuse me, I need to get past you to gather my books. It will get dark soon, and I'm already late."

"Do you need help?" he offered.

"No. If you need to buy a book before I move them inside, let me know."

Faisal withdrew quietly, feeling awkward and inappropriate. Whoever she was, she was as suspicious as she was mysterious.

A man appeared from the bookstore next door and scrutinized Faisal. He was twice Faisal's age and size. "Is there a problem?"

Amani quickly turned to him and said, "No, not at all. Faisal here is thinking about working for my uncle, and I'm trying to see if he'd be a good fit."

That may have been just an excuse Amani used to send the man back and to avoid a confrontation. And yet she remembered his name!

A month later and after many more uneventful and low-key trips to Mutanabbi and to Amani's book stand in particular, he finally asked her, "Do you or whoever owns this store and stand need someone to work for you? I am looking for a job."

To his amazement, she said she might be able to offer him a part-time job to help out while her uncle, the owner, was unwilling or unable to work. She arranged for him to meet her uncle and insisted that it take place somewhere away from Mutanabbi Street, which Faisal agreed to without much thought, but he later considered it puzzling enough to mention at some point if he did get the job. And Faisal did get the job.

"My uncle is the primary source of books, new and used. They arrive here, and we sell them. Or we package them, and he arranges for them to be shipped off to various parts of the country."

The job brought in just enough money for Faisal to add to his other gig to make ends meet without having to sell anything else.

Amani spoke about little beyond business. Faisal, however, wanted to learn more about her. He saw her as a closed book, mysterious, and he wondered what made her so edgy, direct, and suspicious.

"So, why is it that your uncle never comes here?" he asked.

She looked around as if expecting someone to be watching or eavesdropping. Faisal was used to her ways by now and let the process take its course until she felt comfortable enough to answer.

"His son was killed here, in front of him."

Faisal felt his face drop.

"My cousin's name was Omar. A group of sectarian religious extremists thought he was named after a religious figure they didn't approve of, so they killed him. Right here." She pointed to the long concrete pole next to the door.

"Just like that?" Faisal asked.

"It started with an argument, when they asked my uncle why he named his son Omar. Of course my cousin stood up to them, and that's when one of them took out his gun and shot him. They ran away, and since then my uncle has not been able to bring himself to come back here. Omar was an only child."

Amani pulled her hair back as she had done countless times. Without looking at him, she asked, "Are you Sunni or Shia?"

"I thought that on this street in particular sectarian divides didn't matter."

He expected her to feel embarrassed, but she coldly replied, "Sure, before my cousin was killed here. Nothing makes sense anymore."

"My father was Sunni, and my mother is Shia. How about you?"

"Does it matter if I'm Shia or Sunni?"

Faisal blinked a few times. "You just asked me the same question!"

"I don't care if you're Shia or Sunni, but does it matter to you?"

Faisal shook his head and smiled. "Only one thing matters to me."

"What's that?"

"Not now. You will learn in due time." Then he helped her take the books back inside after a long day with little to show for it.

Something was brewing between Faisal and Amani. Something that he didn't fully understand yet, but he suspected that if she felt the same way, he'd tell her the only thing that truly mattered to him. But not yet.

54

Baghdad
2018

Two more months passed before Amani opened up to Faisal about anything. All she'd told him about was her cousin getting killed, but Faisal had detailed his entire family history, offering detailed accounts of everything and everyone except Sami. He had no more to say about his brother after obliquely mentioning that he'd disappeared after a run-in with the law. Amani never asked follow-up questions, but she listened attentively even if she pretended to be uninterested.

Then one day he asked her why she seemed so suspicious all the time. She answered with a dismissive shrug, but a few hours later, seemingly out of nowhere, she said, "When you're a girl in this jungle and with no real support, you have to be suspicious of everything, even the air you breathe, if you want to live."

Faisal listened attentively and was not about to interrupt now that she was finally opening up.

"You may have lost your father," she said, "but I never met mine." She looked him in the eye but showed no emotion. Her eyes were distant, as if searching for something or someone.

"My father was drafted during the Kuwait war in 1991. My mother was seven months pregnant with me, and he never came back."

Her words were cold, but they hit Faisal like a boiling volcano. He felt dwarfed by Amani's composure. The tragedy, pain, and loss he had endured were nothing compared with growing up and never meeting your father. "Have you—"

"My father's entire unit was destroyed when they were retreating from Kuwait."

"I am so sorry, Amani. I didn't mean to open up wounds from the past."

"It's OK. You can't feel the loss of something you never had."

"But you can feel the empty space," Faisal said.

Her eyes were getting watery now. She turned away from him and got busy arranging some books, but she kept talking. "My mother and I have been living in a separate section on the second floor of my uncle's house. He's been my guardian since I was little. He was always pleasant and positive." She paused for a few seconds. "But ever since his son was killed, he's been a different person."

Faisal stepped next to Amani and gently took the three books that she'd been holding for some time. There were tear drops on the covers, and Faisal, despite all his efforts, could not make himself look up at her. He didn't want to see the expression on her face. He gently put the books down. "Allah tests us all in different ways. I just want you to know that I'm here if you need anything."

"Can you rearrange the rest of the books? I just remembered I have to check with the Department of Education and see if they have any openings for a teacher."

She'd been looking for a teaching job ever since she graduated from the College of Education with an emphasis on foreign languages in 2014. Like thousands of other young Iraqi graduates, she'd been dumped onto the street without any job opportunities. Faisal was nearly certain that her attempts were not going to be fruitful. Social media platforms were flooded with unhappy young people and their families despairing over the lack of jobs for college graduates. There were no indications that anything would improve or that Iraq's leaders cared a whit about what young people needed.

By the summer of 2018, everyone in Faisal's family had heard about Amani. His mother wanted to meet her, and after Faisal said that was impossible, she brought him a plate for lunch at work at the bookshop. The next day she came with two plates of food in case "someone else" might be hungry too. When Faisal's sisters found out what their mother had done, he thought the questions and teasing would never end.

Over time he felt like the space between him and Amani was getting warmer and the distance shorter. He was pretty sure that she was growing attached to him, but they never spoke about it, choosing to enjoy it at a distance in diplomatic and sensitive silence.

He was almostl certain that she didn't have an emotional commitment to anyone else. And after six months of almost daily interaction, he thought he understood her personality and way of thinking quite well. He and Amani were similar, yet also different. They had both endured tragedy and loss. Both were looking for a door into another world, but what world? They were both quarantined in Baghdad with all its sorrows.

After Amani's cousin was shot and killed out front, a wave

of chaos broke over the entire street, and a group of hooligans showed up one night and looted and damaged the inside of the store. It was their way of silencing Amani's uncle and telling him to move on without pursuing any further action. With the owner of the bookstore keeping his distance, the store remained damaged.

"I have an idea," Faisal said one day as he and Amani stepped out of the store and stumbled upon scattered boxes and abandoned furniture.

"Oh no," Amani said and chuckled. "God help us!"

"I think it's time to fix up the inside of the bookstore."

"My uncle will never agree to return here."

Faisal was aware of that. He had met her uncle on numerous occasions, all far from Mutanabbi Street. Faisal was now his trusted worker and a hungry would-be manager who wanted to turn things around for the wounded owner.

As it turned out, while Amani's uncle may not have been ready to physically return to the store, he was ready to restore the inside so that his niece wouldn't have to sell books on the street. Reconstruction would of course be a lengthy process, and a shortage of money would make it even more challenging.

They decided to go about it slowly, using whatever extra money the store had left each month after salaries and expenses.

"With our limited resources, this could take anywhere from one to two years," Faisal told Amani.

"Business is slowly picking up," Amani said, "and we have nowhere else to go. So let it take as long as it takes!" It was one of the few times Faisal heard any real emotion in her words.

Her attempts to get a job were still going nowhere. She was active on social media, adding her voice to tens of thousands of frustrated Iraqi men and women demanding reforms that would bring an end to the political deadlock inside the Green Zone and all the failed policies that had crippled the nation's foundation.

"You're wasting your time," Faisal said as she wrote post after post. She ignored him, and he continued. "The corrupt leaders are barricaded in the Green Zone, and their families are enjoying themselves overseas. Yet here you are, stressing yourself out on the internet. They don't know you and will never care."

Her face turned red, but she continued typing her rant. She took a deep breath, put down her phone, and turned to him. "Our problem is that we have too many people who are willing to sit back and watch the country burn. The corrupt don't see us now, but they will when we all get together. They may not hear us individually, but if we collectively speak up in a single, uniform voice, we can shake their very foundation."

Faisal sat there and watched her in silence with a smile on his face.

"What are you laughing at?" she said, still angry.

"I'm not laughing. Just smiling."

"Whatever. It's the same thing."

"OK. You've got a point there. What can I do to show you I actually care?"

Now she looked relieved, almost excited, as if she'd been waiting all along for Faisal to ask her that question. "There's a protest planned this Friday at Tahrir Square. A simple gathering to showcase our displeasure."

The last time Faisal had been to Tahrir Square was when the Americans first entered Baghdad. His memories of Tahrir Square, Firdos Square, and the subsequent destruction of the nation had blurred together in his mind and made him unwilling to even think about, let alone talk about, either of those places. But this was Amani asking, and he was now deeply in love with her. Her passion and depth were only two of the great qualities that had stolen his mind just as her beauty stole his eyes and heart.

"Certainly!" he said. "I'll join just because you said so."

A wide smile overtook her face as she tried hard to contain her excitement.

"But I won't take part in any sectarian movements," Faisal said firmly.

"Trust me," she said, still smiling, "this is as far as it gets from sectarian narratives. Also, keep in mind that while we have a majority Shia government, the Shia-populated areas are the most miserable. Have you been to Sadr City? And our Sunni leaders have been sitting around and piling up fortunes while poverty is growing deeper in their own cities. They're all corrupt, and that's why we will go out and protest."

It was the last night of 2018, and the clouds were rushing across the sky, one after another, periodically letting loose rain showers. It was not Faisal's habit to spend extra time outside, but his first job at the electronics warehouse was experiencing an uptick in business due to the cold winter forcing people to purchase electric heaters or repair their broken ones. At the same time, fewer people frequented Mutanabbi due to the recurrent rains, short days, and cold weather. Faisal was offered extra pay to stay and finish the repairs that had been waiting for days. He had already checked on his mother and told her that he would be late. On his way, he purchased two kilos of oranges and one small cake to celebrate the new year with her.

When he arrived home, sometime after ten, he heard his mother sobbing in her room. His hands shook, and he dropped the plastic bag, sending oranges rolling all over the floor. The plate of cake nearly fell as well, and he quickly set it on the nearest table by the kitchen and headed to his mother's room.

The door was halfway open, and as Faisal slowly stepped closer, the crying grew louder. He now heard his mother repeatedly hitting her head against the headboard. His throat was dry, and his knees were weakening. He gently pushed the door open and stepped into the room. He stood there, confused, and his mother, now sobbing louder, held up her phone and waved it at him to show him the image displayed on her screen.

55

Baghdad
2019

F aisal stared at the screen on his mother's phone, zoomed in, then out, and focused even more, all while his mother repeatedly said, "It's him. It's Sami. I know my son's face from a mile away." She was weeping and slapping her hands against her knees.

The person in the picture was obviously dead. His hair was long and dirty. A blood stain covered the left side of his beard, and his left shoulder was drenched in blood. As much as he wanted to tell himself otherwise or convince his mother that she was wrong, Faisal knew Sami before he was even born, and he knew.

"Where did you find this picture?" Faisal asked, barely able to form words.

"Does it matter? My son is dead!"

He took a screenshot of the picture, then backtracked to the front page of the website. It chronicled the defeat of ISIS and was living proof of the death of their soldiers. The picture was reportedly taken in Mosul during its liberation the previous year. His mother was mourning the death of her son in Mosul, but Faisal showed less emotion. Deep inside, he believed that his twin brother had died inside the walls of Abu Ghraib fifteen years ago.

Fatima visited with her husband and the kids. The family held a quiet funeral inside the small house. No one else would host a funeral for an ISIS fighter. And nobody could deny that the dead man in the picture was Sami. They'd all been living with the Sami nightmare for years. It was time to put it behind them and mourn the loss of their brother in the darkness of night, each of them alone.

For nearly two months, Faisal's mother remained inside the house, refusing to go outside even for a short walk. Faisal was getting daily calls from both of his sisters and had to give them each the same update: she was not eating, and she refused to take her medicine. Amani came over twice to help Faisal bathe and groom his mother, but beyond that she had no further contact with the outside world.

"Take her to a psychiatrist," Hadeel said over the phone, with Fatima also joining in on the group call.

Faisal scoffed. "You want to get off your comfortable sofa in Amman and magically come here and help?"

"Why do you always have to attack me?" Hadeel yelled through the phone. "If you were actually here, you wouldn't make such a ridiculous suggestion."

"OK, you two," Fatima scolded. "Stop the bickering. We need to find a solution."

There was silence for a few moments.

"Can't we just get her some depression medicine?" Fatima said.

Hadeel sighed and said, "You can't just force her to take it."

"I'll mix it with food or do whatever I have to. If you think it's going to help her, I'll make it happen."

∾

The scariest thing about death is that the living slowly get used to mourning. Death is forever foreign to the living and should never become part of daily life. But in Baghdad, people saw their loved ones get shot, stabbed, blown up, and executed right in front their eyes. They had to bury them—or whatever was left of them—mourn, and get up and go on. As much as Faisal wanted his mother to move past the grieving stage, he was afraid that he'd lose whatever connection he still had with his twin the moment her eyes dried.

But she slowly got back up again, and she was even more strongly opposed to depression medicine now that she was feeling better and well enough to know which medicine was which. But Hadeel took it upon herself to push their mother to continue her treatment.

She started leaving the house more often, at times accompanying Faisal to the bookstore. She would only smile at Amani, who was convinced that it was because the depression medicine was working, but Faisal kept telling himself that his mother's face glowed each time she saw the girl with whom he seemed to be deeply in love. It was the kind of love that could fill the Tigris and turn its water red. Not the red of blood but the color of heartful love that Faisal finally decided to express on a warm day of spring 2019.

He didn't have the courage to tell her face to face. Whether that was because she was taller than him or too beautiful, he wasn't sure. But he'd never once told a woman or girl that he had affection for them. And of course he was afraid of rejection. It was a lot easier to reject someone by ignoring a note than having to express it in facial features and words.

So he wrote it down: "I'm going to ask for your hand from your uncle and from your mother. We're going to build a beautiful life together. Agree?"

That was all he could say. To him, it was enough, and it was for Amani as well, because when he gave her the note on the sidewalk outside and asked her to read it later, she immediately stepped inside the bookstore, unfolding the paper at the door. She came back out moments later, a wide smile covering her blushing face as she pressed her lips against each other in excitement. She nodded her head, then carefully placed the folded paper back in her pocket and carried on with her job.

Two weeks later, Faisal had just opened the bookstore, and Amani had not arrived yet. Summer was knocking on the door, and that meant it was time to prepare for what would hopefully be a busier season. Amani's uncle had scored a major victory in his war against grief by visiting the store a few times, but only briefly. But that was enough for the time being.

Faisal had left his mother at home after the two ate breakfast, and she returned to her room to get some rest. She had been up the previous night, she said, scrolling through her phone and catching up with her daughters. Faisal heard her moving about the house until the very late hours. When he left for work that morning, she was still in her room, in bed, but in a tired voice she told him she'd think about stopping by the bookstore later. She wanted to go with Faisal and Amani for a walk, she said.

The phone call came as Faisal had just finished laying down the last set of books on the ground stand. "*Marhaba,* hello, who is this, please?" a frantic male voice said.

Confused, Faisal pulled the phone away from his ear, inspected the screen, and checked the name. It said "Mama."

He put the phone back against his ear and said, "Hello? Mama?"

"Is this Faisal?" the man said again, more urgently this time.

"Yes, who is this?"

"We picked up this phone on the street. The lady who had this phone was hit by a car. Your number was the last on her list. Are you related to her?"

"Yes! That's my mother's phone. Where is she?"

"Ibn Sina Hospital."

Faisal's breathing was labored, his heart was beating rapidly, and his knees were getting weak. Amani had just arrived and was greeting the bookstore owner next door and rushed to Faisal when she saw the look of horror on his face. He slowly dropped down to his knees with the phone in his hand.

"What's wrong?" Amani called out while hurrying over to him.

"My mother. She had an accident. I think it's bad." He got up, shook his head and regained his focus. "I have to go. They said she's at Ibn Sina Hospital."

His mother died at the scene and was pronounced dead at the ambulance's time of arrival. They still took her to the hospital, but the staff who first inspected her and saw the gruesome injuries on her face, chest, and pelvis made them question the ambulance staff's decision to push her stretcher all the way to the emergency room hallway. They wouldn't allow Faisal to see her at first, and he got into an altercation with hospital security, but when Amani finally arrived, she calmed him down. The police also arrived to make a formal report.

A man was being questioned in the hallway as he frantically tried to explain himself. "She jumped in front of my truck. I had no time to react." After every time he explained himself, he hid his horrified face in his hands.

A police officer approached Faisal and asked, "Are you the son?"

Before Faisal could answer, the man who was being questioned jumped at Faisal and hugged him. He started sobbing and said repeatedly, "May Allah forgive me. I didn't mean to hit your mother."

Faisal freed himself from his grip, still numb and lightheaded with his stomach on the verge of expelling its contents. The police officer tried to take the man aside, but he continued. "It's like she did it on purpose. There was a smaller car in front of me, and she seemed to intentionally wait for it to pass, then ran in front of my truck. I am sorry. I am really sorry."

Faisal was finally able to see and identify his mother's body. He passed out, and when he came back, Amani and her uncle were both standing above him next to a hospital bed that someone had placed him on. His mother's body had already been taken away to the morgue.

Fatima and her husband arrived that evening, followed by Mr. Hamdan and his wife plus a few other members of their extended family. There was no point speculating about her motives or describing the accident beyond what the police had decided to write in the report: "The victim was crossing the street, miscalculated the traffic, and was accidentally hit by the oncoming truck."

They buried their mother next to her husband, finishing the story of a couple who had met decades ago with dreams of nice jobs, a house full of children, a car, and the Tigris River as company. They lived to see all of it, but they also lived to watch it collapse.

Of the three siblings, Faisal had the hardest time dealing with the loss of their mother. He had spent the most time with her and witnessed her pain up close. Over the course of the following months of summer, he reduced his hours at the bookstore and avoided interactions with people. Even when it came to Amani, he maintained just enough communication to prevent their relationship from breaking too. Faisal had suffered so much sorrow and loss that he didn't even know where he was in life or how to return to normalcy—if such a thing even existed in Iraq in 2019.

56

Baghdad
2019

Faisal and Amani finally met up one evening after she was able to convince her uncle to mind the bookstore so she could run some errands. They rendezvoused down the street near his home, and the two took a slow stroll toward the river. The line outside Falafel Abu Nawara was as long as Faisal had ever seen. When they got to the window, Faisal didn't see Abu Nawara there, and the guy taking orders was new. He wondered if the food might be different too.

"Is Abu Nawara off today?" he said at the window. "Quite unusual!"

"He's off for good," the man at the window said as he looked at Faisal, waiting for his order. He kept tapping the edge of the window with his pen until Faisal gave him his order. "He ran off, far away. Out of the country. One of his kids did his paperwork for Europe, and he's been gone since last month. We own the place now."

Faisal and Amani received their order, then walked toward the river near the place he'd sat with his sisters on Hadeel's graduation day.

Even Abu Nawara was gone? Faisal slowly unwrapped his falafel sandwich, feeling distant from Amani. He saw out of the corner of his eye that she was watching him closely.

He ate in silence, his eyes fixed on the water.

Amani finally broke the silence. "What are you thinking?"

He ate the last bite of his sandwich, shrugged his shoulders as he swallowed, then looked back to the river. "What happened to us? To our lives? Our nation? This river? Even Abu Nawara. What happened?"

"The war took everything away."

Faisal crossed his arms over his chest. "Why didn't it take us away too?"

"Maybe we're the lucky ones."

He sighed deeply. "Or the unfortunate ones left behind to mop up the mess."

Amani gently slapped his arm. "Enough of the sadness and gloom."

When she finished her sandwich, Faisal threw the trash away and motioned for her to walk with him to the edge of the river. When they were as close as they felt comfortable with, Faisal stopped and looked deeply into the river. "What do you think the Tigris is saying to us?"

Amani chuckled. "Probably that Faisal needs to chill and enjoy his time with a girl who granted his wish to join him on a walk."

Faisal turned to her, smiled, and nodded. "My grandfather always said we Iraqis don't know how to be at peace with ourselves. We murder each other, then cry over the corpses."

Amani said nothing.

"I think this river is tired of us and all the hatred we've

dumped into it over the years. The waters under our city have poisoned our trees and rotted the fruit we eat."

Amani took a step back. "*Wallah*, I've worked the books of Mutanabbi Street for years and never heard such dark philosophy. Let's go back. It will be night soon."

On the way back, Faisal looked at Amani and said, "You're the beautiful light in a dark world, and I'm grateful for your support and for standing beside me in my hard times and—"

"And in your craziness," she said and laughed.

Faisal thought of only one thing the entire way back. Abu Nawara! The last man Faisal ever thought would pack his bags and leave the country behind.

He sat at home in the evening. The cool autumn breeze forced him to close the window where he'd spent so much time since his mother passed. It was the only place in the house where he could see beyond the darkness that had engulfed him. Every time he looked around, he expected to see his mother preparing tea or setting dinner plates on the floor. Her presence had shielded him from the hurricane of loneliness and loss. Now that Mama was gone, it was all laid bare. The tiny house felt like an empty, haunted castle.

But Amani was the light. He loved her. He was certain she loved him even more, but he had a hard time finding the capacity in his impoverished, grief-stricken life to make room for another, to provide the love and commitment she deserved. He felt detached from his surroundings, detached from the land that he understood now was a graveyard.

Outside the window, people of all backgrounds and beliefs reeled in poverty while their land floated on an ocean of oil. He was seeing more demonstrations by young people across the country against politicians and their bankrupt ideologies. He thought back to something Baba Faisal had told him about years past when he was young. Coups followed demonstra-

ZAID BRIFKANI

tions, and wars followed coups. The best-case scenario one could expect in such a world was getting dragged off to war on a full stomach.

He picked up the phone and dialed Fatima. It rang multiple times without an answer. He hung up, waited a few minutes, then tried her number again. Still no answer. She must be busy since she had yet another baby on the way with no signs of slowing down. When she didn't call him back, he dialed Hadeel. She picked up after two rings.

As usual, she asked about his well-being, health, work, his relationship with Amani, any new jobs, and if he was keeping up with Fatima. Faisal went through the motions, answering Hadeel's questions without any follow up. Then he abruptly asked her, "Do you have some money to lend me?"

"How much? What do you need it for?"

Faisal's voice turned stiff. "Why do you always have to question me? I need some money, so the answer is either yes or no."

"OK, Faisal. How much are we talking about?"

"Three to five thousand dollars."

Hadeel giggled.

"Did I say something funny?"

"No, brother, but if you knew our financial situation here, you would think twice about asking me for even two hundred dollars."

"You and your husband are both doctors."

"We're still not allowed to legally work in Jordan, and we're spending whatever money we can spare on lawyers and immigration paperwork."

"OK, sister. I'm sorry to bother you this late at night." He looked at his watch. Half past eleven.

"Wait, Faisal. You didn't tell me why you needed the money. Are you in some sort of trouble?"

"No. I just need the money, OK?"

Fatima was calling him, so he excused himself and hung up while Hadeel was still halfway through another question.

He asked Fatima the same question, to which she sighed deeply and said, "Our finances are down the drain, and my husband is already looking for another part-time job."

Faisal regretted making both phone calls, knowing very well that neither of his sisters would be able to give him five thousand dollars just like that. He needed more, and that was just a start. Fatima was not going to leave him alone or let him hang up without getting to the bottom of it.

Faisal finally relented and told her: "I'm leaving."

Fatima's kids were screaming in the background, and she yelled a few times then asked him, "What? Did you say you're leaving?"

"Yes, leaving. I'm leaving Iraq."

She did not react. She didn't protest. It was as if she'd been expecting it all along or at the least unsurprised with her brother's decision to pack up and hit the road.

Fatima promised him that she would work on it, but Faisal knew she had little to offer, so he told her to kiss the kids and say hi to the husband.

Two weeks later, Fatima called him again. "Finally, you chose to answer after I've been calling you for over a week."

"I'm sorry, sister. I've been busy."

"With what? Preparing to leave? What are your plans? I need to know."

"What is there to know? I've asked around, and there are smugglers who can take me to Europe, and then I could turn myself in."

"Who are these smugglers? Where? Don't foolishly trust someone only to end up in the sea. I won't let that happen." Fatima was now breathing fast through the phone.

"Relax, Fatima. I'm not stupid. I've looked at all my options. If I have to sell a kidney, I'll do it. I'm not staying here."

"Sell a *kidney*? Are you crazy?"

"I'm not crazy. You don't need both kidneys to survive. I've asked around. I could get twenty thousand dollars for one kidney."

"Listen, Faisal. I'm your sister, and I'm older than you. I'm taking the place of our parents now. You won't take a single step without me. Understood? Wait for me to sort things out. I'll talk to Hadeel, and we'll get you what you need."

Faisal said nothing.

"Am I clear?" Fatima shouted. "Tell me you won't do anything crazy!"

"OK, Fatima, OK. Just don't overburden yourself. I'm making a backup plan for every step."

"Just put it on hold for a few more weeks, and I'll help you sort it out."

Faisal hung up and ran his finances through his head. He had a thousand dollars saved up so far and was due three hundred thousand Iraqi dinars from Amani's uncle for a previous month's work. He reached into his pocket and removed his Iraqi passport, which he had picked up earlier that day. The first step had been taken care of.

Protests in Baghdad had picked up in volume and intensity. Tens of thousands of young men and women had been flooding the streets and public squares from the first day of October. The numbers were growing, as was the intensity of violence used by the government forces. Amani had been a regular face there, and she was injured once as she tried to rescue a few girls who were attacked with tear gas. Faisal joined her several times but soon felt a high level of anxiety from daily deaths and injured young men and women. He was terrified of losing Amani and urged her to tone it down a bit and stay home, but she was not having any of it. The two had just left the biggest protest yet, which had included thousands of tok tok cars and hundreds of thousands of protesters from all ideological backgrounds demanding an end to corruption and the formation of a new government free of ideologies and divided interests.

Faisal picked up the phone, and Amani started right away in an excited voice. "Did you see the news? Adil Abdul-Mahdi has resigned. A new government will be formed."

"After what? More than six hundred died?"

"To hell with all of the politicians. The young leaders on the field won't call off the protests until real change is obvious."

Faisal had to tell her, but her excitement was too good to ruin. He listened to her happy voice and contemplated an unknown future and whether or not she had a place in it.

57

Baghdad
2019–2020

Fatima called Faisal a few weeks later and put Hadeel on the line as well. The tone was serious, and the discussion revolved around Faisal's plans to leave the country. It had been established that his decision was beyond discussion. Trying to convince him to stay would be a lost cause.

"I'll sell my gold," said Fatima.

"And I've managed to pull out two thousand dollars from our savings, plus some other money my husband managed to get from his family," added Hadeel.

"I'm not taking money from you," said Faisal, mostly thinking of Fatima.

His two sisters started talking at once, each saying how much he meant to them and how they'd give up their eyes for him if need be.

"I'm not going to allow either of you to sell your gold or take money from your savings."

The conversation dragged on for over an hour, after which the two sisters managed to convince Faisal to take two thousand dollars from each of them and to consider it a loan to pay back later. Oh, and he should also not ask where the money came from. Fatima declared the conversation over, and Faisal realized that after securing a couple more thousand, he'd be ready to take his next steps without needing to sell one of his kidneys.

By February 2020, he'd saved up some additional money. He made a quick trip to Zakho to meet a man representing a smuggler out of Istanbul whom Faisal had been communicating with via texts. Faisal had waited for this last confirmatory step before broaching the subject with Amani, by far the most difficult piece of the plot. Fatima had been pressuring him to talk to her and was threatening to do so herself if Faisal wouldn't do it. She wanted him to propose to Amani and to take her with him wherever he went.

It was cold in Baghdad, and everyone blamed it on the heavy snowstorms that had been battering the Kurdistan region up north. Faisal had rehearsed his talk over and over, but each time he felt speechless when he imagined standing in front of Amani. She was already at the bookstore when he called her on his way from home. He picked up two bowls of hot *lablabi*, chickpea soup, from a nearby stand and gave one to Amani, knowing how much she liked it. They sat down inside the bookstore, half of which had been cleaned and reconstructed during the previous months.

"This lablabi is as good as ever," said Faisal as he nervously held the salt shaker and kept adding more to his bowl.

"There's something in your eyes," Amani said. "Go ahead and say it."

Faisal was amazed by Amani's ability to read him so easily after saying so little and showing so few expressions. He cleared his throat and said, "I've decided to leave the country."

Her face looked like he'd slapped her.

"Leave?" she said, firmly holding her bowl. "And go where?"

For the next hour, Faisal detailed his plan and tried to convince her why he had to go. He was glad that the weather was terrible and that there were no customers inside the bookstore because Amani was now in tears.

"I want you to come with me," Faisal said. "We can get married here and take off together and start our life somewhere far away."

She remained silent, and he moved his chair closer and asked her again.

"What about my mother? I just leave her all alone here and chase you and your dreams?"

Faisal had no answer. Or maybe he had not considered the question. He sighed deeply as Amani wiped tears off her face.

"You should have thought about my situation before coming up with such a drastic plan. Before you got close to me and gained my trust."

"Amani," said Faisal as he tried to get her to look at him. "I only started thinking about it after my mother died. Please understand. I've lost everything I had here. I have nothing left here to live for. Everything reminds me of misery and loss."

"What about me?" she said angrily. "I don't count for anything?"

"Of course you do. You hold a big place in my heart, and it would be my dream to share my life with you. I just can't stay here anymore."

Amani was silent for moments that felt to Faisal like years. Finally she said, "My mother is old and ill. She needs me here.

She sacrificed her youth to stay by my side and raise me. I'm not leaving her behind for anyone or anything."

Amani's uncle arrived at that moment carrying two boxes of books and asked Faisal to help him bring the rest in from outside.

Faisal and Amani continued their conversation over the phone that evening and for several days to follow, but neither was willing to budge despite how much they loved each other. Faisal decided it was best to give the subject a rest for a while and revisit it when Amani had more time to get her emotions in order.

Then the entire world was disrupted by the coronavirus. By May 2020, Faisal had gotten ill with COVID, and it was Amani and her uncle who came to check on him and care for him. Then Amani got sick with COVID, and Faisal blamed himself. It got worse when Amani's mother was hospitalized and nearly lost her life. During his two weeks of isolation and recovery at home, Faisal withdrew to his emotions and memories, contemplating his life and the big decision he had already made.

The lockdowns were intensifying, and a friend from a nearby bookstore suggested to Faisal that if he was serious about leaving the country, it was now or never. The border between Iraqi Kurdistan and Turkey was alternately open and closed. The agent in Zakho said he was taking the last group in July.

Faisal spent one afternoon taking a stroll through the city. He walked over the bridge to the west side of the river, then turned on Haifa Street. His steps felt heavier the closer he got to the old neighborhood. Everyone seemed older, more exhausted, and numb. Fewer people walked around, most of them in masks and with hurried steps. He approached his old street and remembered Sami saying he was going to blow up their old house after it was taken away from them.

Faisal stopped at the edge of the last building before his old street. He recalled the serious look on his brother's face and decided to turn around. He didn't really want to find out what had happened to their old house or the people who took it over. He wanted to preserve his last memory of it, even if it was a memory of leaving it behind. Better than seeing it brought down like a collapsed sandcastle.

His next destination was the National Museum. He stood across from the main gate and remembered the trucks hauling historic pieces out of that building in 2003 when he and Sami stood and watched in horror.

Faisal then arrived at Firdos Square. There was no statue of Saddam and no protesters chanting in happiness for his fall. Everyone was long gone. The square was empty except for a few kids wandering around, probably against their parents' wishes. He wondered how many of the people who helped bring down the statue in 2003 were still alive. What had happened to them? Were they happy now? Did they lose as much as his family did?

By sunset, he had seen enough and felt more than enough. He picked up the phone and dialed his agent in Zakho.

~

Convincing Amani to see him was a challenge. The bookstore had been closed for weeks due to rising COVID cases, and Mutanabbi Street had seen a sharp drop in traffic. But after much insistence from Faisal, Amani showed up. She had lost weight since contracting COVID and still looked pale and had periodic bouts of cough. It had been a while since she had contracted it, but the virus still took its toll on her.

"I didn't bring the keys with me," she said, telling Faisal to get to the point and get it over with.

Faisal looked at her. He saw both love and worry in her eyes even if she went the distance of the galaxy to show otherwise. Only a few stores were open, and Faisal could count the number of people on the street with his fingers. They could have stood there for hours and talked, and no one would pay attention, but Faisal wanted to sit down somewhere and talk in peace. Amani, however, refused.

"I am leaving!"

"I figured!"

"Come with me. It's our chance to go. Please, Amani." He periodically broke eye contact with her when someone passed by and looked at them with interest.

"We've gone over this before," she said, "many times. You know my answer. So why did you bring me here today?"

"I couldn't just leave without seeing you."

"Well, now you saw me. Can I go?"

She started to walk away, but he stopped her. "Amani. I can't just let you walk away from my life like that."

She turned and faced him with a blank face and with her hands in her pockets. "You're the one walking away."

Faisal expected her to turn around again and go, but she stood there in silence, looking at him with sharp eyes, studying his reaction and his next move.

"I will come back for you. Once I settle in Europe, I will return, and we can take your mother with us too."

She shook her head. Faisal couldn't tell if she was questioning what he was saying or if the world had turned her into a person no longer able to dream.

Amani stepped forward and got as close to his face as she

could. "If you walk away and leave me here, don't ever come back for me."

"But I—"

"You won't find me when you return. Even if I am here, you won't find my heart waiting for you."

Faisal stood there in silence, his words stuck in his throat and his thoughts scattered on the empty walkways of Mutanabbi Street. He only snapped out of it when she spoke her final words before walking away for good.

"Take care of yourself wherever you go. Be safe, and delete my number from your phone and my name from your memory."

58

Belarus-Poland Border
Winter 2021

A large truck arrives at dusk carrying blankets, coats, sweaters, and other winter clothes. The freezing night and exhaustion after weeks upon weeks of hopeless anticipation have drained people to the point where the United Nations relief officials have to unload the supplies themselves and personally bring them to our tents. The sentiment is that of despair and letdown. Last night, a child died from freezing temperatures, and the devastated mother still hasn't stopped crying. What has life come to? Running from a burning place we called home to a freezing land that refuses to be anything to us like a home.

For the first time since I left Baghdad, I'm second guessing my decision to leave and seek a better life. Is there any life left to live? What was I thinking? Did I really think crossing the border would free me of burdens? How selfish of me to walk away from the rubble of my hometown, my family, my disabled childhood, and my lost adulthood and to think I could just slip into another life, under a different sky, on different soil, and drink from different waters and expect to not be pulled back into reality. The truth is that we were born to love and live in Baghdad, and we can't just walk away. If Baghdad is bleeding, so are we. If Baghdad is hungry, so are we. If the streets of Baghdad are turned into rubble, so will be the alleys of our individual lives. There is no escape from the city once she claims you as her lover.

I'm still hanging by a thin thread of hope, stubbornness, denial, or whatever you want to call it. I grab a military-style blanket from a UN official and wrap myself in it after I make sure that Gulistan and everyone in her family have what they need. Maybe the warmth of the blanket will bring back some of my determination to cross the fence into Western Europe. Maybe that and maybe many other things, none of which I have seen so far.

Gulistan sits next to me outside the tent. "Faisal, we have a problem. Naza is ill again and can't leave the tent. Her face is pale just like it was the last time, or maybe even worse."

I turn slowly and look in the direction of the small, dirty tent and wonder just how much longer it will be before death looms again.

The young mother steps out, worried and exhausted but fierce and emotionally wide awake. "I'm not taking my children back." Her tone is hesitant but pretentious at the same time.

"Why are you so stubborn, Nasreen?" Gulistan says. She sits as close to me as she can, her lips twitchy and cracked. "Please convince her to go back. Our child will die here."

I remain silent, drowned in my own thoughts. My sister Fatima comes to mind. I've done my best to not think about her, about her worrying about me, or about contacting her.

When I left Iraq, I decided to sever my ties with everything and everyone. But Fatima has always been good to me.

I leave Gulistan and Nasreen to argue among themselves and approach a nearby friend who has a phone with an internet connection. I'm sure he won't forget the time I paid to reload his phone card.

I need to speak with Fatima. She is my weakness, my inspiration to break my own rules. Even after getting rid of my phone and refusing to keep any numbers, my memory refused to let go of her number. I dial it through WhatsApp and bring the speaker to my ear when I hear her voice.

"It's me, Faisal," I say, surprised that she answered a strange number.

Her voice is breathless and anxious. "How are you, my brother? Where are you? Are you OK? Are you safe? Where have you been all this time? Why haven't you contacted us?"

"Listen, sister, my time is limited. The internet is a hot commodity here. I just wanted to hear your voice." Her silence, although brief, tells me all I need to know about how much she understands my pain and why I called her.

"Brother. I have been following the reports and actually saw you on TV twice, which reassured me quite a bit, but things look scary. Why did you put yourself in this position?"

None of what she says surprises me. She never supported my leaving, but I didn't give her a chance to voice her concerns while I was still in Baghdad. While I want her to advise me on whether or not to return, more than anything else I just want to hear her voice. It is the voice of Mother and Father and Baghdad and everything else.

"I'm really sorry, brother. Our financial situation is so difficult. I wish I could help you."

I shift the phone from my right ear to the left. "That's not why I called you."

"I know, I know, but I do wish I could help you financially. Maybe you could pay your way into Western Europe."

How naive, I want to say, but I choose my words better. "Nothing works here. They are determined to stand in our way. It's terrible."

"Have you tried contacting Hadeel? Maybe she can help you in ways I can't?"

I bring the phone against my mouth and angrily say, "Don't mention her name to me. She is the last person I want to think about." I think of Mother and how quickly she deteriorated in front of our eyes, physically and emotionally, after Hadeel told her about Sami and his possible suicide mission.

"Faisal, she is your sister. I've talked to her, and she's worried about you."

"Anyway, let's change the subject. I don't have much time left. The guy is asking me for his phone."

Fatima has always been sharp when it comes to reading people. She clears her throat and yells something at her children, then says to me slowly, "Come back, brother. Come and start your life again."

"I have no life left. It's all gone, whether here or there." I sound more melodramatic than I intend.

"It's not all lost. You have me here."

I want to remind her that her life is a wreck of its own, but I keep silent while she continues.

"And you have a girl that you care about and love. Come back for her."

"That girl is gone," I say. Fatima goes silent for a few seconds, so I decide to keep going. "Amani was a dream, and it evaporated when I chose to leave. I've lost her."

Fatima is still quiet. I can see her face in my mind, broken with sadness, her tearful eyes red and swollen. I tell her I have to go, and she clears her throat. "Just promise me you'll take care of yourself and contact me wherever you end up."

"I will, Fatima. I will."

"God be with you, brother. Please be careful."

"Kiss the kids for me. Much love, my dear." I hang up, more confused than ever, but I can still hear Fatima's voice in my ears and want to keep that going for as long as possible.

When I return to the tent, I hear Gulistan and Nasreen still arguing, but now inside rather than outside. I tap on the tent, and they invite me in. I find Naza's pale face shrunken again, her head resting on her mother's knee while her younger brothers sit and watch their mother cry. Everyone has been through this before many times: Naza's dangling and semi-lifeless head, Nasreen's sobbing, Gulistan's mumbling, and the confused look of the twin boys. I, however, am never going to get used to seeing a child at the edge of death while we stand there and watch.

"We need to take her near the fence and the media," I say. "Maybe someone will take her to the hospital again." But I'm no more convinced of what I'm saying than I am about our prospects of crossing the border without resistance.

Gulistan kneels over and gently rubs Naza's hair. "We took her there. You think we wouldn't? While you were gone, Nasreen carried her around the camp, and none of the journalists, soldiers, or relief personnel wanted anything to do with us."

"They told us we should sign up to be taken back home," Nasreen says, defeated.

Gulistan turns to Nasreen. "Please, my daughter. Let's take the kids back to Kurdistan, and Allah will find a solution."

Nasreen's sobbing is deeper now and more painful to witness. She pulls Naza tighter against her chest. "My daughter will die. No one will do anything for us, not here and not there." She then turns in my direction. "My husband was killed defending our land and saving the world from the Daesh monsters, and now the whole world has turned their backs on us." She pulls her two boys against her as well.

Gulistan approaches Nasreen, gently kisses her on her head, then wraps her motherly arms around her and the kids. The decision has been made. "We will return," Gulistan says, "and as soon as possible. And I *promise* you that I will do whatever needs to be done to get her treatment, even if it means knocking on the doors of every human being on this earth. Just trust me, my daughter."

"Please, don't let my child die." I can't tell if Nasreen is pleading to me, to her mother-in-law, to both of us, or perhaps to the world.

Now that the decision has been made, Nasreen seems somewhat more reassured. They'll be taken back with the very next group of migrants, which could be any time now. Some of Naza's energy returns when she drinks a bag of liquid nourishment and eats a bit of canned beef from one of the United Nations officials. The kids enjoy it, but it's only a matter of time before Naza has another episode and threatens not to come back.

Four buses arrive just before sunset accompanied by two white SUVs flying the blue United Nations flag. Suddenly, the UN personnel are eager to help the migrants on their long-anticipated journey back home, but there is no will to help us cross the border and move through Poland into the rest of Western Europe, where German Chancellor Angela Merkel and company are supposedly willing to open their arms to us. The fence remains tall, the soldiers and guards firm, their guns still silently threatening from afar.

Two men from the Iraqi embassy are also with the United Nations team. One of them was here yesterday to add names to the growing list. There were a few Afghani migrants who actually agreed to be taken back, but one report of some new disagreements between the Taliban and the US caused the migrants to change their minds and stay, with renewed hope or perhaps increased fear of returning home.

I contemplate my own situation, my decision to leave Iraq and the circumstances that led to such a radical plan, leaving everything behind, including family and friends. I review the options I had at the time and whether or not I made a mistake, possibly a dire one, to walk away from hearts that loved me and arms that were willing to hold me. Even in hindsight, I question my decision and my own doubts about it.

Which brings me to my imminent decision: whether to return to the burning home I ran away from or to stay in this open-air freezer, void of the warmth of nature and of humanity. I miss Mother's presence in my life. Her heart was bigger than this world, and her love extended beyond any land one could seek comfort in. Mama made me a refugee in this world the day she packed her sorrowful luggage and took it to another world, where the oppressed and the poor and the weak no longer have to beg for their right to live, where they can just live.

Baba Faisal used to tell me that Baghdad is our mother. We turn to her when we're lost and when we are left motherless. Is it possible that a city where so many of our miseries have been forged, a city that itself is on life support after being neglected by its own sons and daughters, can still provide the love and strength of motherhood?

"You can't want her love but ask for it from afar," Baba Faisal used to say.

59

Baghdad
2022

The plane makes its descent over the city, approaching Baghdad International Airport. Thick clouds cover the city, only allowing narrow beams of sunlight to fall upon the quiet neighborhoods appearing through my window.

I struggled with my decision but found myself submerged in the details without much resistance. When Naza passed out again last night, we took her to the representatives from the Iraqi embassy, and they hurriedly arranged for transport to the nearby Belarussian hospital. They wouldn't allow me to go with her. Only the mother, they said. And they repeatedly emphasized she's only getting a blood transfusion and that she and her mother will be reunited with the rest of the family at the airport. Basically they were saying that this wasn't a way to get into Europe. This morning, when they started loading up the bus, I walked with Gulistan and the twin boys, much to Gulistan's surprise. I guess she thought I had enough will and power to stay there. The officials stopped me at the door and demanded I first write my name on the list and wait my turn with the next round of migrants, but Gulistan's assertive tone reminded them that I was her only help until she reunited with her daughter-in-law and sick granddaughter. I think they just wanted to get rid of us, so the official nodded for me to hop on.

With the plane approaching the ground, I turn to Gulistan, who is sitting in the opposite aisle, also the window, and she nods with a smile. I've only told her a little about Amani, and she didn't mention Amani's name when she urged me to return home. Maybe she's also convinced that Amani is gone, a lost treasure that can't be found again. She just wanted me back in Baghdad.

I wonder what she's seeing out her window. Do her motherly eyes see something I'm missing? I never wanted to be back in Baghdad after Mama died. I turned my back on everything so I wouldn't have to confront emptiness and loss.

The plane touches down, and I'm shaken from the impact. I spent the entire time above the city looking for evidence that Amani is down there somewhere, and I didn't see any, but she obviously wasn't in dark, cold Belarus either.

I turn to my left, and Gulistan is still watching me, her reassuring smile saying more than words. I'm back in Baghdad and with more questions than I have answers for, but at least I'm back with a mother by my side. It was fate that brought this woman to me so she could hold my hand and guide me back home.

Naza is asleep or maybe half dead. She's barely arousable, and Nasreen stands and cries for help as soon as the plane's door opens. I carry Naza over my shoulder and stroll past the passengers and around their luggage until I reach the exit, Gulistan and the rest of the family following me with anticipation. I don't see any ambulances outside. There are no EMS personnel on site to support and resuscitate Naza. Why was I expecting such a thing anyway? I rush toward an airport police officer, and he waves for me to get back in line as an old bus arrives to take us to the terminal.

"She's very sick and needs immediate attention," I say, barely able to catch my breath now.

He points at the bus. "Government officials are waiting for all of you in the terminal and will take the appropriate steps."

Once we enter the terminal, a group of officials, military and civilian, approach us and ask us to line up against the wall. To be counted, to be checked, to be looked at, to be ridiculed, to be stared at! Nasreen screams for help, her eyes fixated on her daughter's head as it dangles from my arms. An official in civilian clothes who's holding a folder walks up to me and asks, "What's wrong with this girl? Is she your daughter?"

"No, I'm only helping them. That is her mother and grandmother over there. She needs urgent help. We were told there would be an ambulance waiting for us at the airport."

He grins and gently inspects Naza's head then says, "Follow me!"

We leave the other crowd of migrants behind and head toward the exit, a group of spectators curiously watching our anxious sprinting. The official makes a few calls on his cell phone, and when we reach the exit door, we find two military personnel in front of us directing us to the sidewalk. A cameraman emerges a few feet to my right, and a few seconds later a female journalist brings her microphone near my face and asks, "Are you part of the group of migrants who just returned?" I nod.

Gulistan jumps in the picture and says a few words in

Kurdish before switching to Arabic. "My granddaughter is dying. She needs help. Please, someone help!"

Two more cameras arrive, and a dozen or more spectators surround us while Gulistan gives her emotional address as Nasreen cries.

"My son, her father, died protecting us, you, the world against Daesh. Now everyone has turned their backs on us."

Nasreen takes Naza from me and holds her tight against her, and the cameras shift away from me, which I don't mind a bit.

Another journalist asks, "What's wrong with the girl? What does she need?"

Gulistan produces a piece of paper from her pocket and waives it at the cameras. It's all in English. "This is the doctor's report. My baby has something they call aplastic anemia and needs a bone marrow transplant. We are from Erbil, and my son died serving his country. Where are the men of honor and religion? Where are the big hearts of this country?"

I'm impressed with Gulistan's power of persuasion, but as they say, desperation is the mother of creativity and strength.

An ambulance arrives, and the police start dispersing spectators to make room. One of the journalists moves closer to Nasreen and asks, "Why did you return? Did you try to get help at the border?"

How stupid and how foolish! I want to grab his microphone and shove it down his throat and let me be the talk of the news and social media. Gulistan does the job for me, though, and yells, "Instead of asking us these questions, why aren't you asking the government why thousands upon thousands of people are risking their lives to flee to foreign lands? Our daughter is one of millions of Iraqi children who need medical care in a country that sits on an ocean of oil."

Gulistan is now visibly upset and breaks down crying.

Commotion builds up, and a few men shout obscenities at corrupt officials. They load Naza into the ambulance, her mother close by her side. Gulistan insists on accompanying them, but they refuse.

A taxi driver nearby quickly opens the door and asks Gulistan to get in. "I'll take you to the hospital behind the ambulance, *khala.*"

I follow Gulistan, and before the ambulance takes off, she points to me while looking at the camera and says, "This young man saved us. He's an example of bravery and patriotism. Men like him should hold positions of responsibility in this country."

All eyes turn to me, and I quickly climb into the passenger seat, suffocated by the attention. With the twin boys seated next to her in the back seat, Gulistan closes the door, and the taxi speeds off behind the ambulance.

At the entrance to Yarmouk General Hospital, two armed security personnel stop the taxi as they motion for the ambulance to pass through. We get out, and I apologize to the taxi driver for not having any money to give him. His face turns red, and he says, "Come on, brother, what are you talking about? I take money from you?"

I thank him, and he turns around and disappears into the sea of yellow cabs. They inform us that Naza and her mother have already been taken inside and that we are not allowed to enter. All visitation has been suspended due to COVID-19. Gulistan fights back, and security is called. Soon, a government crew arrives and interrogates us about our identity. After a few phone calls, they inform us that we're to be taken to a nearby hotel for now. Gulistan refuses to leave. There's no indication that she's going to give in, so they surrender to her wishes and allow her and the two boys inside. As for me, they show no leniency whatsoever. I need rest and a good shower, so I won't say no to the hotel. I'm also not going to tell them I am from Baghdad so they don't think I am a local with housing arrangements. Gulistan kisses my head and repeatedly thanks me for my help. I'm not willing to part ways without any way to contact her later, but neither of us has a phone. I write Fatima's number on a piece of paper and hand it to her.

"This is my sister's number. As soon as you have a phone, please contact her and give her your information, and wherever I am, I will contact you." I turn and follow the government officials before Gulistan sees my tearful eyes.

They drop me off at a small hotel, hand me a hundred thousand dinars, and tell me I'm now on my own.

The next morning, when I go downstairs to check out of the hotel, a TV in the lobby is playing a local news broadcast. It turns out that some wealthy private donors and government officials in both Baghdad and Erbil have stepped up to sponsor an overseas bone marrow transplant for Naza in Germany. Apparently, Gulistan's rant in front of the cameras yesterday went viral on social media. I remember telling Amani that nobody in power would ever care about us. Might things finally be turning around in this country?

60

Baghdad
2022

My grandfather used to say that Baghdad is where everything converges, past and present, longing and belonging, where the waters flow into the deepest of roots and cleanse the remnants of the foul, still waters that don't belong and never have.

The city is just like I left it. Busy traffic is on full display on both narrow and wide roads in the early morning hour. The Tigris sits in calmness and solemnity, its water quietly making its way through without being a nuisance. I'm back because throughout history, the Tigris has always found its way under the earth to flush out the bad seeds and replace them with new life, the real sons and daughters of this land.

It's still too early for the bookstore to be open, so I treat my deprived stomach to the popular Baghdad breakfast plate of geymar and kahi at the nearest cheap place I can find. Three rounds of tea after breakfast and the malnutrition of many months is suddenly a page from the distant past. I look at my wristwatch after I pay the restaurant manager with the little bit of money the government officials gave me yesterday, and then I set out.

My heart races as I step onto Mutanabbi Street. There are a lot more people wandering about than the last time I was here. Most people are not wearing masks, so I feel less estranged in my maskless face as I slowly walk through the crowds, absorbing every image, every sign, and every book stand as if I have not worked here long enough to memorize every corner, recognize every business, and feel at home. And yet I somehow feel foreign, and that feeling intensifies the closer I get to the bookstore.

I hear a voice behind me. "*Marhaba*, Faisal. Where have you been, brother?" It's one of the bookstore owners I've dealt with on many occasions.

"In this world," I say, continuing my pace, wondering if he actually realized how long I had been gone or if he knew where I had gone away to.

My feet slow down against my will when I first see the bookstore from far away. It has been renovated, and the overhead sign is now laminated and more alive. An old woman wearing two masks and carrying more plastic bags than she can handle bumps into me. "Young man, you can't just stop and stand there in the middle of the street. Move over."

But I don't move over. Instead, I walk straight toward the bookstore, and with each step I take, my heart feels heavier. The store is closed, the stand out front empty. The exterior paint is new. Have they sold it? Did Amani and her uncle move away or move on from this business?

Most of the other stores are open now, and street vendors

have set up their stands. Across from the bookstore, a young man is playing some tunes on a black guitar, moving his head in harmony with music that I can't tell if it's Eastern or Western or some combination of the two.

It's now close to noon, and no one has come to open the bookstore yet. I take a seat on a small wooden chair next to the empty book rack like I had done so many times before. I watch the hands of the young musician expertly play the strings of the guitar, a slow version of a popular folk song, and I must have gotten too involved in its melodies to notice two people approaching the bookstore. They must have also not noticed me. Amani is standing behind her uncle while he inserts a key into the front doorknob.

I get up and greet them, and he runs in my direction and hugs me. Over his shoulders, I see that Amani won't look at me. She just stands there, silent and still as her uncle pats my back and asks me a dozen questions. "How have you been?" "Where did you go?" "When did you get back?"

But now I can't hear anything except Amani's silence. Her uncle invites me in, but Amani says in a cold voice, "Uncle, we have a lot of work to do, and I need to leave soon."

"Don't worry," I say. "I'll leave you two alone and let you do your work. I just got back yesterday and wanted to drop by and say hello."

Amani steps inside without turning, and her uncle smiles and nods at me before following her in. I look back to the street, and the musician is gone. I sit down again, put my hands inside the pockets of my jacket, and rest my head against the book rack. I need to make sense of where I am, where I've ended up, and what's next in my life.

I don't know how much time has passed, but there she is, Amani, with a puzzled but calm look on her face. I quickly stand up and face her, looking her in the eye.

"My uncle thinks we still need someone to help manage the bookstore. He wants to talk to you inside." She motions for me to go in front of her and says, "If it were up to me, I wouldn't make this offer." I can't tell if she's being sarcastic or serious.

"Well, is it also not up to you whether to smile or not?"

Before she answers, I push the door open and go inside, again to be greeted by her uncle with a warm hug and words of excitement.

Amani walks to the opposite side of the store and begins sorting some books on the top shelf.

"This place looks amazing now," I say. "It's lovely and truly alive."

"And we're very happy to have you back."

I step closer to him. I'm not going to let another moment pass by. I clear my throat and say to Amani's uncle, "I'm here to ask for Amani's hand."

His face widens in excitement, but he doesn't say anything, as if he's waiting for me to say more, so I do.

"I know there's a proper way to do this formally, but I can't wait another minute to propose to the most wonderful girl a man can dream of."

I can see her in the corner of my eyes. She still hasn't turned around. She's standing, but she isn't moving.

"*Inshallah, khair,*" her uncle says with a smile. "Whatever is best will happen. Life will unfold as it should."

"As soon as possible, I'll bring my family to make this formal."

He nods. "We will discuss it among ourselves at home and give you an answer. We would be proud to have someone like you in our family."

I inhale a deep sigh of relief.

"At the end of the day," he says, "it will be her decision after she consults with her mother."

"Of course. I totally understand."

I turn and look in her direction. With her back to me, I am certain she's smiling. I know she is.

AUTHOR'S NOTE

Across history, people came and left. Armies invaded and retreated. Rulers conquered, and others defended. Civilizations collided, and kingdoms and empires rose and collapsed. New parties formed, and others dissolved. Prison walls were built, while others were broken down. Lies circulated, some truths were buried, and other truths were uprooted.

During all these periods, the Tigris River flowed through Baghdad, watering the seeds planted by all who claimed that Iraq belonged to them. But Iraq does not belong to anyone. They belong to Iraq.

Made in the USA
Middletown, DE
15 October 2023

40853051R00223